£ 30.00

Debt Securities

Debt Securities

A. J. FROST BSC., FIA

and

D. P. HAGER MA, FIA, FPMI

Published for the
Institute of Actuaries and
the Faculty of Actuaries

HEINEMANN PROFESSIONAL PUBLISHING

Heinemann Professional Publishing Ltd
Halley Court, Jordan Hill, Oxford OX2 8EJ

OXFORD LONDON MELBOURNE AUCKLAND
SINGAPORE IBADAN NAIROBI GABORONE KINGSTON

First published 1990

British Library Cataloguing in Publication Data
Frost, Alan J.
Debt securities.
1. Great Britain. Investments. Securities
I. Title II. Hager, David P.
332.63'2

ISBN 0 434 90588 7

Typeset by August Filmsetting, Haydock, St Helens
Printed in Great Britain by Billings, Worcester

Contents

Preface

This book was commissioned by the Institute of Actuaries and the Faculty of Actuaries as a replacement for two volumes of the textbooks written by Day and Jamieson in the middle of the 1970s. It is a companion volume to our *General Introduction to Institutional Investment*. The book has had a long gestation. There is no doubt that the pace of change has frustrated our efforts to complete the volume in a shorter time. The 'Big Bang' of 1986 in the London securities markets has led to many changes of practice which we have tried to describe. Government policy and Bank of England innovation has created a constantly changing backdrop of circumstances in which we have amended our thoughts on the role of gilts in the UK economy; the role of the PSDR as distinct from a PSBR; the use of auctions by the Bank of England; and so on.

The chapters on traditional UK fixed-interest stocks and preference shares are drawn directly from Day and Jamieson's original volume subject to minor editing and updating. The remainder of the text was written by us to reflect the conditions of the late 1980s and, in particular, to include overseas bond markets. The inelegant title *Debt Securities* is accurate in terms of context.

We are indebted to a great number of people. Robert Clarkson and Paul Meins were the official 'actuarial' scrutineers and were most helpful. Special thanks are due to Gerard Wherity and Derek McLean, two experienced practitioners in the marketplace, who read through the text and made useful points on matters of current practice. We would also like to give our thanks to Bill Truckle; Mr K. L. Gardner, his successor as Director of Education at the Institute of Actuaries; Kathryn Grant of Heinemann for her patience and encouragement; to the many companies that gave permission for use of their charts and tables; to our wives; and, finally, to the various secretaries that have 'word-processed' our manuscripts with such fortitude.

We apologize for any inaccuracies that may still be in the text despite our best endeavours and wish you, the reader, success in your careers. If this volume helps a little we shall have achieved our objective.

1

The economic background

Introduction

1.1

The economies of the major countries of the world are complex and interlinked. Economists have produced many theories on how such economies can be managed, from Keynesian approaches to a strict control of the money supply, but in practice it has been necessary to evolve complicated methods of economic management on a wide variety of variables.

1.2

There are a number of key variables which are likely to be important to any country – exchange rates and their stability, currency reserves, balance of payments position, external capital flows (inward and outward), economic growth, capital investment level, government income and expenditure, taxation, money supply, domestic credit expansion and interest rates. Control of some of these variables may be attempted, and it is likely that debt securities will, in one form or another, be a strong feature of economic management.

1.3

Fluctuating exchange rates introduced in 1972/73 have been a common feature of the 1980s as large capital flows take place between the major currencies. If a currency is perceived as strong, investors which are free to move their funds between the major markets may exchange their assets into short-dated debt securities in the favoured currency. Their willingness to carry out the transaction will depend on the expected exchange rate movement and on the interest rates available, and capital flows can be encouraged or discouraged according to the interest rates available elsewhere. The rates of interest will also affect the cost of borrowing in the country concerned, and may have some impact upon the rate of economic growth and perhaps the level of consumer spending. Exchange rate movements can affect the money supply and the ability of exporters to sell overseas. They may also have an impact on the goods imported. The investor may decide to purchase securities issued by the government which may assist the funding of government spending. While it is possible to operate on many variables to manage an economy, interest rates are likely to be one of the prime variables, since they have an extensive effect throughout the economy.

Fluctuating exchange rates can have a destabilizing effect on economic activity and a number of moves have been made in an effort to produce a more stable environment. Certain European Economic Community (EEC) countries operate within the exchange rate mechanism of the European Monetary System (EMS) where currencies fluctuate within small bands, but since this does not cover transactions in three major currencies (sterling, US dollar and the yen), there are informal arrangements between seven major countries which have some impact upon foreign exchange markets. These countries are known as the Group of Seven and comprise Canada, France, Germany, Italy, Japan, UK and USA. Attempts to reduce exchange rate fluctuations may require foreign exchange intervention by central governments but these arrangements to moderate exchange rate movements will probably mean that since countries will not have the freedom to move exchange rates, interest rates will have increased importance as an economic variable.

1.4

A country with a balance of payments deficit on its trade can usually be expected to see its exchange rate fall over time. The mechanism is complex but a decline in the value of the currency increases the costs of imports and decreases the foreign currency cost of producing goods for export. Alternatively, the trade imbalance can remain if the country can offset this by capital flows, and the use of interest rates can be important in ensuring an orderly depreciation of the currency over time.

1.5

In the mid 1970s, there was an oil crisis and a dramatic rise in oil prices. This led to the huge transfer of resources from the oil-consuming countries to the oil producers. The oil producers could not initially utilize all the money which they were receiving and hence it found its way back into the worldwide banking system and into financial markets. Such balances can move from market to market and could have a dramatic effect on the economy concerned. The consequences of the oil crisis further emphasize the role of interest rates and debt securities in the world economy.

1.6

The interest rate on debt securities will depend on a number of factors. Some aspects will relate to the supply of securities (i.e. if the government reduces the securities available by net repayments of stock, the yields on the stocks are likely to be lower than would be the case if the government were a net issuer of securities) while other aspects will be influenced by the demand side (i.e. the levels of liquidity available to buyers of securities such as private individuals, corporate bodies, institutions and foreign governments). Supply and demand are important factors for fixed interest markets, but the increasing internationalization of securities markets makes the ramifications more difficult to determine. For example, it may be thought that UK institutions have low cash balances and would be reluctant to sell other assets to fund a gilt issue, but this may be irrelevant if there are international investors in the wings who see the UK as an attractive place for their excess liquidity.

1.7

Investors which lend their assets can expect, in theory, to receive a payment to compensate them for the loss of purchasing power in their cash while it is lent, plus some premium for actually giving someone else the use of the money. Furthermore, the longer the money is lent, the greater the risks to the lender and hence lending for longer periods could be expected to be at higher rates of interest than for shorter periods. In practice, interest rates on securities may or may not reflect these factors and in the UK there has been a higher rate of interest on short-dated stocks in recent years compared with the rates available on similar long-dated securities. This may mean that investors expect short-term rates to decline, or may just mean that short-term economic management requires a particular level of short-term rates, which may have little or no relevance for the factors which usually influence longer-term rates or on the demand for long-dated stocks, (see Section 1.9). The variation of interest rates on securities against time to maturity can be plotted graphically and is known as a yield curve. The curve is described as upward sloping if theoretical considerations apply but recent UK experience is of mainly downward sloping curves. Figure 1.1 shows three different types of curve experienced recently in the UK.

Figures 1.2—1.5 show the yield curves for the UK, US, Japan and Germany as at the end of 1988.

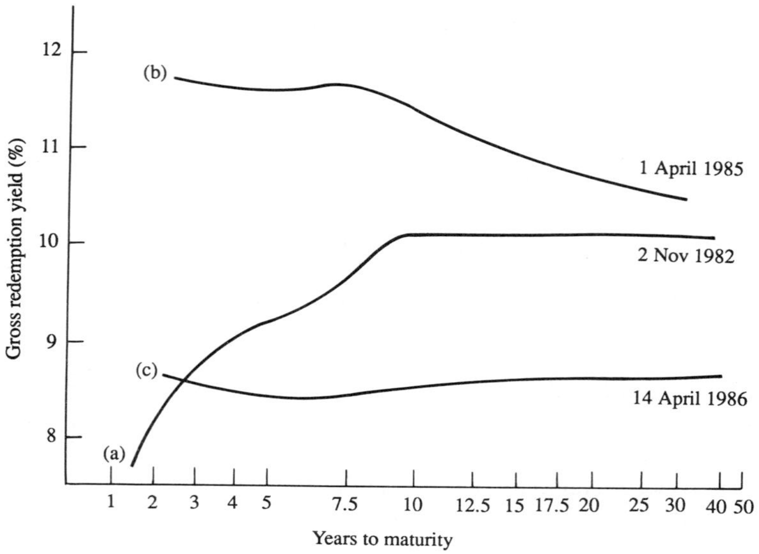

Figure 1.1 *Yield curves for British government securities*
Source: James Capel Gilts Limited

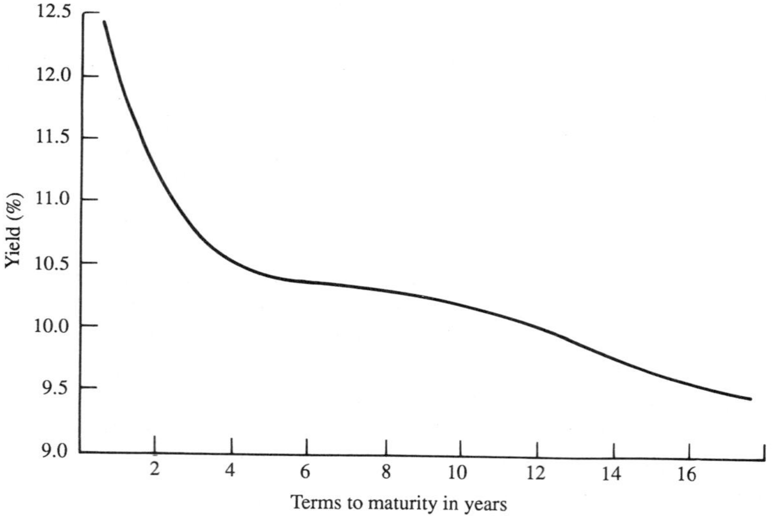

Figure 1.2 *UK gilt yield curve as at 30 December 1988*

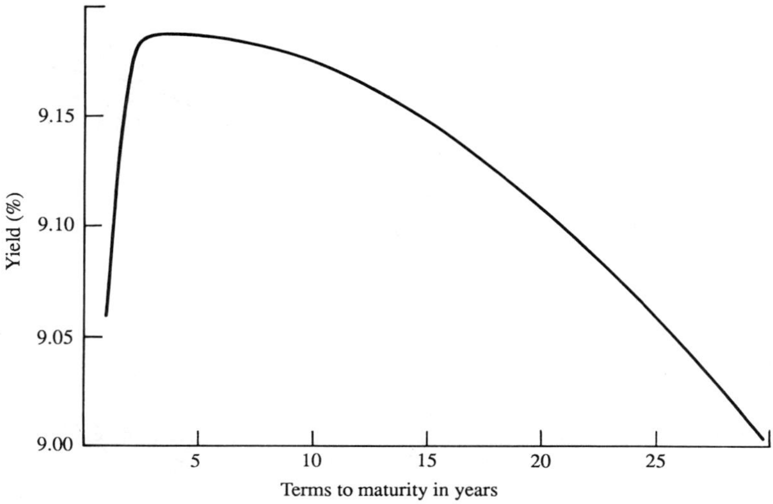

Figure 1.3 *US treasuries yield curve as at 30 December 1988*

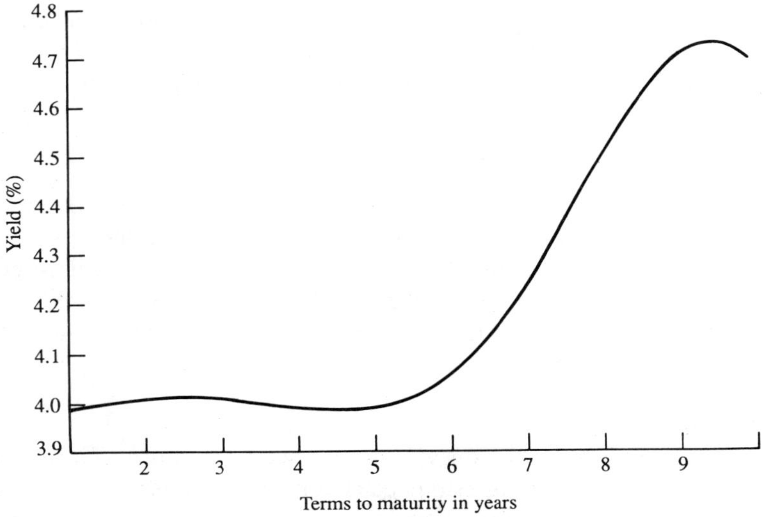

Figure 1.4 *Japanese government yield curve as at 30 December 1988*

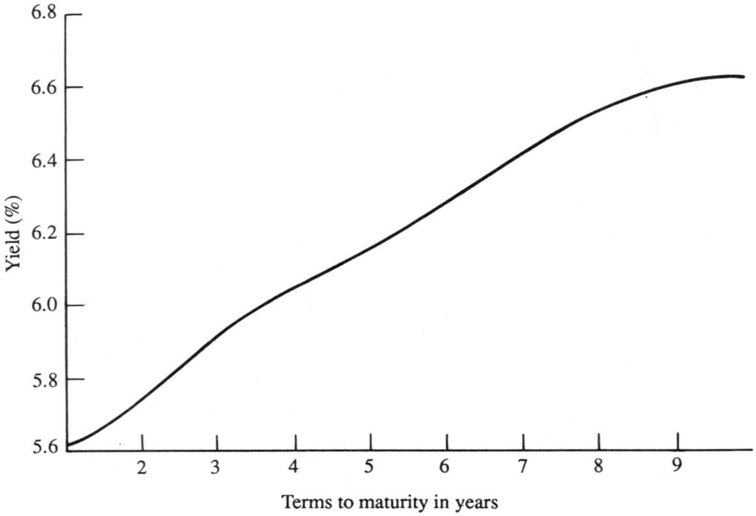

Figure 1.5 *Bundesrepublik yield curve as at 30 December 1988*

1.8

The way in which each government operates its economic policy varies but usually involves the central bank of each country. In the UK it is usually the Bank of England which operates interest rate policy in conjunction with the Treasury. In the US it is the Federal Reserve which is the dominant force for official interest rate policy, while in Germany it is the Bundesbank.

1.9 Factors affecting interest rates

There are a large number of factors which can influence the level of interest rates and the factors which have an impact on short-term rates may not be those which have a dominant effect on long-term rates. Nevertheless, both types of influence will be considered together at this stage. Many of the influences are interrelated but where possible the effects are shown on the basis of moving one factor in isolation.

1.9.1 INFLATION

In theory if someone lends money, he should receive a return which should compensate him not only for estimated changes in the purchasing power of the money while the lender is without his cash, but also an additional amount above this as a payment for the actual lending. In practice inflation does not appear to be a dominant force for very short-term rates in any clear way in that rates at any time do not seem to be close to the expected short-term

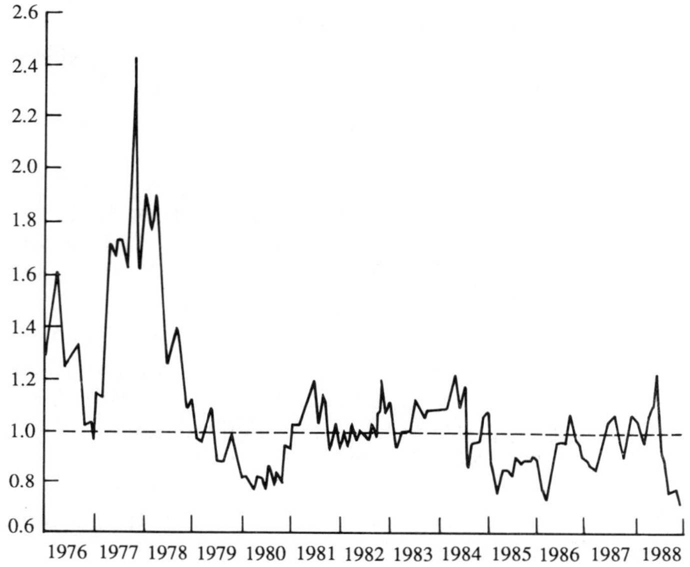

Figure 1.6 *Long/short interest rate ratio 1976 to 1988*
Source: Datastream International

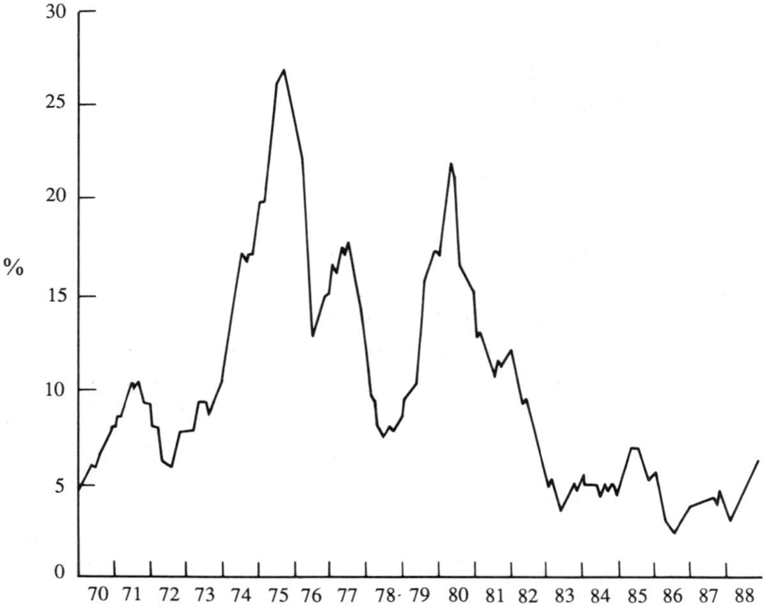

Figure 1.7 *Inflation since 1970*

inflation level at that time. However, if an investment in short-term investments such as cash deposits on the interbank market, or Treasury bills which are continually rolled over when they reach maturity, is examined in the UK over periods of more than fifteen years the overall return on this type of investment has been usually very close to the rate of inflation over the same period.

The influence of inflation on long-term interest rates should in theory be stronger than on short-term rates, but in practice over periods of time short-term rates have been a closer match to inflation, perhaps because long-term rates are more influenced by expectations than by actual rates. In theory in the long term the investor should receive a rate of return to at least compensate for changes in money values due to inflation. In stable low-inflationary conditions the redemption yield on fixed-interest securities may be loosely based on a continuation of current inflation levels, plus some risk premium against an upward move in inflation levels. In high-inflation conditions such as in the 1970s, redemption yields tended to be below the levels of price inflation and investors in fixed-interest securities were generally not compensated for the erosion in purchasing power of their money. Indeed except over

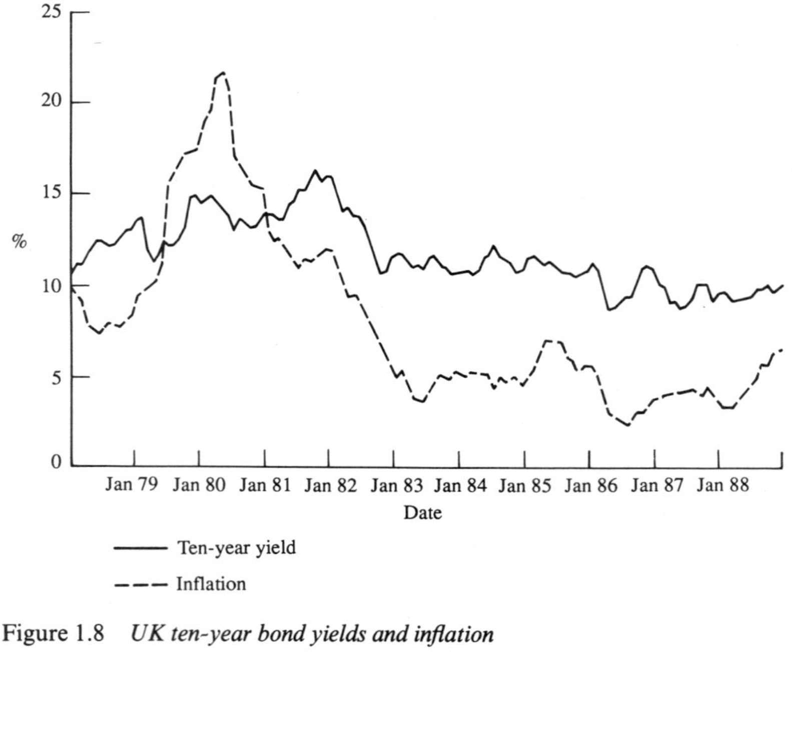

Figure 1.8 *UK ten-year bond yields and inflation*

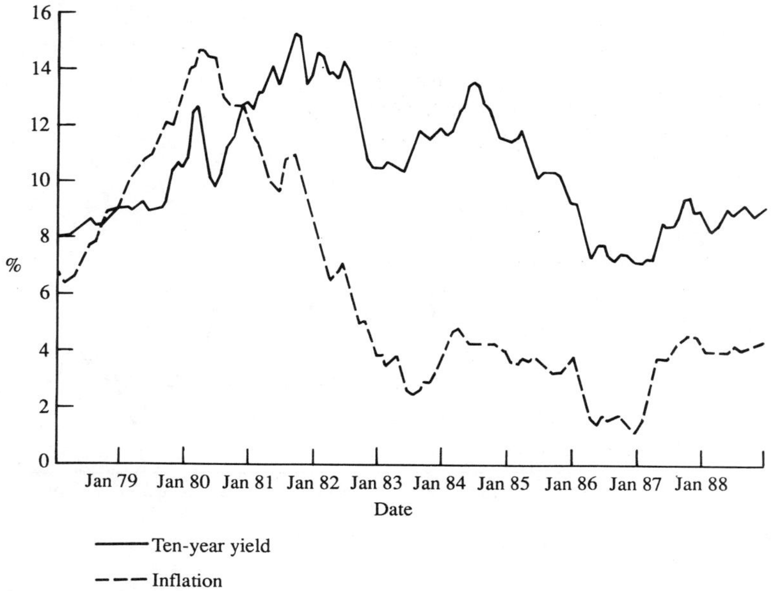

Figure 1.9 *US ten-year bond yields and inflation*

Figure 1.10 *German ten-year bond yields and inflation*

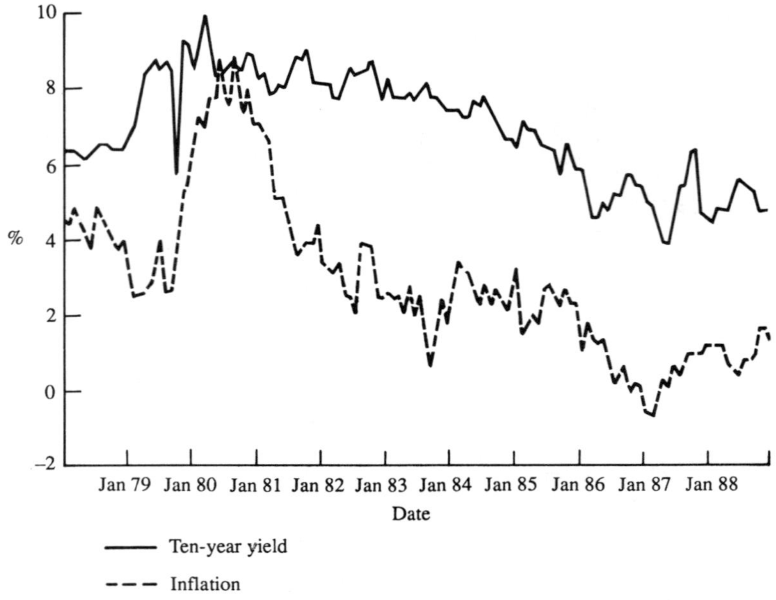

Figure 1.11 *Japanese ten-year bond yields and inflation*

the last ten years or so, with the benefit of hindsight, investors in fixed-interest securities in the UK have not received sufficient returns over long periods to offset for the loss in purchasing power of their investment, but the experience in other markets such as the USA shows a different picture. Hence in the UK long-term interest rates have not correctly reflected future inflation rates, but investors in other markets need to examine the position for that country.

1.9.2 WORLDWIDE INTEREST RATES

Investors are able to move large sums of money from country to country without penalty or difficulty, according to their views on the relative strength of each currency and the interest rates available. The sums of money which can be moved are substantial and no major country can isolate its interest rate policy from the interest rates available elsewhere. The effect occurs both on long-term and short-term rates although the type of investor would be different. If interest rates in other major centres are low, then it is likely that a country may also be able to sustain a low interest rate policy unless its currency is under pressure or expected to become weak relative to other currencies.

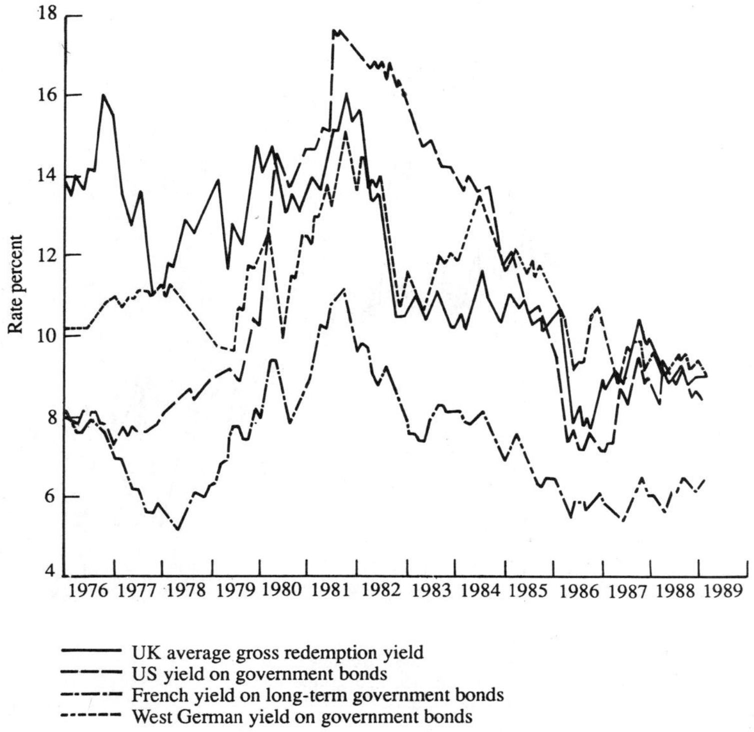

Figure 1.12
Source: Datastream International

Figures 1.12 and 1.13 show the yields in some major government bond markets since 1976 (UK, US, France, Germany, Japan, Holland and Switzerland).

1.9.3 CURRENCY EFFECTS

If the currency of a country comes under pressure then one defence to this is to raise interest rates, or if the currency is too strong making exporting difficult then interest rates can be reduced to try to decrease the strength of the currency. The logic behind this is that investors may be attracted by higher interest rates, provided that they do not consider that the move in the currency will still be so large that the interest rate change is small in comparison. Upward moves in interest rates of this type are not generally small and usually operate on short-term rates such as the official bank rate or its equi-

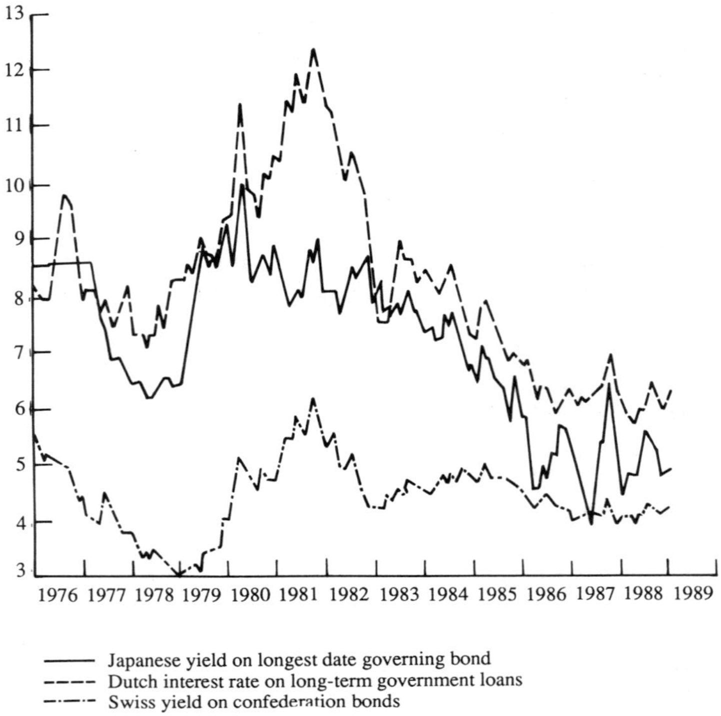

Figure 1.13
Source: Datastream International

valent such as interbank dealing rates. This may have a knock-on effect into longer-term rates if there is a continuing expectation of currency weakness (or strength).

1.9.4 BALANCE OF PAYMENTS POSITION

The balance of payments position can affect interest rates in an indirect way. Adverse payments positions usually need correction at some stage and this can be done in a variety of ways. However, high interest rates may be needed if there is an expectation of future adverse balance of payments trends if currency stability is to be attempted, but no change to rates may be appropriate if the currency is to depreciate to offset the payments deficit. If the payments position is in surplus, interest rates may be reduced to avoid an overstrengthening of the currency. Most of the effect will be on short-term rates, but longer-term investors will be attracted to areas where there is no balance of payments problem and no expectation of a change in this situation so that there will be some effect on longer-term rates.

1.9.5 ECONOMIC CYCLE

When economic demand is low, interest rates (if determined by domestic forces) are likely to be low. As economic activity increases the demand for borrowing increases and with an unchanged supply of finance, the price of borrowing (i.e. the interest rate) will rise. The cycle can in theory be regulated by a number of factors including the interest rate.

1.9.6 GOVERNMENT POLICY

Government policy can have a dramatic effect on both long and short-term rates. If there is a Public Sector Borrowing Requirement (PSBR), it may be necessary for interest rates to rise so that sufficient investors are attracted to lend money to the government. Alternatively, when government revenue exceeds expenditure a Public Sector Debt Repayment (PSDR) occurs and interest rates can be reduced over the levels otherwise prevailing. Funding of government spending can be done by selling assets, as in the UK and France. This reduces pressure to fund in fixed-interest markets, thus keeping interest rates down. Funding in this way or when a PSDR occurs may have the effect of reducing longer-term interest rates since investors may feel that there should be a scarcity value placed on government fixed-interest stocks as their future may be limited.

If recessionary pressures occur and unemployment threatens, a government may decide to increase the supply of money in the economy as well as directly operating on interest rates to try to engineer even larger falls in interest rates. This hopefully may stimulate economic activity, but will only do so if investment and spending plans are closely related to the cost of finance. Similarly, if inflationary pressures are causing concern, interest rates may be raised and the supply of money may also be reduced to accentuate the effect.

Some countries use interest rates as their main regulator of the economy on a macro basis. This means that interest rates may be subject to more pressures than if a currency and monetary policy are also in operation. The way in which a government carries out the regulation of its economy is important for investors and should be thoroughly understood.

1.10 A historic look at the 1970s and 1980s

Figures 1.8–1.11 show the trend of interest rates and inflation for each of the four main economies for debt securities, for the period since 1978. The 1970s saw periods of relatively high inflation of each of the economies, together with the Oil Crisis. By contrast, the 1980s have seen much lower levels of inflation in most countries and lower nominal interest rates.

In the UK and US there have been substantial periods of negative real interest rates as the rate of depreciation of monetary assets by inflation has been greater than the interest rate received, but in the mid/late 1980s the real interest rates were high by historic standards. Japan and Germany have maintained real interest rates during most of the period considered, and the greater stability of these economies compared with the UK and US can be seen in Figures 1.10 and 1.11 showing their interest and inflation rates.

1.11 Returns achieved on asset classes

Table 1.1 shows the real rates of return from capital and income combined in excess of retail price rises to a gross investor in UK shares, UK long-dated gilts and in cash for periods to 31 December 1988. The figures for cash have been derived from Treasury bills (to provide consistency over a forty-year period).

Table 1.1.

Period in years to 31 December 1988	*UK equities (%)*	*Long-dated gilts (%)*	*Cash (%)*
5	13.9	5.7	5.4
10	12.1	5.8	3.8
15	8.3	3.1	0.9
20	4.3	1.1	0.5
25	5.4	0.3	0.7
30	6.4	0.3	1.0
35	7.4	−0.2	0.8
40	6.8	−0.7	0.5

Source: Barclays de Zoete Wedd

If Table 1.1 is produced for periods ending in other years as well as to the end of 1988, the conclusions are as follows:

1. UK equities have tended to produce a real rate of return (above retail prices) of around 5 per cent to 7 per cent per annum over long periods.
2. UK gilts have produced high real returns over the shorter terms, but the longer-period returns have been close to, or below, the rate of price inflation.
3. Apart from the last five and ten-year periods cash has usually produced a return close to the rate of price inflation.

4 The index-linked gilt real return (currently in the 3 per cent to 4 per cent range) looks attractive against other asset classes on a historical basis.

1.12 Returns achieved on bonds

Table 1.2 shows the returns on an investment by a sterling investor in each of the main bond markets, assuming performance in line with the domestic bond market and after adjusting for currency changes. Although it can be theoretically expected that all these rates would be fairly similar as currency movements would compensate for interest rate differentials, this has not turned out to be the case in practice. The tables are shown in nominal and real terms.

1.13 Indices

Given the amount of money invested in debt securities worldwide, it is somewhat surprising that there is no universally accepted series of bond indices. Part of the reason for this may be the lack of sophisticated performance measurement of fixed interest portfolios. Another reason is that fixed-interest investors often concentrate on interest yield or redemption yield, and make the comparisons that they require with similar returns on, say, a ten-year bond. Hence a full performance analysis including capital changes and income may seem superfluous for some investors.

Figure 1.14 shows the FT Government Securities Index since 1982.

In the UK the development of the FT Actuaries All Share Index and constituent indices took place in the early 1960s, but it was not until the early 1980s that investors had a complete set of indices covering gilts as well which were suitable for performance purposes. Comprehensive indices were also produced for representative redemption yields for various maturities within the fixed-interest markets. There are, therefore, two types of index according to the purpose of the calculations. Performance comparisons on a time-weighted rate of return basis with a fixed-interest portfolio taking into account both changes in capital values and income accrued figures can be made for the maturity bands and investment categories shown below:

- Conventional gilts
  - Up to five years to maturity
  - Five to fifteen years to maturity
  - Over fifteen years to maturity
  - Irredeemables
  - All stocks

Table 1.2 *Market statistics in sterling*

Annual returns % pa end year	*1979*	*1980*	*1981*	*1982*	*1983*	*1984*	*1985*	*1986*	*1987*	*1988*	*1979–1988 Nominal returns*	*AAI% Real returns (UK CPI)*
							Bonds					
USA	−10.7	−9.7	26.4	69.0	11.6	43.7	5.6	21.1	−26.8	12.6	11.3	3.2
Japan	−30.1	17.1	30.4	22.0	24.1	30.0	11.1	36.3	11.2	4.3	13.9	5.6
UK	4.5	21.3	1.4	54.5	16.2	7.2	11.0	12.7	15.9	9.2	14.6	6.3
Germany	−4.1	−17.0	13.3	37.8	1.8	25.2	15.4	34.2	−0.6	−3.7	8.9	0.9
Switzerland	−8.6	−16.4	22.8	17.9	4.5	9.2	7.0	35.3	4.7	−9.6	5.6	−2.1
France	−9.1	−14.8	1.6	20.7	8.1	31.3	21.8	39.3	−4.3	11.1	9.3	1.3
Netherlands	−4.0	−14.3	13.7	43.5	2.6	24.2	17.9	36.9	3.2	−3.0	10.7	2.6
Italy	1.6	−16.6	−8.5	29.9	15.6	40.7	8.5	57.6	−2.7	6.9	11.3	3.2
Canada	−10.4	−7.6	21.5	65.0	20.2	36.5	−6.2	16.3	−14.6	24.1	12.1	4.0
Australia	−14.7	−10.5	13.4	36.6	11.7	31.8	−30.8	14.6	0.0	38.9	6.7	−1.1
World – GDPppp	−10.7	−5.1	18.7	49.6	13.2	34.9	8.1	28.0	−10.2	9.7	12.1	3.9
							Money					
USA	2.3	6.6	47.2	33.5	21.9	39.0	−13.5	3.4	−15.5	12.0	11.9	3.7
Japan	−21.3	22.8	24.3	18.6	20.1	23.3	6.9	29.5	7.4	5.2	12.7	4.5
UK	14.6	18.6	15.0	13.0	10.5	10.2	12.4	11.2	10.3	11.0	12.7	4.4
Germany	2.4	−9.7	21.5	22.3	2.4	14.7	8.9	29.7	0.3	−3.7	8.2	0.3
Switzerland	−5.7	−14.4	28.0	8.1	3.4	7.1	5.5	29.1	3.7	−8.8	4.8	−2.9
France	4.2	−6.5	14.4	17.2	1.7	22.8	13.1	23.9	2.3	−0.8	8.8	0.8

Table 1.2—*continued*

						Money						
Netherlands	3.5	−7.6	20.3	20.6	0.5	14.8	9.7	30.0	2.9	−3.5	8.5	0.6
Italy	5.7	−5.6	16.0	24.4	8.8	26.2	6.9	38.0	1.6	3.4	11.8	3.7
Canada	3.9	2.9	50.2	31.0	20.5	31.6	−17.0	7.9	−9.0	24.4	13.0	4.7
Australia	−4.8	9.6	34.6	18.2	12.6	28.0	−24.1	9.8	−1.6	39.8	10.6	2.6
World – GDPppp	0.1	5.9	33.4	25.9	15.7	28.8	−2.9	15.4	−5.1	8.6	11.8	3.7
						Currency movements relative to sterling						
USA	−8.5	−6.7	25.0	18.2	11.3	25.4	−20.0	−2.6	−21.1	3.9	1.2	
Japan	−25.7	10.1	15.4	10.6	12.6	16.0	0.3	23.3	2.9	0.9	5.8	
UK	0.0	0.0	0.0	0.0	0.0	0.0	0.0	0.0	0.0	0.0	0.0	
Germany	−3.4	−17.6	8.6	12.1	−2.9	8.5	3.0	23.9	−3.5	−7.8	1.5	
Switzerland	−6.2	−16.4	22.6	6.6	1.9	5.8	0.4	24.4	−0.1	−11.8	2.0	
France	−4.9	−17.0	−1.8	1.0	−10.3	9.2	2.4	14.6	−5.8	−8.3	−2.5	
Netherlands	−5.5	−16.5	7.8	11.2	−4.7	8.3	3.0	22.6	−2.4	−8.0	1.0	
Italy	−5.6	−19.5	−3.0	3.5	−8.1	7.5	−7.3	21.5	−9.3	−7.3	−3.3	
Sweden	−5.2	−11.6	−1.9	−9.7	1.5	11.6	−5.1	9.3	−7.8	−1.8	−2.3	
Spain	−3.0	−22.2	1.6	−8.3	−10.8	13.3	−9.4	13.0	−3.3	−1.2	−3.6	
Belgium	−6.1	−17.0	2.4	−3.1	−6.1	10.6	0.9	21.7	−4.1	−7.9	−1.4	
Denmark	−13.2	−16.8	2.6	3.3	−5.5	10.0	1.0	18.3	−4.5	−7.9	−1.8	
Norway	−6.7	−11.3	11.5	−2.7	1.7	6.6	−4.1	0.3	−6.6	16.3	0.2	
Austria	−1.6	−16.0	8.7	12.5	−4.0	10.0	2.5	23.8	−3.5	−7.9	1.9	
Canada	−7.1	−8.8	25.9	14.0	10.0	18.1	−24.4	−1.4	−16.1	13.2	1.1	
Australia	−12.2	−0.4	19.4	2.8	2.4	15.1	−34.0	−5.1	−14.3	22.9	−1.8	
Singapore	−8.3	−3.8	27.8	14.8	10.3	22.5	−17.1	−5.5	−14.1	6.6	2.3	
Hong Kong	−11.2	−10.0	13.0	3.3	−7.1	24.7	−19.8	−2.4	−20.7	3.3	−3.6	
SDR	−7.5	−9.7	14.1	12.0	5.6	17.4	−10.3	8.5	−9.2	−0.9	1.5	
ECU	−3.7	−15.3	3.6	5.4	−4.8	7.5	0.2	17.4	−3.9	−6.5	−0.4	

Source: *UBS Phillips & Drew*

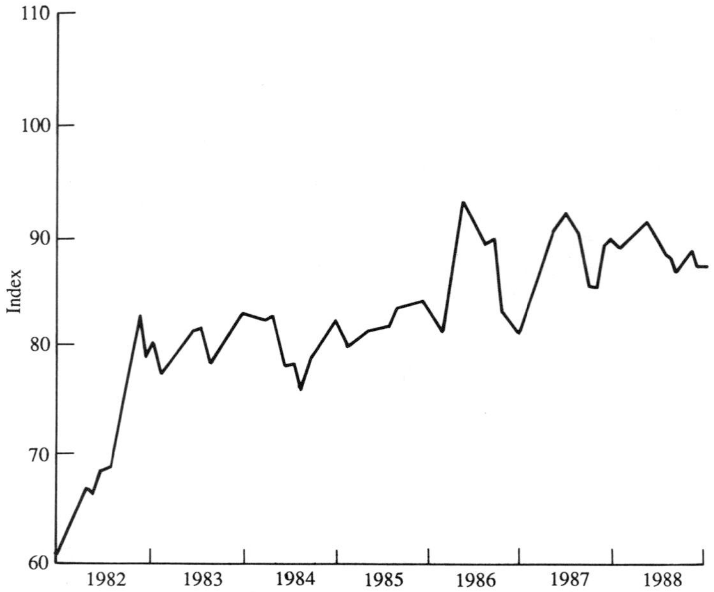

Figure 1.14 *Financial Times Government Securities Index*
Source: Copyright 1989 International Stock Exchange of the United Kingdom and the Republic of Ireland

- Index linked { Up to five years to maturity / Over five years to maturity / All stocks }
- Debentures and loans
- Preference shares

The index return for a period can be calculated, for short periods, such as a month or quarter, as:

$$\frac{I_2 + a_2 - a_1}{I_1}$$

Where I_1 is the index figure at the start of the period
I_2 is the index figure at the end of the period
a_1 is the accrued interest figure at the start of the period
a_2 is the accrued interest figure at the end of the period.

The complexity of the return calculations can be increased if it is decided to take account of the fact that there is a time delay of about five weeks between the time that a stock goes ex-dividend and the time of receipt of the dividend payment. Further refinements can also be made for the tax deducted at source on gilt-edged holdings. Calculations for longer periods are usually done by chainlinking the monthly (or quarterly) returns.

The other series of indices relates to representative redemption yields for various maturity bands for the gilt market. Although not designed for performance measurement, investors can use these figures to see the approximate shape of the yield curve.

Further details of the method of construction of the indices can be found in Dobbie and Wilkie, 'The FT-Actuaries Fixed Interest Indices' *JIA*, **105**, page 15, and subsequent notes published in *JIA*.

2

Government funding and the money markets

2.1 Public Sector Borrowing Requirement (PSBR) and Public Sector Debt Repayment (PSDR)

The PSBR is the difference between the expenditure of the public sector and its income. When public sector income exceeds expenditure then there is a negative PSBR or rather a PSDR. It will be described for the UK but the same broad principles apply for other countries. It is necessary for investors to appreciate the importance of the public sector on investment markets, and the factors which lead to changes in the impact of the state funding programme.

In the UK the PSBR is an amalgam of the differences between revenue and expenditure for central government, local government and public sector corporations and industries, adjusted to take account of any lending by central government to local authorities. The PSBR is, therefore, the borrowing requirements of central government, the local authorities and that of public corporations and industries. Creative accounting may lead to a number of problems with examining trends in PSBR and PSDR over time, and a good example at the present time is the substantial privatization programme which is effectively a depletion in the assets held by central government. The proceeds of the asset sales have been used in the past to decrease the PSBR and now to increase the PSDR by including these as part of government revenue.

2.2

The PSBR and PSDR are merely based on the difference between income and expenditure. Each pound the state spends is deemed to have the same effect and there is no differentiation between expenditure on salaries for troops and investment in new infrastructure such as motorways or airports. Similarly, income from asset sales is treated in the same way as tax receipts.

This means that considerable care is needed in evaluating whether the public sector finances as described by the PSBR and PSDR are giving a correct picture. Three key points should be borne in mind:

1 No differentiation is made between current and capital expenditure.
2 No balance sheet is given showing how the value of public sector assets has altered.
3 No allowance is made for the actuarial liabilities which are built up in the state pension scheme.

2.3 Methods of financing the PSBR

The government could borrow this from the commercial banks. If it does this, the amount of the government's overspending (the PSBR) increases the supply of money in the UK, since there is no corresponding reduction in another bank account to compensate.

The government could sell securities in one form or another to the non-bank public. If it does this there is a reduction in the bank balances of the public caused by the purchase of the securities which exactly offsets the increase in the money in the hands of the public as a result of the government overspending. These securities can take the form of gilt-edged stock, Treasury bills, National Savings and tax certificates. In addition the government can fund the PSBR by increasing the notes and coin in circulation, by borrowing from the Bank of England, by borrowing overseas, by operating the public sector debt or the commercial bill markets and by decreasing the official reserves. The PSBR can also be funded by making asset sales and treating the proceeds as revenue.

Over the past few years when the PSBR existed the most important of these items has tended to be net sales of gilt-edged stock, followed by asset sales. The government has been the dominant issuer of stock in domestic fixed interest markets due to the need to complete its funding requirements. Since 1984 there have been increasing levels of privatization of state-owned companies, and in effect the government has switched from funding its deficits by means of fixed-interest securities to funding by equity sales.

If a PSDR exists debt can be repaid and the process is in essence the opposite of funding a PSBR. The government has in the year 1988/89 made substantial repurchases of existing debt, particularly in long-dated gilt issues, and has reduced the average outstanding term of government debt. This process is expected to continue in 1989/90.

2.4 The relationship between PSBR/PSDR and GDP

The PSBR or PSDR is, in effect, the difference between two very large num-

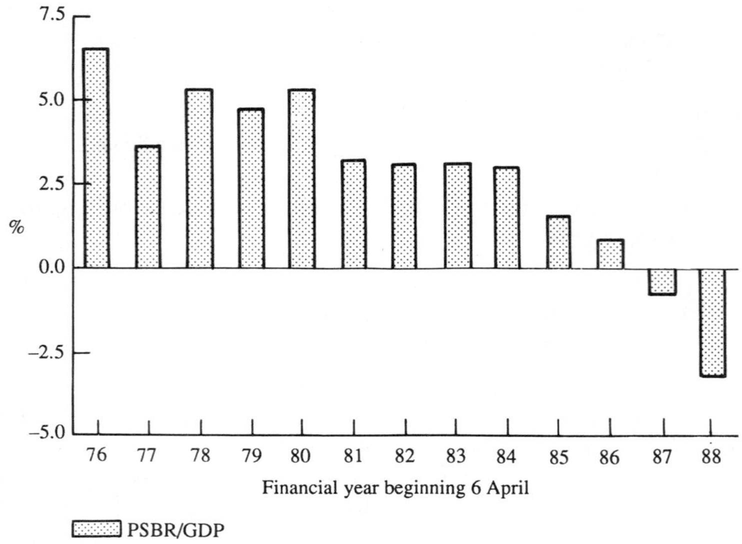

Figure 2.1 *PSBR as percentage of GDP*

bers and is, therefore, difficult to control precisely. What is important though is the size of the PSBR or PSDR in relation to the size of the total economy. If the PSBR or PSDR is only a small percentage of the Gross Domestic Product (GDP), then there should be little difficulty in funding it in the case of a PSBR or spending it if there is a PSDR, whereas if it is large, it is possible that the PSBR funding may crowd out or dominate other economic activity.

Government revenues exceeded expenditure in 1969 and 1970, but since then there have mostly been sizable levels of PSBR. From a nil position in 1970, the PSBR constituted over 7½ per cent of GDP by 1974 and 9½ per cent of GDP by 1975. Since then it has been reduced and in 1987 it was close to 1 per cent of GDP, although it should be remembered that the figure was artificially reduced by the privatization of state industries. In the 1987/88 and 1988/89 financial years, government revenues exceeded expenditure and the Chancellor has said that he intends to maintain this position. The funding of continual PSBRs has meant that National Debt has increased in absolute terms as has the cost of debt servicing. The size of the National Debt has been kept reasonably constant as a percentage of GDP and has usually been within a couple of percentage points of 45 per cent of GDP for the last decade. The debt service cost has been much larger in absolute terms than the PSBR and has been maintained in the range 5–5½ per cent of GDP in recent years. The return to government income exceeding expenditure should result in a reduction in this figure from 1988 onwards and there is now a real prospect of substantial reduction of the National Debt and the costs of debt service.

In the USA, Federal Government expenditure has also exceeded revenue, but when the Federal Budget Deficit (FBD) is expressed as a percentage of Gross National Product (GNP), the figures tend to be lower than the UK equivalent. The highest percentage was 6.3 per cent reached in 1982, and although the FBD has been cited by some as a reason for the October 1987 worldwide stockmarket crash, it was only 3.4 per cent of GNP for the year to September 1987, and on a decreasing trend in real terms.

2.5 Liquidity

Economists have held various views on the impact of liquidity and the money supply on the economy. At times it has been the cornerstone of economic policy – the so-called monetarist view – but today the money supply is one of many important economic variables that are closely monitored and where possible controlled.

There is no single measure of the money supply which can encapsulate monetary conditions and provide a basis for the control of the monetary growth, prices and nominal incomes. This is because of the substitutability between forms of money and liquidity. Various definitions have been used in the past, but those in use in the UK at the end of 1988 are:

M0 Notes and coins in circulation plus banks' till money and bank balances with the Bank of England.

M1 Notes and coins in circulation plus private sector sterling sight deposits.

M3 M1 plus private sector holdings of time deposits with banks and bank certificates of deposit (CDs).

M4 M3 plus building society holdings of M3 categories plus non-bank private sector holdings of building society shares and deposits and building society CDs and time deposits.

M5 M4 plus non-bank non-building society private sector holdings of money market instruments and national savings.

The relationship between money supply, inflation rates and interest rates is complex and not clear cut. However, in simplistic terms, if there is excessive money in the economy, interest rates may be low, but the excess money pumped into the economy may fuel future inflation and could overheat the economy. Conversely, tight monetary conditions may be accompanied by high interest rates.

The government's ability to control the money supply will depend on the way in which it sells or repays securities and how it borrows. If the government sells securities to the (non-bank) public, the amount placed in the public hands by government spending equals the amounts paid by the public for the securities. If the government spending is financed by bank borrowing, the money supply is effectively increased by the amount of borrowing.

Money market operations

2.6 Historical background

In the environment of the 1980s discussions on money market operations must reflect the fact that although the first monetary targets in the UK were set in the mid-1970s the attitude of the authorities has changed considerably. The first monetary targets were informal and specified guidelines and anticipated outturns for broad money growth and domestic credit. These followed a period of rampant inflation. Denis Healey (the Chancellor of the Exchequer) referred to a published target for M3 in his budget statement of April 1976. This was partially a policy response to a crisis of confidence in sterling at a time when discussions were taking place with the International Monetary Fund (IMF).

After the election in May 1979 of the Conservative Government economic and financial policy was changed radically. Significant changes in taxation policy were announced and the money supply became a crucial part of economic and financial management. The stated goal was, and is, a reduction in the rate of inflation. Sterling M3 (£M3) was the initial measure of money. Simultaneously minimum lending rate (MLR) had been raised from 12 per cent to 14 per cent.

In the second Conservative budget of March 1980 the Medium-Term Financial Strategy (MTFS) was introduced. The budget suggested that control of monetary growth was to be linked to control of the size of the Public Sector Borrowing Requirement (PSBR) in relation to GDP. The whole strategy was clearly monetarist relying on the relationship $MV = PT$. Over the years the objectives changed little but the role of monetary policy in their achievement shifted substantially.

By 1981, during a period of sterling weakness, structural changes had begun to have their effect in the money markets. Exchange controls had been abolished in 1979 and the Supplementary Special Deposits scheme known as the 'corset' was abolished finally in June 1980. The scheme imposed penalties on the banking system for expanding their interest-bearing eligible liabilities at a rate faster than that prescribed by the Bank of England. One consequence of the change was that the banks began to lend significantly for residential mortgages. During the same period of 1979–81 the demand for liquid balances as a means of saving appeared to increase and in response to all these factors more stringent targets were introduced not only for M3 but also for M1 and a wide monetary definition called PSL2. By the 1984 and 1985 Budgets M0 had joined M3 as a chosen target indicator. By the 1988 Budget the monetary motorway had extended to favour M4 but by 1989 target ranges were set for M0 only. The wider monetary aggregates have grown for several years at rates well above the rate of inflation, and until late 1988, this has not involved adverse inflationary implications. The narrow monetary aggregates (M0) growth has, however, been kept to single figures.

The main expansionary stimulus in the UK throughout the period of monetary targets has come from bank lending to the private sector. In order to reduce the effect of this on M3 the authorities have on occasions chosen to overfund the PSBR. Overfunding occurs when the non-bank private sector purchases more public sector debt than the size of the PSBR. One consequence of overfunding has been a shortage of liquidity in the money market. The Bank has relieved this shortage by buying bills from discount houses. The ensuing 'bill mountain' had reached a size of £12 billion by December 1986. The government subsequently ceased its policy of overfunding and also benefited from inflow over the foreign exchanges. During the spring of 1987 the Bank was a net seller of bills whereas previously it had been buying in aggressively.

2.7 Treasury bills

Earlier we referred to MLR which was first introduced on 13 October 1972 and replaced Bank Rate. MLR was defined at 0.5 per cent above the average rate of discount for Treasury bills at the most recent tender, rounded to the nearer 0.25 per cent above. On 20 August 1981 it ceased to be used. This reflected a change in the role the Bank played in the money market. The Bank's principal objective is to ensure the clearing banks reach their desired operational balances. The Bank controls the amount of cash in the banking system by selling bills to relieve a cash surplus or buying bills when the system needs cash. The Bank produces a daily forecast of the money market and makes this known to the participants at 9.45 a.m. daily. The estimate cannot be accurate because money at call with discount houses can be withdrawn by the banks at any time up to midday and even after midday the London clearing banks cannot be sure of their final cash position because of the impact of the Town Clearing System. The Bank expresses forecasts in actual figures. They reflect the high likelihood of variation to the total forecast and the contribution of Exchequer flows are described approximately. Thus the expression 'about £200 million' means an initial shortage or surplus in the range '£175–225 million'. If the figures move by more than £25 million outside that range a revised figure will be announced later in the day. The Bank's subsequent actions will reflect the primary objective above and, on occasion, wider government policy. The Bank intervenes taking into account reported positions of the discount houses and the major banks, and the behaviour of short-term interest rates. The latter have become, as we noted above, a central thrust of government policy.

The Bank will intervene in one of three ways. It may buy or sell bills. Treasury bills usually have a life of ninety-one days but often have been issued with other maturities. There is no interest or coupon rate and instead the bills are issued at a discount and redeemed at par. The price to be paid is determined by a weekly tender each Friday and they are issued on each working day by the Bank. The highest tenders are satisfied and a proportion of the discount market's application is allotted. Although not quoted, Treasury Bills are highly marketable British government securities and their return is a key rate of risk-free interest at the very short end of the market. The rate of discount is determined by simple interest.

Once issued, bills are classified as falling into one of four maturity bands.

- Band 1 – up to 14 days
- Band 2 – 15–33 days
- Band 3 – 34–63 days
- Band 4 – 64–91 days

It is thought the Bank keeps Band 1 bills within an unpublished range.

In the last quarter of 1988, a monthly series of ECU Treasury bill tenders commenced with maturities of one month, three months and six months. The sums involved are fairly small and ECU 1.9 billion was outstanding on 13 January 1989. The discount houses have a traditional undertaking to underwrite the whole of the UK Treasury bill tender. The mechanism traditionally enables the government to finance its floating debt. The bill mountain was a temporary aberration showing the flexibility of the UK government to meet contingencies. Broadly speaking, sales of longer-term government debt including gilts to the non-bank private sector have become more important since the mid 1970s than using bills to finance needs. The privatization policy of the Conservative Government has moved the funding policy even more towards the non-bank private sector and the move to a PSDR is likely to keep the size of the Treasury bill issue fairly small.

The second method of Bank intervention is by purchase and resale (repo) agreements. The Bank buys bills but agrees to sell them back to the market at an agreed price in the future. The technique will be used to smooth out a known, future market position, to prevent a particular interest rate structure from becoming too entrenched or when the market is reluctant to sell bills outright because of interest rate expectations. The third form of intervention is through straightforward lending. By refusing to relieve market shortages through bill operations the Bank can force the discount houses to borrow from it.

The interplay between the Bank, the discount houses and the other members of the banking system has evolved gradually. The rules and relationships now in place are very different from those only a decade ago. London's role has developed as a base for international banks. Banks which are short of deposits to match loan commitments may bid for the surplus deposits. Demand for retail funds to lend on for mortgage loans or credit purchases has intensified as the banks and building societies compete more actively for retail savings.

The wholesale money markets have offered a mechanism for acquiring such funds. Since the demise of MLR as a benchmark the London Interbank Offered Rate (LIBOR) is widely used to price money. The banks still refer to their own base lending rates but these too are closely linked to money market rates.

3

The conventional gilts market

Introduction

3.1

The gilt-edged market provides about 70 per cent of Stock Exchange trading measured in terms of value. The UK market in government stocks is very large, having total market holdings of £139.8 billion as at 31 December 1988. There is ease of dealing and marketability even for very large transactions. Turnover in 1988 was £1,129 billion, including intra-market business, with a daily average of £4.46 billion. The market also offers a large number of stocks with great variety in their length of life and in their coupon rates. At the end of 1988 there were forty-seven 'shorts' with durations up to seven years; thirty-four 'mediums' with maturity between seven and fifteen years hence; twenty-two 'longs' with maturity dates up to the year 2017; and six 'undated' stocks which for practical purposes are regarded as irredeemable. There are thirteen index-linked gilts which are explained in Chapter 4. A full list of stocks is given in Table 3.3. Turnover is shown in Table 3.4. All stocks are denominated in sterling and are dealt for cash settlement on the next day after dealing. They carry an absolute guarantee in money terms by Her Majesty's Government.

Operations in the market for government stocks by the authorities play an important part both in the execution of monetary policy and in the management of the National Debt. The growth of funded debt in the UK since 1695 is shown in Figures 3.1 and 3.2. Official operations are conducted by the Bank of England's gilt-edged department.

A number of changes have been made in recent years in the types of British government stock and their methods of issue. In 1973 a convertible stock, offering a short-dated stock with an option to convert at a given date into a long-dated stock, was first issued. Another new type of instrument – Treasury variable rate stock – was introduced in 1977 and was issued on three occasions, with six-monthly interest payments based on the average discount rates for Treasury bills over the preceding six months. This particular experi-

Table 3.1 *Classification of market values for quarter by International Stock Exchange Securities Group at 31 December 1988*

	SE Group	*Listed UK and Irish (£m)*	*Listed Overseas (£m)*	*Total listed (£m)*	*USM (£m)*	*Third market (£m)*
Fixed interest						
British funds	1	139,814.6	–	139,814.6	–	–
Corporation and county stocks	2	434.5	–	434.5	–	–
Public boards	3	101.1	–	101.1	–	–
Commonwealth government etc	4	–	22,085.1	22,085.1	–	–
Foreign bonds	5	32,306.5	63,113.3	95,419.8	–	–
Fixed-interest stocks excluding preference and any stock with an equity element	6	7,570.3	1,063.1	8,633.4	–	–
Preference	7	2,021.1	102.7	2,123.8	0.3	2.5
Convertibles	8	12,909.5	2,856.0	15,765.5	197.5	3.4
Waterworks	9	407.7	–	407.7	–	–
Total fixed interest		**195,565.3**	**89,220.2**	**284,785.5**	**197.8**	**5.9**

Source: The International Stock Exchange

Table. 3.2 *Nominal and market value of all securities at 31 December 1988*

	No. of securities	*Nominal value (£m)*	*Market value (£m)*
Public sector: UK and Ireland			
Short (0–7)	47	53,668.6	53,393.8
Medium (7–15)	34	45,112.8	47,460.3
Others (over 15)	28	26,351.5	25,111.3
Index-linked	13	12,651.7	13,849.2
Sub total British funds etc.	122	137,784.6	139,814.6
Short (0–7)	42	6,437.4	6,376.7
Medium (7–15)	16	2,609.0	2,779.5
Others (over 15)	34	1,622.0	1,678.9
Sub total Irish government	92	10,668.4	10,835.1
Corporation and county stocks – Great Britain and Northern Ireland	106	1,079.3	434.5
Public boards etc. – Great Britain and Northern Ireland	40	158.0	97.4
Public sector: overseas			
Commonwealth and provincial securities	13	7.1	3.7
Commonwealth corp stocks	2	4.0	3.7
Foreign stocks bonds etc.	151	3,583.0	3,728.1
Corporation stocks: foreign	16	1.5	1.3
Sub total public sector	**542**	**153,285.9**	**154,918.4**
Eurobonds			
UK companies	261	23,888.5	23,385.3
Irish companies	6	306.0	306.0
Overseas companies	1,197	85,142.2	84,289.9
Sub total Eurobonds	**1,464**	**109,336.7**	**107,981.2**

Source: The International Stock Exchange

Table 3.3 *British funds*

1989			*Price*	*+ or*	*Yield*	
High	*Low*	*Stock*	*£*	*–*	*Int.*	*Red.*
'Shorts' (Lives up to five years)						
$99\frac{1}{2}$	$97\frac{3}{16}$	Treas 3pc 1989	$99\frac{1}{2}$xd	....	–	–
$99\frac{3}{4}$	$99\frac{1}{32}$	Treas $10\frac{1}{2}$pc 1989	$99\frac{3}{4}$	$+\frac{1}{32}$	10.53	12.38
$99\frac{7}{16}$	$98\frac{21}{32}$	Exch. 10pc 1989	$99\frac{7}{16}$	$+\frac{1}{16}$	10.06	12.14
$99\frac{7}{16}$	$99\frac{1}{32}$	Exch 11pc 1989	$99\frac{13}{32}$	$+\frac{1}{32}$	11.06	12.21
$97\frac{25}{32}$	$95\frac{5}{8}$	Treas 5pc 1986–89	$97\frac{25}{32}$	$+\frac{5}{32}$	5.11	9.98
$99\frac{1}{2}$	$99\frac{1}{16}$	Exch $10\frac{1}{4}$ pcCv '89	$99\frac{1}{4}$xd	....	10.29	11.07
$101\frac{21}{32}$	$100\frac{1}{8}$	Treas 13pc 1990‡‡	$100\frac{11}{16}$	$+\frac{1}{8}$	12.91	11.88
$99\frac{31}{32}$	$98\frac{23}{32}$	Exch 11pc 1990‡‡	$99\frac{13}{32}$	$+\frac{1}{8}$	11.07	11.81
$101\frac{7}{16}$	$99\frac{25}{32}$	Exch. $12\frac{1}{2}$pc 1990	$100\frac{7}{16}$	$+\frac{5}{32}$	12.45	11.96
$93\frac{25}{32}$	$91\frac{5}{16}$	Treas. 3pc 1990	$93\frac{3}{4}$xd	$+\frac{1}{8}$	3.20	9.64
$96\frac{13}{16}$	$95\frac{5}{8}$	Treas $8\frac{1}{4}$pc 1987–90‡‡	$96\frac{3}{8}$	$+\frac{1}{8}$	8.56	11.80
$98\frac{13}{16}$	$95\frac{13}{16}$	Treas. 8pc Cv 1990 ‡‡	$96\frac{1}{2}$	$+\frac{1}{16}$	8.29	11.23
$98\frac{11}{16}$	$97\frac{1}{16}$	Treas. 10pc Cv 1990	$97\frac{3}{4}$	$+\frac{3}{16}$	10.23	11.69
$90\frac{3}{16}$	$87\frac{15}{16}$	Exch $2\frac{1}{2}$pc 1990	$90\frac{5}{32}$xd	$+\frac{7}{32}$	2.77	9.43
$101\frac{23}{32}$	$99\frac{9}{16}$	Treas $11\frac{3}{4}$pc 1991	$100\frac{1}{4}$	$+\frac{1}{8}$	11.72	11.54
$91\frac{7}{8}$	$89\frac{7}{8}$	Funding $5\frac{3}{4}$ pc '87–91‡‡	$91\frac{5}{8}$	$+\frac{1}{8}$	6.28	10.68
$88\frac{1}{2}$	$86\frac{3}{16}$	Treas. 3pc 1991	$88\frac{5}{16}$xd	$+\frac{1}{4}$	3.40	9.48
$100\frac{5}{16}$	$96\frac{13}{16}$	Treas 10pc Cv '91‡‡	$97\frac{3}{4}$	$+\frac{3}{16}$	10.24	11.24
$101\frac{3}{16}$	$98\frac{7}{16}$	Exch. 11pc 1991	$99\frac{3}{16}$	$+\frac{5}{32}$	11.09	11.38
$94\frac{1}{8}$	$91\frac{23}{32}$	Treas. 8pc 1991	$92\frac{19}{32}$	$+\frac{3}{32}$	8.643	11.34
$106\frac{7}{16}$	$102\frac{31}{32}$	Treas $12\frac{3}{4}$pc 1992‡‡	$103\frac{27}{32}$	$+\frac{1}{16}$	12.27	11.03
$99\frac{1}{2}$	$96\frac{1}{2}$	Treas 10pc 1992	$97\frac{3}{8}$	$+\frac{1}{4}$	10.26	11.08
$94\frac{1}{32}$	$91\frac{1}{2}$	Treas. 8pc 1992‡‡	$92\frac{1}{2}$	$+\frac{9}{32}$	8.65	11.06
$100\frac{3}{4}$	$97\frac{11}{16}$	Treas $10\frac{1}{2}$pc Cv 1992‡‡	$98\frac{21}{32}$xd	$+\frac{1}{32}$	10.64	11.01
$85\frac{3}{16}$	$82\frac{1}{4}$	Treas. 3pc 1992	84	$+\frac{3}{8}$	3.57	9.02
$105\frac{27}{32}$	$102\frac{3}{32}$	Exch. $12\frac{1}{4}$pc '92	$103\frac{1}{8}$	$+\frac{1}{32}$	11.87	11.06
$109\frac{3}{4}$	$105\frac{25}{32}$	Exch $13\frac{1}{2}$pc 1992	$106\frac{25}{32}$	$+\frac{1}{32}$	12.63	10.99
$94\frac{3}{16}$	$90\frac{15}{16}$	Treas $8\frac{1}{4}$pc 1993	$92\frac{1}{32}$	$+\frac{1}{32}$	8.96	10.83
$100\frac{7}{32}$	$96\frac{11}{16}$	Treas 10 pc 1993‡‡	$97\frac{23}{32}$	$+\frac{1}{32}$	10.23	10.70
$108\frac{3}{4}$	$104\frac{9}{16}$	Treas $12\frac{1}{2}$pc 1993‡‡	$105\frac{5}{8}$	....	11.84	10.80
$87\frac{3}{4}$	$84\frac{3}{4}$	Funding 6pc 1993‡‡	$85\frac{1}{4}$	$-\frac{1}{16}$	6.99	10.08
$113\frac{3}{4}$	$109\frac{9}{32}$	Treas $13\frac{3}{4}$ pc 1993‡‡	$110\frac{19}{32}$xd	....	12.44	10.75
$94\frac{3}{8}$	$90\frac{25}{32}$	Treas. $8\frac{1}{2}$pc 1994	$91\frac{23}{32}$	$+\frac{3}{32}$	9.26	10.75
$117\frac{25}{32}$	$113\frac{19}{32}$	Treas $14\frac{1}{2}$pc 1994‡‡	$114\frac{11}{16}$	$+\frac{1}{8}$	12.66	10.56
$113\frac{11}{16}$	$109\frac{13}{32}$	Exch $13\frac{1}{2}$pc 1994	$110\frac{5}{16}$	....	12.23	10.75

Table 3.3 — *continued*

1989 High	Low	Stock	*Price* £	+ or −	*Yield* Int.	Red.
Five to fifteen years						
$100\frac{5}{8}$	$96\frac{25}{32}$	Treas. 10pc Ln. 1994‡‡	$97\frac{3}{4}$xd	$+\frac{1}{8}$	10.23	10.57
$110\frac{1}{4}$	$106\frac{1}{32}$	Exch. $12\frac{1}{2}$pc 1994	$106\frac{29}{32}$	....	11.69	10.73
$96\frac{19}{32}$	$92\frac{7}{8}$	Treas 9pc 1994‡‡	$93\frac{3}{4}$xd	....	9.60	10.51
$108\frac{11}{16}$	$104\frac{7}{16}$	Treas 12pc 1995	$105\frac{7}{16}$	....	11.38	10.69
$79\frac{7}{8}$	$74\frac{1}{2}$	Exch 3pc Gas 90–95	$75\frac{3}{4}$xd	$+\frac{1}{2}$	3.96	8.20
$101\frac{11}{16}$	$97\frac{1}{2}$	Exch. $10\frac{1}{4}$pc 1995	$98\frac{1}{2}$	....	10.40	10.57
$113\frac{11}{16}$	$109\frac{5}{32}$	Treas $12\frac{3}{4}$pc 1995‡‡	$110\frac{3}{32}$xd	....	11.58	10.55
$119\frac{15}{32}$	$114\frac{19}{32}$	Treas. 14pc '96	$115\frac{9}{16}$	....	12.12	10.68
$97\frac{1}{2}$	$93\frac{1}{8}$	Treas. 9pc 1992–96‡‡	$94\frac{1}{4}$	....	9.54	10.15
$126\frac{15}{16}$	$121\frac{7}{16}$	Treas $15\frac{1}{4}$pc 1996‡‡	$122\frac{9}{16}$	$+\frac{3}{16}$	12.44	10.59
$117\frac{5}{16}$	112	Exch $13\frac{1}{4}$pc 1996‡‡	$113\frac{3}{16}$xd	$+\frac{3}{16}$	11.71	10.55
$101\frac{7}{16}$	$96\frac{11}{16}$	Conversion 10pc 1996	$97\frac{7}{8}$xd	$+\frac{1}{8}$	10.22	10.40
$118\frac{1}{2}$	113	Treas $13\frac{1}{4}$pc 1997‡‡	$114\frac{1}{4}$	$+\frac{3}{16}$	11.60	10.51
$104\frac{7}{32}$	$99\frac{9}{32}$	Exch $10\frac{1}{2}$pc 1997	$100\frac{7}{16}$	$+\frac{3}{16}$	10.46	10.41
$95\frac{15}{32}$	$90\frac{3}{4}$	Treas $8\frac{3}{4}$pc 1997‡‡	$91\frac{29}{32}$	$+\frac{3}{16}$	9.52	10.20
$128\frac{5}{8}$	$122\frac{7}{8}$	Exch 15pc 1997	$124\frac{1}{16}$	$+\frac{3}{16}$	12.09	10.62
$100\frac{11}{16}$	$95\frac{25}{32}$	Exch $9\frac{3}{4}$pc 1998	97	$+\frac{3}{16}$	10.05	10.27
$84\frac{7}{8}$	$80\frac{1}{2}$	Treas $6\frac{3}{4}$pc 1995–98‡‡	$81\frac{3}{4}$xds	$+\frac{3}{16}$	8.26	9.85
$134\frac{7}{16}$	$128\frac{1}{2}$	Treas $15\frac{1}{2}$pc '98‡‡	$129\frac{13}{16}$	$+\frac{1}{4}$	11.94	10.43
$113\frac{15}{16}$	$108\frac{13}{32}$	Exch. 12pc 1998	$109\frac{3}{4}$xd	$+\frac{7}{32}$	10.93	10.35
$100\frac{3}{4}$	$95\frac{7}{16}$	Treas $9\frac{1}{2}$pc 1999‡‡	$96\frac{7}{8}$	$+\frac{3}{16}$	9.81	10.00
$115\frac{7}{8}$	$110\frac{3}{8}$	Exch. $12\frac{1}{4}$pc 1999	$111\frac{9}{16}$	$+\frac{3}{16}$	10.98	10.34
$105\frac{5}{8}$	$100\frac{13}{32}$	Treas. $10\frac{1}{2}$pc 1999	$101\frac{19}{32}$xd	$+\frac{5}{32}$	10.33	10.23
$104\frac{3}{16}$	$98\frac{15}{16}$	Conversion $10\frac{1}{4}$pc 1999	$100\frac{1}{8}$xd	$+\frac{1}{8}$	10.23	10.22
$94\frac{3}{16}$	$89\frac{3}{16}$	Treas. $8\frac{1}{2}$pc Ln 2000‡‡	$90\frac{9}{16}$	$+\frac{3}{16}$	9.39	9.94
$97\frac{7}{16}$	$92\frac{5}{16}$	Conversion 9pc 2000‡‡	$93\frac{5}{8}$	$+\frac{3}{16}$	9.62	9.97
$122\frac{3}{16}$	$116\frac{3}{16}$	Treas 13pc 2000	$117\frac{7}{16}$	$+\frac{3}{16}$	11.07	10.33
$103\frac{5}{8}$	$98\frac{7}{16}$	Treas 10pc 2001	$99\frac{5}{8}$	$+\frac{1}{8}$	10.03	10.04
$124\frac{13}{32}$	$118\frac{17}{32}$	Treas 14pc '98–01	120xd	$+\frac{1}{8}$	11.66	10.51
$102\frac{3}{16}$	$97\frac{1}{8}$	Conversion $9\frac{3}{4}$pc 2001	$98\frac{3}{8}$	$+\frac{3}{16}$	9.92	9.99
$113\frac{15}{16}$	$108\frac{3}{8}$	Exch 12pc '98–02	$109\frac{11}{16}$	$+\frac{1}{16}$	10.94	10.38
$104\frac{17}{32}$	$99\frac{7}{16}$	Conversion 10pc 2002	$100\frac{11}{16}$	$+\frac{3}{16}$	9.93	9.90
$102\frac{15}{16}$	$97\frac{7}{8}$	Treas $9\frac{3}{4}$pc 2002	$99\frac{1}{8}$	$+\frac{3}{16}$	9.84	9.87
$97\frac{23}{32}$	$92\frac{13}{16}$	Exch 9pc 2002	$94\frac{1}{16}$xd	$+\frac{1}{8}$	9.57	9.80
$126\frac{15}{16}$	$120\frac{7}{8}$	Treas $13\frac{3}{4}$pc 2000–03	$122\frac{1}{16}$	$+\frac{1}{8}$	11.26	10.37
$105\frac{5}{8}$	$100\frac{3}{8}$	Treas 10pc 2003	$101\frac{9}{16}$	$+\frac{1}{8}$	9.85	9.78
$113\frac{15}{32}$	$107\frac{13}{16}$	Treas $11\frac{1}{2}$pc 2001–04	109	$+\frac{1}{8}$	10.55	10.16
Over fifteen years						
$106\frac{9}{16}$	$101\frac{1}{4}$	Treas 10pc 2004	$102\frac{9}{16}$xd	$+\frac{1}{8}$	9.76	9.68
$59\frac{7}{8}$	$57\frac{1}{8}$	Funding $3\frac{1}{2}$pc '99–04	58	$+\frac{1}{16}$	6.05	8.49
$102\frac{15}{16}$	$97\frac{31}{32}$	Conversion $9\frac{1}{2}$pc 2004	$99\frac{5}{16}$	$+\frac{1}{8}$	9.56	9.58
$103\frac{3}{16}$	$98\frac{9}{32}$	Conversion $9\frac{1}{2}$pc 2005	$99\frac{9}{16}$	$+\frac{1}{8}$	9.54	9.55

Table 3.3 — *continued*

1989 High	*1989* Low	*Stock*	*Price* £	*+ or −*	*Yield* Int.	*Yield* Red.
$111\frac{3}{4}$	$106\frac{7}{16}$	Exch $10\frac{1}{2}$pc 2005	$107\frac{11}{16}$	$+\frac{1}{8}$	9.74	9.54
$125\frac{5}{32}$	$119\frac{3}{16}$	Treas $12\frac{1}{2}$pc 2003–05	$120\frac{7}{16}$xd	$+\frac{1}{8}$	10.38	9.82
$90\frac{7}{8}$	$86\frac{3}{8}$	Treas 8pc 2002–06‡‡	$87\frac{9}{16}$	$+\frac{1}{8}$	9.14	9.47
$105\frac{7}{8}$	$101\frac{1}{16}$	Conversion $9\frac{3}{4}$pc 2006	$102\frac{3}{16}$xd	$+\frac{1}{8}$	9.54	9.48
$118\frac{23}{32}$	$113\frac{1}{8}$	Treas $11\frac{3}{4}$pc 2003–07	$114\frac{3}{8}$	$+\frac{1}{8}$	10.27	9.81
$96\frac{7}{32}$	$91\frac{1}{2}$	Treas $8\frac{1}{2}$pc 2007 ‡‡	$92\frac{23}{32}$	$+\frac{5}{32}$	9.17	9.33
$134\frac{5}{8}$	$127\frac{27}{32}$	Treas $13\frac{1}{2}$pc '04–08	$129\frac{3}{16}$	$+\frac{3}{16}$	10.45	9.73
$101\frac{1}{16}$	$96\frac{1}{8}$	Treas 9pc 2008‡‡	$97\frac{7}{16}$	$+\frac{3}{16}$	9.24	9.28
$92\frac{3}{16}$	$87\frac{5}{8}$	Treas 8pc 2009	$88\frac{7}{8}$	$+\frac{3}{16}$	8.99	9.20
$102\frac{1}{16}$	$97\frac{1}{8}$	Conv 9pc Ln 2011 ‡‡	$98\frac{7}{16}$	$+\frac{3}{16}$	9.16	9.18
$68\frac{7}{8}$	$65\frac{5}{16}$	Treas $5\frac{1}{2}$pc 2008–12‡‡	$66\frac{3}{16}$	....	8.33	9.00
$89\frac{7}{8}$	$85\frac{3}{8}$	Treas $7\frac{3}{4}$pc 2012–15‡‡	$86\frac{5}{8}$	....	8.95	9.10
$132\frac{7}{32}$	$126\frac{1}{16}$	Exch 12pc '13–'17	$127\frac{5}{16}$	$+\frac{3}{16}$	9.42	9.17
Undated						
$45\frac{5}{8}$	$42\frac{3}{4}$	Consols 4pc	$43\frac{3}{4}$	....	9.14	–
$40\frac{3}{8}$	$38\frac{1}{8}$	War Loan $3\frac{1}{2}$pc‡‡	$38\frac{13}{16}$xd	....	9.02	–
$70\frac{11}{16}$	$60\frac{7}{8}$	Conv. $3\frac{1}{2}$pc '61 Aft	$66\frac{3}{8}$	....	5.27	–
$41\frac{7}{16}$	$31\frac{15}{16}$	Treas 3pc '66 Aft	$36\frac{1}{2}$	....	8.22	–
$30\frac{1}{4}$	$26\frac{3}{4}$	Consols $2\frac{1}{2}$pc	$27\frac{11}{16}$	$-\frac{1}{8}$	9.03	–
$29\frac{1}{2}$	$26\frac{3}{4}$	Treas. $2\frac{1}{2}$pc	$27\frac{3}{8}$	$-\frac{1}{8}$	9.13	–
Index-linked		**(b)**			**(1)**	**(2)**
$128\frac{9}{16}$	124	Treas 2pc IL '90(84.6)	$128\frac{1}{2}$	$+\frac{1}{8}$	–	2.63
107	$103\frac{7}{16}$	Do. 2pc '92‡‡(97.8)	107	$+\frac{3}{16}$	2.63	3.56
$99\frac{9}{32}$	$94\frac{27}{32}$	Do. 2pc '94(102.9)	99xd	$+\frac{3}{16}$	2.98	3.50
145	$139\frac{1}{8}$	Do. 2pc '96(67.9)	$144\frac{11}{16}$	$+\frac{1}{4}$	3.20	3.57
$124\frac{13}{16}$	$118\frac{7}{16}$	Do. $2\frac{1}{2}$pc '01(78.3)	$123\frac{5}{8}$	$+\frac{3}{8}$	3.40	3.65
$122\frac{19}{32}$	$115\frac{5}{8}$	Do. $2\frac{1}{2}$pc '03(78.8)	$121\frac{1}{4}$xd	$+\frac{3}{8}$	3.44	3.66
$125\frac{13}{16}$	$117\frac{11}{16}$	Do. 2pc '06(69.5)	$124\frac{1}{4}$	$+\frac{5}{16}$	3.47	3.65
$117\frac{7}{8}$	$110\frac{1}{4}$	Do. $2\frac{1}{2}$pc '09(78.8)	$116\frac{1}{4}$xd	$+\frac{5}{16}$	3.48	3.65
$123\frac{1}{32}$	$114\frac{13}{16}$	Do. $2\frac{1}{2}$pc '11(74.6)	$121\frac{1}{16}$	$+\frac{5}{16}$	3.48	3.64
$102\frac{1}{2}$	$95\frac{1}{4}$	Do. $2\frac{1}{2}$pc '13(89.2)	$100\frac{3}{4}$	$+\frac{5}{16}$	3.46	3.61
$110\frac{27}{32}$	$101\frac{1}{8}$	Do. $2\frac{1}{2}$pc '16(81.6)	$108\frac{15}{16}$	$+\frac{5}{16}$	3.43	3.57
$108\frac{5}{8}$	$100\frac{7}{8}$	Do. $2\frac{1}{2}$pc '20(83.0)	$106\frac{5}{8}$	$+\frac{5}{16}$	3.39	3.52
$91\frac{9}{16}$	$84\frac{13}{16}$	Do. $2\frac{1}{2}$pc '24‡‡(97.7)	$89\frac{13}{16}$	$+\frac{5}{16}$	3.36	3.48

Prospective real redemption rate on projected inflation of (1) 10% and (2) 5%. (b) Figures in parentheses show RPI base month for indexing, (ie 8 months prior to issue) and have been adjusted to reflect rebasing of RPI to 100 in January 1987. Conversion factor 3.945. RPI for August 1988: 107.9 and for March 1989. 112.3.

Source: The Financial Times, 4 May, 1989

Table 3.4 *Turnover by security groups – British government*

● **Annually (£m)**

	Short (0–5 years)	**Customer business** *Medium (5–15 years)*	*Others (over 15)*	*Total*	*Total bargains*	**Business days**
*1964	2,718.9	–	2,064.1	4,783.0	112,757	87
1965	10,593.8	–	5,401.8	15,995.6	362,629	255
1966	10,581.4	–	6, 025.5	16,606.9	372,203	254
1967	16,524.2	–	11,447.8	27,972.0	450,527	252
1968	14,502.1	–	6,532.5	21,034.6	392,497	257
1969	11,620.5	–	7,839.3	19,459.8	439,780	257
1970	12,940.2	–	14,409.6	27,349.8	476,203	255
1971	22,061.8	–	25,335.4	47,397.2	530,051	253
1972	15,619.4	–	17,124.0	32,743.4	452,277	254
1973	20,859.1	–	14,551.8	35,410.9	471,418	253
1974	20,060.1	–	18,202.3	38,262.4	536,945	255
1975	41,216.2	–	26,027.9	67,244.1	688,998	254
1976	47,510.4	–	34,413.6	81,924.0	768,150	255
1977	78,888.0	–	56,871.1	135,759.1	979,916	252
1978	62,664.1	–	41,014.7	103,678.8	752,060	252
1979	65,457.6	–	63,491.1	128,948.7	878,829	253
1980	75,177.7	–	76,520.5	151,698.2	996,505	254
1981	75,305.4	–	70,750.2	146,055.6	949,487	252
1982	100,000.5	–	103,388.5	203,389.0	1,076,518	253
1983	105,918.1	–	104,837.4	210,755.5	867,298	252
1984	156,587.0	–	112,092.2	268,679.2	849,248	253
1985	124,019.5	–	137,509.5	261,529.0	757,364	253
1986	186,404.2	–	238,010.6	424,414.8	797,092	253

*Figures for 1964 are Sept-Dec. only.
Figures prior to April 1973 are for London Unit only.
Aggregate of purchases and sales.

	Customer business					**Intra**	
	Short (0–7 yrs)	*Medium (7–15 yrs)*	*Others (over 15 yrs)*	*Total*	*Total bargains*	*Short (0–7 yrs)*	*Medium (7–15 yrs)*
1987	190,066.3	153,719.5	230,692.0	574,477.8	720,944	243,765.2	176,473.3
1988	254,412.0	122,184.1	170,704.7	547,300.8	611,668	271,485.8	153,856.4
● **Quarterly (£m)**							
1987							
Jan–March	45,136.1	40,099.7	58,897.4	144,133.2	207,427	65,778.5	45,431.0
Apr-June	40,516.0	39,501.1	72,625.7	152,642.8	191,384	62,527.5	49,047.8
July–Sept	43,614.6	30,074.7	43,705.5	117,394.8	163,106	40,837.5	34,979.0
Oct–Dec	60,799.6	44,044.0	55,463.4	160,307.0	159,027	64,621.7	47,015.5
1988							
Jan–March	66,461.5	38,774.2	48,155.9	153,391.6	177,663	71,264.9	44,509.3
Apr–June	72,688.3	28,152.1	36,221.3	137,061.7	158,065	72,350.0	33,955.8
Jul–Sept	59,064.8	24,914.2	39,511.6	123,490.6	145,956	67,047.7	37,151.3
Oct–Dec	56,197.4	30,343.6	46,815.9	133,356.9	129,984	60,823.2	38,240.0
● **Monthly (£m)**							
1988							
Jan	19,660.4	12,228.5	12,924.6	44,813.5	54,761	23,206.5	14,756.4
Feb	18,070.2	11,791.3	16,746.0	46,607.5	57,607	20,747.6	13,369.0
March	28,730.9	14,754.4	18,485.3	61,970.6	65,295	27,310.8	16,383.9
April	27,590.0	9,231.4	10,313.6	47,135.0	55,459	26,439.3	11,065.2
May	21,918.2	7,055.7	10,284.6	39,258.5	50,174	21,099.6	9,055.9
June	23,180.1	11,865.0	15,623.1	50,668.2	52,432	24,811.1	13,834.7
July	20,297.8	7,637.0	13,868.3	41,803.1	57,340	23,128.4	11,386.1
Aug	20,273.8	7,253.8	12,113.4	39,641.0	47,504	20,871.7	11,134.2
Sept	18,493.2	10,023.4	13,529.9	42,046.5	41,112	23,047.6	14,631.0
Oct	19,127.7	10,944.1	19,136.8	49,208.6	47,908	22,363.5	12,053.8
Nov	18,827.2	9,987.4	16,175.0	44,989.6	46.418	21,047.4	16,040.3
Dec	18,242.5	9,412.1	11,504.1	39,158.7	35,658	17,412.3	10,145.9

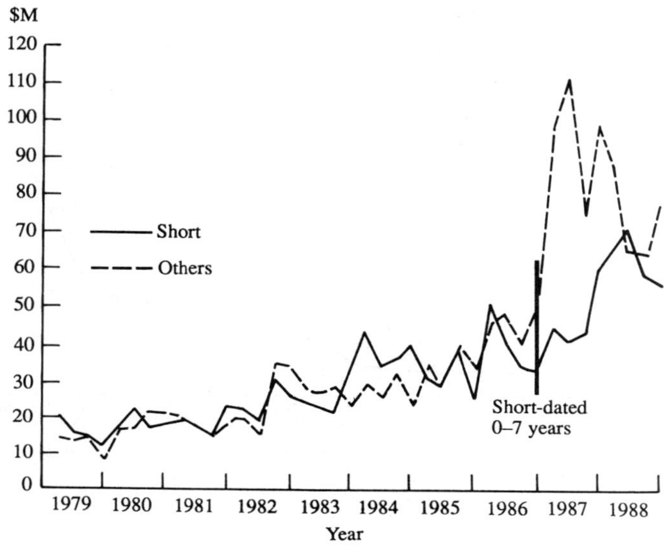

Market						
Others (over 15 yrs)	*Total*	*Total bargains*	*Total value*	*Total bargains*	*Business days*	
181,135.1	601,373.6	396,731	1,175,851.4	1,117,675	253	1987
156,468.2	581,810.4	299,036	1,129,111.2	910,704	253	1988
						1987
44,485.7	155,695.2	113.909	299,828.4	321,336	63	Jan–March
48,763.6	160,338.9	103,956	312,981.7	295,340	61	Apr–June
40,706.4	126,522.9	84,349	243,917.7	247,455	65	July–Sept
47,179.4	158,816.6	94,517	319,123.6	253,544	64	Oct–Dec
						1988
46,212.2	161,986.4	92,901	315,378.0	270,564	64	Jan–March
36,626.1	142,931.9	72,715	279,993.6	230,780	61	Apr–June
34,961.9	139,160.9	66,944	262,651.5	212,900	65	July–Sept
38,668,0	137,731.2	66,476	271,088.1	196,460	63	Oct–Dec
						1988
12,499.6	50,462.5	31,095	95,276.0	85,856	20	Jan
17,281.7	51,398.3	30,396	98,005.8	88,003	21	Feb
16,430.9	60,125.6	31,410	122,096.2	96,705	23	March
11,542.4	49,046.9	25,204	96,181.9	80,663	19	April
10,426.5	40,582.0	21,192	79,840.5	71,366	20	May
14,657.2	53,303.0	26,319	103,971.2	78,751	22	June
10,734.4	45,248.9	22,084	87,052.0	79,424	21	July
13,650.9	45,656.8	22,218	85,297.8	69,722	22	Aug
10,576.6	48,255.2	22,642	90,301.7	63,754	22	Sept
14,834.5	49,251.8	25,752	98,460.4	73,660	21	Oct
12,623.3	49,711.0	22,643	94,700.6	69,061	22	Nov
11,210.2	38,768.4	18,081	77,927.1	53,739	20	Dec

Source: The International Stock Exchange

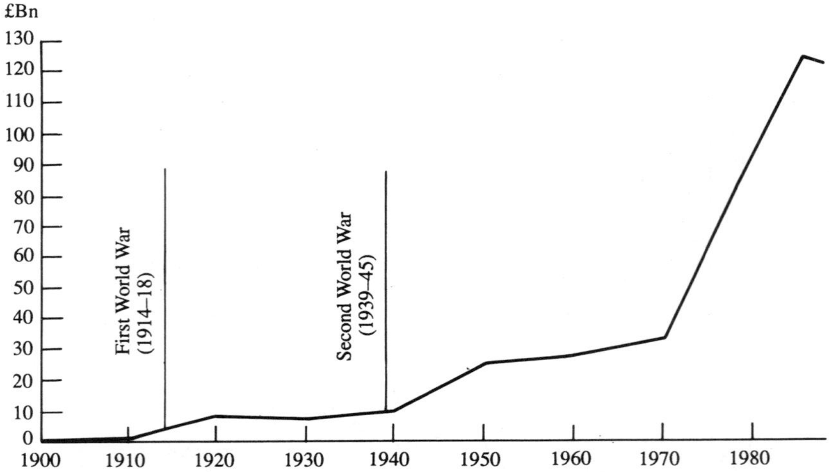

Figure 3.1 *Growth of funded debt 1900–88*
Source: James Capel Gilts Limited

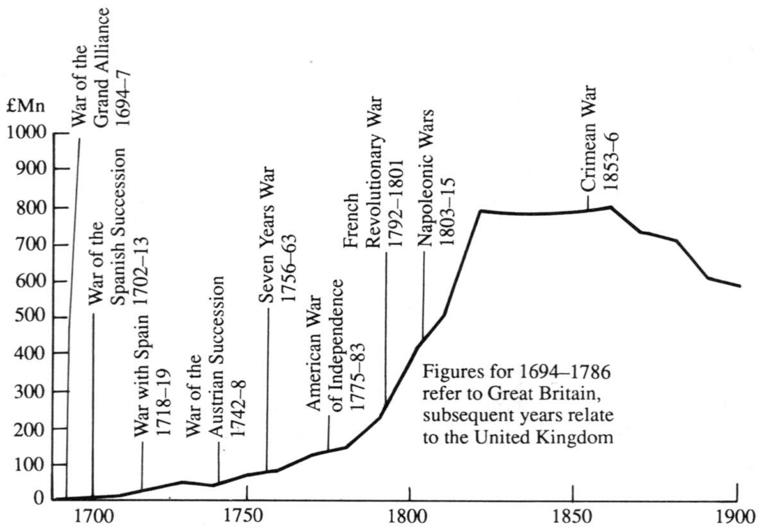

Figure 3.2 *Growth of funded debt 1694–1899*
Source: James Capel Gilts Limited

ment was not a success. In 1977 the government adapted their issue technique to provide for only part of the subscription money for a new issue to be paid at the time of application, with the balance being payable in instalments timed by reference to the government's expected financing needs. Partly-paid stocks have since been used frequently.

Since March 1979 many issues of stocks to the public have been made by tender. A further innovation has been the introduction of 'taplets' which allow the Bank of England to issue small further issues of existing stocks. This method has also been used for issues of new stocks. In May 1987 the Bank of England held its first auction of short-dated gilts and there have been further issues since.

The methods of issue of gilt-edged securities are discussed in more detail in Chapter 9.

In 1981 the government issued the first of its index-linked stocks. Initially, only approved pension funds were allowed to hold this stock but since 1982 there has been no limitation on the status of the holder. These have many of the features of conventional stocks but the coupons payable and the redemption values are linked to movements in the Retail Price Index. They offer a yardstick for measuring the rate of real return (in price terms) for a risk-free asset in the UK, and are discussed further in Chapter 4.

The main features of UK government or quasi-government quoted borrowings as investment can be summarized as follows:

1 They are highly marketable when compared with most other securities and the difference between buying and selling prices is small. Figure 3.3 shows the average number of daily bargains since 1970. Figure 3.4 shows recent turnover including intramarket dealings. Figure 3.5 shows the average daily value of bargains.
2 They comprise a wide range of stocks to suit most investors' requirements in terms of life and coupon.
3 Dealing costs are low and it is usually possible to deal in large size without affecting the market.
4 They may bear tax or statutory privileges for investors non-resident in the UK. In particular, overseas investors may be able to receive coupons tax free on certain stocks. Gains from gilts are not subject to capital gains tax by UK residents.
5 They have a high degree of security in monetary terms. This is not always the case, however, for UK local authorities or public boards.
6 There is an efficient 'stock lending/borrowing' system available to market makers through the 'money-brokers' who are regulated by the Bank of England.
7 Settlement is straightforward, particularly since the introduction of the Central Gilts Office (CGO).

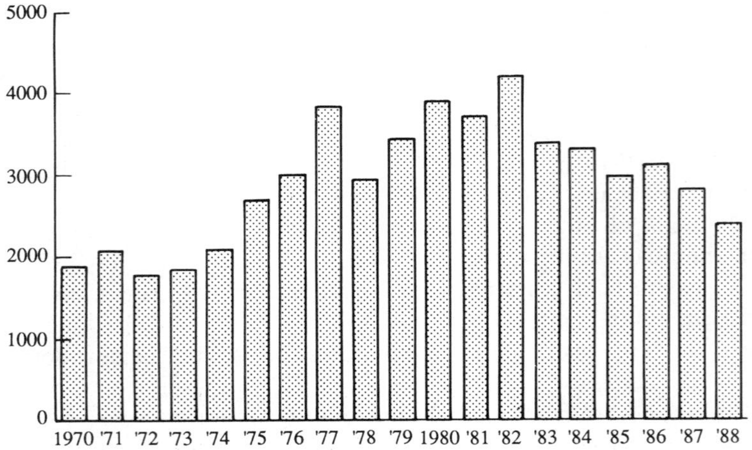

Figure 3.3 *Government stocks – average number of daily bargains*

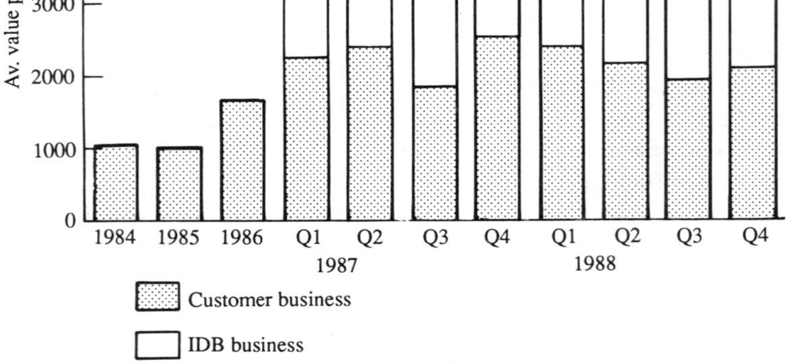

Figure 3.4 *Gilt market – average daily turnover*

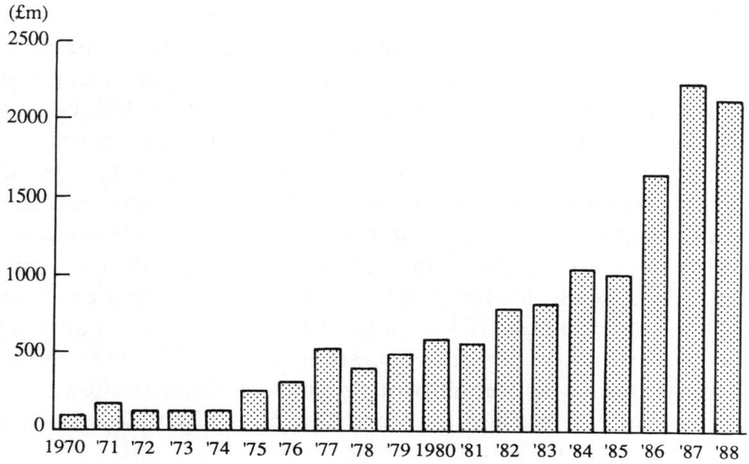

Figure 3.5 *Government stocks – average daily value of bargains*

3.2 Titles

Most modern issues carry the name 'Treasury' or 'Exchequer'. Sometimes names indicate the purpose of the stock, e.g. 'Conversion' is a stock which has been offered by way of conversion from a previous issue. A particular group of stocks was created on the nationalization of certain industries and were named after those industries. For example, 'British Transport' is one such relic which disappeared in 1988. Recent privatization issues have reversed the policies of the past and the ordinary shares issued bear equally graphic titles, such as 'British Gas'. Other stock names in common use are 'funding', 'redemption', 'consols' and the large issue known as 'War Loan'. Most issues are termed 'stocks' which are not usually available in bearer form, whereas a 'loan' is normally obtainable in bearer form.

Apart from a name the simplest gilt-edged stocks have in their description a nominal interest rate, called the coupon, and a redemption date. Undated stocks do not bear a redemption date. They have been in existence for many years and the government's obligation is the payment of interest. There is an option to repay at par at any time on giving due notice. It is unlikely that such an option would be exercised as long as the general level of interest rates remains above the nominal rates on the stocks, which are in the range of $2\frac{1}{2}$ to 4 per cent. Their total market value is only around £1 billion.

3.3 Interest

The nominal rate of interest represents the annual amount of interest paid per £100 of nominal stock. In the UK it is the practice to pay equal amounts of interest semi-annually on fixed dates six months apart e.g. 15 January and 15 July. The one exception to this rule is Consolidated $2\frac{1}{2}$ per cent Stock which pays four coupons of $\frac{5}{8}$ per cent on the fifth day of January, April, July and October each year. Incidentally, the word 'coupon' is an anachronism, referring to the time when in order to receive a dividend it was necessary to cut (French – *couper*) a coupon from the bond itself and present it to a paying agent in order to obtain interest due. Some other markets still use this mechanism of 'clipping' interest. The word 'gilt-edged' is also archaic alluding to the days when bills were described figuratively as such if of the best quality. This was at a time when certain writing paper or books could have been literally gilt-edged. Gilt-edged is a word now used in the UK lexicon as a synonym for the phrase 'safe as the Bank of England'.

Stocks which are newly issued and/or in partly-paid form may not necessarily pay the standard rate of interest on the first due date and in such cases it will be made known that a special payment will be made.

The Chancellor of the Exchequer announced on 28 February 1985 provisions which altered significantly the whole basis of taxation of income derived from gilt-edged stocks and indeed many other fixed interest stocks. The full provisions came into effect on 28 February 1986. The new arrangements apply to residents and to non-residents of the UK if they are trading in the UK through a bank or agency.

In order to ensure prompt payment of dividends to stockholders, the Bank of England 'closes the books' for qualification for dividends five weeks and two days before the payment date. At this point the stock goes 'ex-dividend' or 'ex-interest'. In the three weeks prior to going 'ex-dividend' stocks, except for stocks with less than five years to maturity and War Loan, can be traded in both 'cum dividend' form and 'special ex-dividend' form. For example, $5\frac{1}{2}$ per cent Treasury 2008/12 has interest dates of 10 March and 10 September. For the 10 March payment it goes 'ex-dividend' about 2 February and can be dealt 'special ex' or 'cum' in the days 12 January to 1 February.

Until 28 February 1986 the whole of the consideration of any gilt-edged bargain was considered to be a capital item. Only the actual dividends received were treated as income for the purposes of taxation. From that date interest on gilt-edged securities has been treated as accruing on a day-to-day basis between interest payment dates. Thus only the 'clean price', that is market price less accrued interest, is used in determining the capital value of a transaction. Income tax is now levied on the sum of dividends received plus the gross accrued interest at the date of sales minus the gross accrued interest at the date of purchase.

Under the old system, because of the 'cum' and 'special ex' period, it was possible for certain institutions to artificially generate 'dividends' which were actually capital items and subject to a lower rate of tax than income at that time. The Chancellor thus plugged a loophole in gilt taxation but was also able to announce later a total abolition of capital gains tax on gilts and most other fixed-interest stocks on 2 July 1986.

When going 'ex' a gilt-edged stock should theoretically fall by a proportion of the instalment of gross coupon next due. In practice, the 'clean price' in ex-dividend form will be a small fraction *higher* than the previous day's cum dividend clean price.

This increase in price can be explained theoretically as the sum of two components. The first is the value of the interest on the net dividend discounted from the date of dividend payment back to the ex-dividend date. The second component is the present value to gross funds of the interest on the tax deducted at source from the dividend that they will eventually reclaim. Market-makers trade gross and these considerations are not insignificant when dealing in huge sums. Similar logic can be applied to pension funds.

In summary, stocks quote a price which is the 'clean price'. Accrued interest is added to the consideration unless the stock is ex-dividend in which case accrued interest is deducted from the clean price.

3.4 Redemption dates

The date on which a stock is due to be repaid by the government is called its redemption date. These range from the current year to 2017. Some stocks have a single date for redemption, e.g Treasury 10 per cent 2001. Others have a spread of dates and providing the government gives the necessary notice, often three months, it may redeem at any time between the two stated dates e.g. Treasury $5\frac{1}{2}$ per cent 2008/12 may be redeemed between 2008 and 2012. All conventional stocks are redeemable at par, which is £100 for £100 nominal of stock. It is conventional to assume in yield calculations that if the clean price is under par the stock will be redeemed at its latest date. This is because the government would have to borrow at more expensive terms to replace it. If the clean price stands above par it can be assumed that a stock will be redeemed at the first opportunity because the government could borrow more cheaply. A change in general interest rate levels will alter assumptions concerning the life of a stock and care should be exercised in calculations. Coupons on mediums and longs with spread redemption dates vary from 3 per cent to 14 per cent and, given that interest rates in future are very likely to lie between these extremes, the assumed redemption date is not insignificant. This would be particularly so if the calculations were being performed for matching or immunization purposes. The practice of issuing stocks with spread redemption dates has been discontinued in recent years.

The list of stocks in Table 3.3 shows stocks varying in 'length' from a few months to nearly thirty years as well as the undated issues. The coupons vary from $2\frac{1}{2}$ per cent to $15\frac{1}{2}$ per cent. There is thus a great variety of stocks available for institutional investors wishing to match particular liabilities. Short-dated stocks are held principally by investors such as discount houses, banks and building societies which need 'short' assets to match liabilities or potential liabilities. Some institutions are obliged to observe liquidity rules in relation to their reserve assets and such assets are typically short-term money instruments including short-dated gilts.

Mediums, longs and undateds suit investors with longer horizons. These investors will include life assurance companies and pension funds. In particular, they favour ultra-longs with maturity dates more than twenty years away. Only a few such stocks exist including a recent tap stock, Treasury 9 per cent Loan 2008 and the longest dated stock Exchequer 12 per cent 2013/17. The longer-dated stocks have become popular with more speculative investors. The higher response of these stocks to a change in overall market yields and thus the potential for capital gain in a rising market have made them very popular. Tap stocks and recent issues are favoured especially because marketability is high, market-makers' quotes are narrow and issues in partly-paid form offer increased gearing (exposure to price movements is enhanced per pound of investment).

3.5 Taxation

There is a large number of stocks which are exempt from all UK taxation to non-residents of the UK. The advantage is that dividends are paid gross, whereas normally tax at the basic income tax rate would be deducted at source. War Loan (technically War $3\frac{1}{2}$ per cent 1952 or after) is unique in that dividends are paid gross to all holders wherever resident.

Capital gains on gilts are normally free of tax following the changes (in July 1986) referred to earlier.

Individual investors who pay income tax will have a natural preference for lower coupon stocks because more of the redemption yield is in the form of tax-free capital gain.

Institutions classified as dealers in securities including banks, building societies, discount houses and general insurance funds are taxed at the full corporation tax rate on UK income and capital gains. They will, therefore, be indifferent between income and capital gains. Pension funds and charities are not normally subject to taxation on income or capital gains and will, therefore, be indifferent between them. Tax deducted at source can be reclaimed by them from the Inland Revenue.

Life assurance companies and unit trusts are taxed on income but are not usually liable to tax on capital gains on gilts. They would, therefore, normally prefer medium coupon stocks. Private investors bid low coupon stocks to such expensive levels that they are unattractive to institutions.

Different preferences for lower or higher coupons and differing tax bases leads to distortions in gross redemption yields. Lower yields are usually the case for low coupon stocks, higher coupons having the higher yield. Further details of the tax levels and preferences for various sorts of security are given in Section 9.25.

3.6 Futures, options and warrants

3.6.1 FUTURES

The London International Financial Futures Exchange (LIFFE, pronounced to rhyme with wife) opened in September 1982 and traded its first gilt contract in November.

It was one of the first group of contracts to be traded and was based upon a nominal 12 per cent (now 9 per cent) twenty year stock. In September 1985 a short-dated gilt-edged contract ($4\frac{1}{2}$ year 10 per cent coupon) was introduced, together with traded options based upon the long gilt futures contract. Since then a medium contract has been issued (7–10 years, 9 per cent coupon).

Over a similar period the Stock Exchange has introduced traded option contracts on a short gilt (Treasury $11\frac{3}{4}$ per cent 1991), a medium (Treasury 12 per cent 1995) and a long gilt (Treasury $11\frac{3}{4}$ per cent 2003/07). Traded options in gilts were abandoned in February 1989 due to insufficient demand.

In 1987 a number of US investment banks introduced warrants based on UK gilts.

A gilts future is based on a gilt-edged security and such a contract is quite simply an obligation to buy or sell the underlying gilt at a specified price on a specified future date. The market in the underlying gilt is called the *cash* market to distinguish it from the *futures* market. A relationship must obviously exist between the cash market and the futures market and, while mathematically options pricing theory is fairly abstruse, the simplest way of understanding the physical relationship is to consider the day of delivery. On delivery day, sellers of futures have the option of buying back their contracts or of delivering the underlying gilt to those with open bought positions. The option available to the seller on delivery ensures eventual convergence between the cash price and the futures price.

Futures and options within LIFFE are traded under the system of open outcry. Traders meet in trading areas known as 'pits' and by 'crying out' bids or offers a bargain is eventually struck between a willing buyer and a willing seller. Bargains are processed quickly and information on prices struck is published electronically through proprietary informations systems such as Reuters or Telerate. Transactions are cleared through the International

Commodities Clearing House (ICCH) for the LIFFE trades and through the London Options Clearing House (LOCH) for Stock Exchange bargains. The clearing houses accept responsibility for settlement from buyers and sellers once trades have been agreed, which reduces credit risk. The clearing house is also responsible for maintaining the margin system. Dealing on margin means that only a small proportion of the quoted futures price needs to be paid for by the customer. An 'initial margin' provides a cushion against potential losses. 'Variation margin' covers significant moves after the original bargain is struck. ICCH is not only responsible for collecting and holding payments but it also determines initial margin levels.

The use of futures markets and options on both cash gilts and gilts futures is a phenomenon in the UK of the 1980s. Many of the ideas were imported from North America and in their original home were used in hedging strategies. Financial futures are widely believed to improve liquidity in markets and the long-gilt contract is exceptionally liquid. Because it is possible to trade in such instruments on margin there is, of course, a speculative nature to the market which causes on occasions much volatility. The mathematics of futures and options is covered in Chapter 10. We discuss below, however, the purpose of such instruments in investment management.

Clearly it is the unique qualities of gilt futures which the 'cash' market does not have which suggests futures uses. Earlier we referred to the attractions of volatile, long-dated gilts to speculators who find such stocks attractive in a rising market. Because futures are dealt on margin they are even more highly geared (leveraged in US parlance) and are thus even more attractive to speculators. Further advantages are immediately apparent in that the futures market offers an opportunity to sell speculatively in a falling market whereas the cash market may offer more limited scope to do so.

A more temperate long-term investor may use the option facility of futures markets by pre-investing known future cash flows at current yields for a modest outlay. The contrary strategy to this is to use the futures market to 'sell' stock currently held without, in fact, disposing of the cash holding. This might be advantageous because of taxation reasons or other portfolio constraints. This is one example of a hedging strategy. Hedging strategies generally combine the purchase of two investments with negative correlation of return. Theoretically, when a fully-hedged strategy is adopted the total return from the combined investment should be zero. In the simple case above the strategy could be used to 'insure' a fund from a fall in capital values during a period of rising interest rates. A detailed examination of hedging strategies is beyond the scope of this volume.

3.6.2 OPTIONS

Futures contracts in any commodity theoretically are subject to extreme price movements in either direction. Options in the gilt market are a derivative of futures but, as with options in equities, have one crucial difference. It is mandatory for a futures dealer to deliver stock or buy back the contract. An option is the right, but not the obligation, to exercise the option to buy or sell stock on a given date or to allow the option to lapse. Thus there is no unlimited liability. The most the options holder can lose is his options premium.

3.6.3 WARRANTS

In July 1987 several investment houses launched warrants in the gilt market. Warrants are securities and some investors prohibited from dealing in options are able to deal in warrants. These new instruments allow the investor to protect himself against falls in the market, either by buying a put warrant, or by the strategy of buying a call warrant and selling the future or cash market.

3.7 Settlement

The settlement of gilt-edged stock bargains has been simplified recently through the introduction of the Central Gilts Office (CGO) which was established within the Bank of England and is responsible jointly to the Bank and the Stock Exchange. The participants using the CGO are market-makers (known until 1986 as jobbers), interdealer brokers, Stock Exchange money-brokers, discount houses, certain banks, the International Commodities Clearing House (ICCH) and various institutions, such as pension funds and insurance companies. The CGO scheme provides a computerized settlement system with no stock certificates.

Generally, settlements of gilt-edged transactions are for cash, which means on the next working day. Thus a buyer must have sterling available to pay his market-maker or broker before the close of banking hours on the working day after the purchase. Deferred settlement is permitted if arranged at the time of dealing but for specific reasons only and within defined limits. The CGO system works with users having access to a visual display unit and participants have an assured payments system which means that all payments are backed by bank guarantees. The system works on the basis that if stock is transferred between two CGO participants, then there is an equivalent cash payment also between the accounts of the two participants. Participants in this sytem have until 11.15 a.m. each morning to advise each other of the stock that will be delivered that day. Buyers and sellers who do not use the computerized system use a standard stock transfer form and associated certificate. In practice, many contingencies occur which necessitate special settlement procedures. In particular, stock may be either in bearer form, in the form of registered stock or in allotment letter form following a new issue.

3.8 Brokers' lists

Pages 47–49 show the format of one example of a gilt list as used by institutions in the marketplace. One side only is illustrated. Note the reference to 'volatility' of the stock in the first column. Net yields are also quoted. There is a considerable amount of extra information beyond that illustrated in Table 3.3. The list is issued daily.

Greenwell Montagu Gilt-Edged
Member of The International Stock Exchange
Member of The Securities Association
10 Lower Thames Street, London EC3R 6AE
Telephone 01-260 0373 Telex 27783 GMGILT G
Facsimile (Groups 3, 2 & 1) 01-220 7113
TOPIC SERVICE : Key * 2016#
REUTER MONITOR : MGMA TELERATE : 22491
KNIGHT RIDDER : PAGES 182 - 195

BRITISH FUNDS

Tuesday 3rd January, 1989

LONG GILT FUTURE MAR 88	95–14	
Exchange Rates	U.S. 1.8095	D.M. 3.2101
£ Index =	Old = 77.8, New = 97.6	
Treasury Bills (3 mth)	30 Dec	6 Jan
Allotted (£m)	100	100
Maturities (£m)	100	100
Minimum Price		
Average Rate		
Equivalent Yield		
Current R.P.I. Nov 110.0	L.C.B. Base Rate 13%	

Compound Interest Volatility * *	Amount of Loan in Millions	STOCK		Interest dates	Next XD Date (and First Dealing Day)	Gross Accrued Interest (Days)	Price Changes Since 23/12/88 %	Previous day	CLEAN PRICE	Yield	Redemption Yield	1 Tick Variation in price	NET YIELDS Cap Nil Inc. at 35.0	Cap at 35 Inc. at 35.0
0.034	2,250	**TREASURY 11½%**	22 Feb 1989	*22 F.A.*	16 Jan	4.253 (+135)	+0.18	–	**99–22**	**11.536**	**12.965**	.2278	**9.211**	**8.427**
0.070	854	**TREAS. CONV. 9½%**	18 Apr 1989	*18 A.O.*		2.030 (+78)	+0.19	–	**99–01**	**9.593**	**12.810**	.1124	**9.504**	**8.326**
0.087	500	**TREASURY 3%**	15 May 1989	*15 M.N.*		.411 (+50)	−0.08	–	**97–06**	**3.087**	**11.138**	.0927	**10.050**	**7.240**
0.105	1,400	**TREASURY 10½%**	14 June 1989	*14 J.D.*		.604 (+21)	+0.08	−1	**99–02**	**10.599**	**12.700**	.0750	**9.002**	**8.255**
0.132	2,400	**EXCHEQUER 10%**	1 Aug 1989	*1 F.A.*		.767 (−28)	+0.10	−2	**98–22xd**	**10.133**	**12.627**	.0597	**9.027**	**8.207**
0.172	2,000	**EXCHEQUER 11%**	29 Sept 1989	*29 M.S.*	20 Feb	2.923 (+97)	+0.05	−1	**99–04**	**11.097**	**12.226**	.0459	**8.352**	**7.938**
0.185	601	**TREASURY 5%**	15 Oct 1986-9	*15 A.O.*		1.110 (+81)	−0.08	–	**95–28**	**5.215**	**10.602**	.0441	**8.795**	**6.905**
0.201	174	**EXCH. CONV. 10¼%**	15 Nov 1989	*15 M.N.*		1.404 (+50)	+0.17	–	**99–04**	**10.340**	**11.310**	.0392	**7.700**	**7.349**
0.235	1,000	**†TREASURY 13%**	15 Jan 1990	*15 J.J.*		.392 (−11)	−0.19	−3	**101–07xd**	**12.843**	**11.721**	.0328	**7.211**	**7.614**
0.254	1,400	**†EXCHEQUER 11%**	12 Feb 1990	*12 F.A.*	6 Jan	4.370 (+145)	−0.22	−3	**99–07**	**11.087**	**11.700**	.0310	**7.848**	**7.606**
0.275	1,250	**EXCHEQUER 12½%**	22 Mar 1990	*22 M.S.*	13 Feb	3.562 (+104)	−0.22	−4	**100–27**	**12.395**	**11.737**	.0282	**7.380**	**7.615**
0.315	550	**TREASURY 3%**	8 May 1990	*8 M.N.*		.468 (+57)	+0.12	+2	**91–14**	**3.281**	**9.990**	.0271	**8.868**	**6.554**
0.329	600	**†TREASURY 8¼%**	15 Jun 1987-90	*15 J.D.*		.452 (+20)	−0.12	–	**96–06**	**8.577**	**11.182**	.0247	**8.214**	**7.297**
0.349	1,000	② **†TREAS. CONV. 8%**	16 July 1990	*16 J.J.*		.263 (−12)	−0.38	−3	**96–21xd**	**8.277**	**10.450**	.0232	**7.576**	**6.819**
0.402	1,887	**TREAS. CONV. 10%**	25 Oct 1990	*25 A.O.*		1.945 (+71)	−0.24	−4	**97–24**	**10.230**	**11.394**	.0199	**7.843**	**7.422**
0.441	500	**EXCHEQUER 2½%**	22 Nov 1990	*22 M.N.*		.295 (+43)	+0.12	–	**88–04**	**2.837**	**9.539**	.0201	**8.589**	**6.297**
0.438	2,200	**TREASURY 11¾%**	10 Jan 1991	*10 J.J.*		.193 (−6)	−0.18	−4	**100–25xd**	**11.659**	**11.312**	.0177	**7.218**	**7.346**
0.507	400	**†FUNDING 5¾%**	5 Apr 1987-91	*5 A.O.*	1 Mar	1.434 (+91)	+0.10	–	**90–08**	**6.371**	**10.738**	.0171	**8.589**	**7.070**
0.545	400	**TREASURY 3%**	13 May 1991	*13 M.N.*		.427 (+52)	+0.06	–	**86–16**	**3.468**	**9.541**	.0166	**8.390**	**6.320**
0.542	645	① **†TREAS. CONV. 10%**	12 July 1991	*12 J.J.*		.219 (−8)	−0.31	−8	**98–18xd**	**10.146**	**10.685**	.0146	**7.147**	**6.959**
0.590	1,550	**EXCHEQUER 11%**	25 Oct 1991	*25 A.O.*		2.140 (+71)	−0.13	−3	**99–27**	**11.017**	**11.062**	.0132	**7.201**	**7.183**
0.631	1,350	**TREASURY 8%**	10 Dec 1991	*10 J.D.*		.548 (+25)	−0.29	−3	**92–22**	**8.631**	**10.978**	.0134	**8.044**	**7.207**
0.624	900	**†TREASURY 12¾%**	22 Jan 1992	*22 J.J.*		.629 (−18)	−0.28	−7	**104–30xd**	**12.150**	**10.814**	.0119	**6.483**	**6.986**
0.655	1,600	**TREASURY 10%**	21 Feb 1992	*21 F.A.*	16 Jan	3.726 (+136)	−0.33	−6	**97–21**	**10.240**	**10.880**	.0122	**7.334**	**7.092**
0.695	1,550	**†TREASURY 8%**	13 Apr 1992	*13 A.O.*	7 Mar	1.819 (+83)	−0.46	−7	**92–09**	**8.669**	**10.848**	.0122	**7.910**	**7.126**
0.689	1,288	**†TREAS.CONV.10½%**	7 May 1992	*7 M.N.*		1.668 (+58)	−0.32	−6	**99–04**	**10.593**	**10.813**	.0114	**7.118**	**7.035**
0.783	500	**TREASURY 3%**	11 Jun 1992	*11 J.D.*		.197 (+24)	+0.44	–	**82–12**	**3.642**	**9.085**	.0121	**7.906**	**6.067**
0.727	1,350	**EXCHEQUER 12¼%**	25 Aug 1992	*25 F.A.*	19 Jan	4.430 (+132)	−0.19	−4	**104–04**	**11.765**	**10.823**	.0103	**6.651**	**6.997**
0.730	1,757	**EXCHEQUER 13½%**	22 Sept 1992	*22 M.S.*	13 Feb	3.847 (+104)	−0.19	−4	**108–04**	**12.486**	**10.768**	.0099	**6.275**	**6.925**
0.845	800	**TREASURY 8¼%**	18 Feb 1993	*18 F.A.*	12 Jan	3.142 (+139)	−0.25	−4	**92–10**	**8.937**	**10.576**	.0100	**7.550**	**6.948**

0.851	1,850	†**TREASURY 10%**	15 Apr 1993	*15 A.O.*		2.219 (+81)	−0.18	−3	**98−12**	**10.165**	**10.467**	.0093	**6.935**	**6.817**
0.860	1,100	†**TREASURY 12½%**	14 July 1993	*14 J.J.*		.342 (−10)	−0.25	−5	**106−17xd**	**11.734**	**10.650**	.0085	**6.443**	**6.865**
0.981	600	†**FUNDING 6%**	15 Sept 1993	*15 M.S.*	**6 Feb**	1.825 (+111)	+0.18	−	**86−02**	**6.972**	**9.762**	.0093	**7.465**	**6.477**
0.899	1,250	†**TREASURY 13¾%**	23 Nov 1993	*23 M.N.*		1.582 (+42)	−0.19	−4	**111−18**	**12.325**	**10.640**	.0078	**6.152**	**6.817**
0.994	1,800	**TREASURY 8½%**	3 Feb 1994	*3 F.A.*		.699 (−30)	−0.26	−5	**91−27xd**	**9.255**	**10.619**	.0086	**7.485**	**6.983**
0.928	600	†**TREASURY 14½%**	1 Mar 1994	*1 M.S.*	23 Jan	4.966 (+125) 2.225 (−56)	−0.27	−4	**115−06** 115−10xd	**12.588** 12.575	**10.594** 10.578	.0073 .0073	**5.956** 5.940	**6.760** 6.753
0.959	1,100	**EXCHEQUER 13½%**	27 Apr 1994	*27 A.O.*		2.552 (+69)	−0.16	−3	**111−05**	**12.145**	**10.679**	.0073	**6.264**	**6.845**
1.024	1,400	†**TREASURY 10%**	9 June 1994	*9 J.D.*		.712 (+26)	−0.28	−4	**98−07**	**10.181**	**10.430**	.0078	**6.893**	**6.796**
1.013	1,550	**EXCHEQUER 12½%**	22 Aug 1994	*22 F.A.*	16 Jan	4.623 (+135) 1.678 (−49)	−0.18	−3	**107−16** 107−22xd	**11.628** 11.608	**10.676** 10.665	.0072 .0072	**6.502** 6.485	**6.874** 6.867
1.105	1,600	†**TREASURY 9%**	17 Nov 1994	*17 M.N.*		1.184 (+48)	−0.30	−4	**94−04**	**9.562**	**10.352**	.0075	**7.084**	**6.782**
1.074	2,350	**TREASURY 12%**	25 Jan 1995	*25 J.J.*		.690 (−21)	−0.26	−4	**106−05xd**	**11.304**	**10.598**	.0068	**6.553**	**6.836**
1.168	2,100	**EXCHEQUER 10¼%**	21 July 1995	*21 J.J.*		.477 (−17)	−0.27	−5	**99−07xd**	**10.331**	**10.422**	.0067	**6.816**	**6.782**
1.162	1,000	†**TREASURY 12¾%**	15 Nov 1995	*15 M.N.*		1.747 (+50)	−0.20	−5	**110−30**	**11.493**	**10.467**	.0061	**6.293**	**6.713**
1.159	900	**TREASURY 14%**	22 Jan 1996	*22 J.J.*		.690 (−18)	−0.18	−4	**116−09xd**	**12.040**	**10.650**	.0058	**6.209**	**6.794**
1.282	750	†**TREASURY 9%**	15 Mar 1992-96	*15 M.S.*	**6 Feb** (16 Jan)	2.737 (+111)	−0.30	−4	**93−30**	**9.581**	**10.206**	.0065	**6.931**	**6.688**
1.173	1,400	†**TREASURY 15¼%**	3 May 1996	*3 M.N.*		2.590 (+62)	−0.20	−5	**123−19**	**12.339**	**10.542**	.0054	**5.897**	**6.676**
1.209	800	†**EXCHEQUER 13¼%**	15 May 1996	*15 M.N.*		1.815 (+50)	−0.22	−4	**114−00**	**11.623**	**10.468**	.0057	**6.209**	**6.693**
1.333	1,109	**CONVERSION 10%**	15 Nov 1996	*15 M.N.*		1.370 (+50)	−0.24	−4	**98−06**	**10.185**	**10.335**	.0060	**6.796**	**6.732**
1.280	1,500	†**TREASURY 13¼%**	22 Jan 1997	*22 J.J.*		.653 (−18)	−0.16	−4	**115−01xd**	**11.519**	**10.437**	.0053	**6.208**	**6.669**
1.351	3,100	**EXCHEQUER 10½%**	21 Feb 1997	*21 F.A.*	16 Jan	3.912 (+136) 1.381 (−48)	−0.22	−3	**100−25** 100−30xd	**10.419** 10.402	**10.340** 10.332	.0057 .0057	**6.689** 6.678	**6.714** 6.709
1.460	3,600	†**TREASURY 8¾%**	1 Sept 1997	*1 M.S.*	23 Jan	2.997 (+125) 1.342 (−56)	−0.28	−3	**92−04** 92−06xd	**9.498** 9.492	**10.131** 10.125	.0058 .0058	**6.906** 6.902	**6.653** 6.651
1.320	1,000	**EXCHEQUER 15%**	27 Oct 1997	*27 A.O.*		2.636 (+69)	−0.20	−4	**124−26**	**12.018**	**10.587**	.0047	**6.065**	**6.705**
1.466	2,850	**EXCHEQUER 9¾%**	19 Jan 1998	*19 J.J.*		.401 (−15)	−0.25	−3	**97−08xd**	**10.026**	**10.222**	.0055	**6.748**	**6.668**
1.620	1,000	†**TREASURY 6¾%**	1 May 1995-98	*1 M.N.*		1.184 (+64)	−0.35	−3	**81−26**	**8.251**	**9.758**	.0059	**7.080**	**6.508**
1.396	1,100	†**TREASURY 15½%**	30 Sept 1998	*30 M.S.*	**21 Feb** (31 Jan)	4.077 (+96)	−0.11	−3	**130−15**	**11.880**	**10.431**	.0043	**5.908**	**6.579**
1.483	2,500	**EXCHEQUER 12%**	20 Nov 1998	*20 M.N.*		1.479 (+45)	−0.21	−3	**110−10**	**10.878**	**10.301**	.0048	**6.370**	**6.619**
1.579	1,250	†**TREASURY 9½%**	15 Jan 1999	*15 J.J.*		.286 (−11)	−0.26	−3	**97−05xd**	**9.778**	**9.948**	.0051	**6.562**	**6.489**
1.508	2,900	**EXCHEQUER 12¼%**	26 Mar 1999	*26 M.S.*	**17 Feb** (27 Jan)	3.356 (+100)	−0.20	−3	**112−08**	**10.913**	**10.276**	.0046	**6.311**	**6.590**
1.570	1,252	**TREASURY 10½%**	19 May 1999	*19 M.N.*		1.323 (+46)	−0.26	−3	**102−00**	**10.294**	**10.181**	.0049	**6.554**	**6.602**
1.622	1,548	**CONVERSION 10¼%**	22 Nov 1999	*22 M.N.*		1.208 (+43)	−0.26	−3	**100−16**	**10.199**	**10.167**	.0048	**6.593**	**6.604**
1.710	1,200	†**TREASURY 8½%**	28 Jan 2000	*28 J.J.*		.559 (−24)	−0.29	−3	**90−21xd**	**9.376**	**9.909**	.0050	**6.737**	**6.517**
1.698	1,554	†**CONVERSION 9%**	3 Mar 2000	*3 M.S.*	25 Jan (4 Jan)	3.033 (+123)	−0.30	−4	**93−23**	**9.603**	**9.942**	.0049	**6.654**	**6.512**
1.590	1,817	**TREASURY 13%**	14 July 2000	*14 J.J.*		.356 (−10)	−0.22	−3	**118−04xd**	**11.005**	**10.283**	.0042	**6.225**	**6.563**
1.739	1,050	**TREASURY 10%**	26 Feb 2001	*26 F.A.*	20 Jan	3.589 (+131) 1.452 (−53)	−0.32	−3	**99−30** 100−03xd	**10.006** 9.991	**9.992** 9.986	.0045 .0045	**6.497** 6.489	**6.496** 6.491
1.391	1,250	**TREASURY 14%**	22 May 98-2001	*22 M.N.*		1.649 (+43)	−0.14	−3	**120−22**	**11.600**	**10.477#**	.0047	**6.160#**	**6.662#**
1.782	802	**CONVERSION 9¾%**	10 Aug 2001	*10 F.A.*	4 Jan	3.927 (+147) .988 (−37)	−0.36	−3	**98−14** 98−19xd	**9.905** 9.889	**9.963** 9.953	.0045 .0044	**6.517** 6.506	**6.488** 6.480
1.496	1,600	**EXCHEQUER 12%**	22 Jan 99-2002	*22 J.J.*		.592 (−18)	−0.19	−3	**110−07xd**	**10.887**	**10.335#**	.0047	**6.402#**	**6.642#**
1.823	716	**CONVERSION 10%**	11 Apr 2002	*11 A.O.*	**6 Mar** (13 Feb)	2.329 (+85)	−0.38	−4	**100−26**	**9.919**	**9.883**	.0042	**6.404**	**6.418**
1.862	1,450	**TREASURY 9¾%**	27 Aug 2002	*27 F.A.*	23 Jan	3.473 (+130) 1.442 (−54)	−0.36	−2	**99−07** 99−13xd	**9.827** 9.808	**9.841** 9.830	.0042 .0042	**6.415** 6.404	**6.403** 6.394
1.911	1,300	**EXCHEQUER 9%**	19 Nov 2002	*19 M.N.*		1.134 (+46)	−0.40	−2	**94−04**	**9.562**	**9.774**	.0043	**6.493**	**6.395**
1.572	1,800	**TREASURY 13¾%**	25 July 2000-03	*25 J.J.*		.791 (−21)	−0.20	−2	**122−25xd**	**11.199**	**10.333#**	.0040	**6.157#**	**6.569#**

Compound Interest Volatility * *	Amount of Loan in Millions	STOCK	Interest dates		Next XD Date (and First Dealing Day)	Gross Accrued Interest (Days)	Price Changes Since 23/12/88 %	Price Changes Since Previous day	CLEAN PRICE	Yield	Redemption Yield	1 Tick Variation in price	NET YIELDS Cap Nil Inc. at 35.0	NET YIELDS Cap at 35 Inc. at 35.0
1.923	1,000	TREASURY 10%	8 Sept 2003	*8 M.S.*	30 Jan (9 Jan)	3.233 (+118)	−0.41	−3	**102−00**	**9.804**	**9.736**	.0040	**6.286**	**6.315**
1.688	1,900	TREASURY 11½%	19 Mar 2001-04	*19 M.S.*	10 Feb (20 Jan)	3.371 (+107)	−0.27	−3	**109−17**	**10.489**	**10.114#**	.0042	**6.336#**	**6.508#**
1.970	900	TREASURY 10%	18 May 2004	*18 M.N.*		1.288 (+47)	−0.44	−3	**102−27**	**9.723**	**9.640**	.0039	**6.209**	**6.248**
2.590	443	FUNDING 3½%	14 July 99-2004	*14 J.J.*		.096 (−10)	−0.17	−	**57−30xd**	**6.041**	**8.399**	.0052	**6.665**	**5.836**
2.020	1,362	CONVERSION 9½%	25 Oct 2004	*25 A.O.*		1.848 (+71)	−0.40	−3	**99−10**	**9.566**	**9.580**	.0039	**6.240**	**6.231**
2.049	1,881	CONVERSION 9½%	18 Apr 2005	*18 A.O.*		2.030 (+78)	−0.40	−3	**99−20**	**9.536**	**9.541**	.0038	**6.209**	**6.204**
2.032	1,050	EXCHEQUER 10½%	20 Sept 2005	*20 M.S.*	13 Feb (23 Jan)	3.049 (+106)	−0.38	−2	**107−27**	**9.736**	**9.546**	.0036	**6.068**	**6.159**
1.851	2,200	TREASURY 12½%	21 Nov 2003-05	*21 M.N.*		1.507 (+44)	−0.44	−4	**121−02**	**10.325**	**9.778#**	.0035	**5.966#**	**6.236#**
2.204	1,800	†TREASURY 8%	5 Oct 2002-06	*5 A.O.*	1 Mar (8 Feb)	1.995 (+91)	−0.41	−3	**87−16**	**9.143**	**9.462**	.0040	**6.384**	**6.233**
2.125	702	CONVERSION 9¾%	15 Nov 2006	*15 M.N.*		1.336 (+50)	−0.42	−2	**102−14**	**9.518**	**9.460**	.0036	**6.109**	**6.135**
1.821	3,150	TREASURY 11¾%	22 Jan 2003-07	*22 J.J.*		.579 (−18)	−0.43	−3	**114−26xd**	**10.234**	**9.783#**	.0037	**6.054#**	**6.269#**
2.226	1,400	†TREASURY 8½%	16 July 2007	*16 J.J.*		.279 (−12)	−0.45	−2	**92−27xd**	**9.155**	**9.316**	.0038	**6.178**	**6.099**
1.852	1,250	TREASURY 13½%	26 Mar 2004-08	*26 M.S.*	17 Feb (27 Jan)	3.699 (+100)	−0.44	−4	**129−31**	**10.387**	**9.687#**	.0032	**5.783#**	**6.138#**
2.263	1,800	†TREASURY 9%	13 Oct 2008	*13 A.O.*	7 Mar (14 Feb)	2.047 (+83)	−0.45	−3	**97−20**	**9.219**	**9.258**	.0035	**6.054**	**6.032**
2.361	1,000	TREASURY 8%	25 Sept 2009	*25 M.S.*	16 Feb) (26 Jan)	2.214 (+101)	−0.47	−2	**89−04**	**8.976**	**9.176**	.0037	**6.130**	**6.028**
2.382	369	†CONVERSION 9%	12 July 2011	*12 J.J.*		.197 (−8)	−0.48	−3	**99−03xd**	**9.082**	**9.097**	.0033	**5.924**	**5.917**
2.689	1,000	†TREASURY 5½%	10 Sep 2008-12	*10 M.S.*	1 Feb (11 Jan)	1.748 (+116)	−0.60	−3	**66−21**	**8.251**	**8.894**	.0044	**6.301**	**5.998**
2.550	700	†TREASURY 7¾%	26 Jan 2012-15	*26 J.J.*		.467 (−22)	−0.54	−3	**87−04xd**	**8.895**	**9.043**	.0035	**6.023**	**5.940**
2.354	1,000	EXCHEQUER 12%	12 Dec 2013-17	*12 J.D.*		.756 (+23)	−0.50	−5	**128−09**	**9.354**	**9.107#**	.0026	**5.666#**	**5.816#**
2.695	276	CONSOLS 2½%	after 5 Apr 1923	*5 J.A.J.O.*		.007 (−1)	−0.19	−	**27−18xd**	**9.173§**		.0105	**5.940§**	**5.940§**
2.818	1,909	†WAR 3½%	after 1 Dec 1952	*1 J.D.*		.326 (+34)	−0.33	−	**39−14**	**8.875**		.0070	**5.752**	**5.752**
2.756	359	CONSOLS 4%	after 1 Feb 1957	*1 F.A.*		.307 (−28)	−0.28	−	**44−03xd**	**9.072**		.0064	**5.911**	**5.911**
2.754	475	TREASURY 2½%	after 1 Apr 1975	*1 A.O.*	23 Feb (2 Feb)	.651 (+95)	−0.19	−	**27−17**	**9.081**		.0103	**5.854**	**5.854**

Compound Interest Volatility	Amount of Loan in Millions	STOCK	Interest dates		Next XD Date (and First Dealing Day)	Gross Accrued Interest (Days)	Price Changes Since 23/12/88 %	Price Changes Since Previous day	CLEAN PRICE	Inflation 5% Redemption Yield	Inflation 5% 1 Tick Var.	Inflation 5% Cap Nil Inc. at 35.0	Inflation 10% Redemption Yield	Inflation 10% Cap Nil Inc. at 35.0
0.246	500r	Index-Linked Treasury 2%	25 Jan 1990	*25 J.J.*		.144 (−21)	−0.07	−	**124−00xd**	**3.875r**	.0244	**3.178r**	**1.379r**	**0.695r**
0.733	650r	†Index-Linked Treasury 2%	23 Mar 1992	*23 M.S.*	14 Feb	.616 (+103)	−0.15	−2	**103−16**	**3.823r**	.0098	**3.100r**	**2.992r**	**2.280r**
0.921	400r	Index-Linked Treasury 2%	16 May 1994	*16 M.N.*		.283 (+49)	−0.16	−2	**94−28**	**3.854r**	.0066	**3.116r**	**3.361r**	**2.633r**
1.674	1,000r	Index-Linked Treasury 2%	16 Sept 1996	*16 M.S.*	7 Feb (17 Jan)	.946 (+110)	−0.10	−2	**139−06**	**3.773r**	.0032	**3.024r**	**3.418r**	**2.679r**
2.542	900r	Index-Linked Treasury 2½%	24 Sept 2001	*24 M.S.*	15 Feb (25 Jan)	.952 (+102)	−0.29	−4	**118−15**	**3.832r**	.0025	**2.883r**	**3.587r**	**2.652r**
2.804	800r	Index-Linked Treasury 2½%	20 May 2003	*20 M.N.*		.424 (+45)	−0.33	−4	**115−20**	**3.869r**	.0023	**2.908r**	**3.654r**	**2.707r**
3.386	1,200r	Index-Linked Treasury 2%	19 July 2006	*19 J.J.*		.125 (−15)	−0.35	−4	**117−22xd**	**3.865r**	.0019	**3.049r**	**3.688r**	**2.884r**
3.652	950r	Index-Linked Treasury 2½%	20 May 2009	*20 M.N.*		.424 (+45)	−0.37	−4	**110−10**	**3.846r**	.0019	**2.854r**	**3.681r**	**2.704r**
3.933	1,350r	Index-Linked Treasury 2½%	23 Aug 2011	*23 F.A.*	17 Jan	1.307 (+134)	−0.32	−5	**114−30**	**3.821r**	.0017	**2.822r**	**3.665r**	**2.681r**
4.158	1,300r	Index-Linked Treasury 2½%	16 Aug 2013	*16 F.A.*	10 Jan	.488 (−50) 1.154 (+141)	−0.40	−4	**115−00xd** **95−08**	**3.816r** **3.803r**	.0017 .0019	**2.818r** **2.794r**	**3.661r** **3.660r**	**2.679r** **2.667r**
4.473	1,700r	Index-Linked Treasury 2½%	26 July 2016	*26 J.J.*		.352 (−43) .196 (−22)	−0.40	−4	**95−10xd** **102−31xd**	**3.797r** **3.756r**	.0019 .0016	**2.790r** **2.739r**	**3.655r** **3.617r**	**2.664r** **2.617r**
4.836	1,400r	Index-Linked Treasury 2½%	16 Apr 2020	*16 A.O.*		.713 (+80)	−0.41	−4	**100−28**	**3.683r**	.0015	**2.659r**	**3.559r**	**2.552r**
5.193	900r	†Index-Linked Treasury 2½%	17 July 2024	*17 J.J.*		.097 (−13)	−0.46	−4	**84−30xd**	**3.635r**	.0017	**2.601r**	**3.519r**	**2.504r**

For next interest payment see over

1. Next Conversion option 12 January 1989 into £99%. Conversion 9½% 2001. G.R.Y. assuming conversion = *9.558*
Next Conversion option 12 January 1989 into £99%. Conversion 9% 2011. G.R.Y. assuming conversion = *9.045*

2. Next Conversion option on 16 January 1989 into £104% Treasury 8½% 2007. G.R.Y. assuming conversion = *9.302*

For Footnotes See Over.
E. & O.E.

For private circulation only.

4

Index-linked gilts and other UK government borrowing

4.1 Index-linked gilts

In their volume on gilt-edged securities published in 1975, Day and Jamieson put forward the arguments for a much more unorthodox stock, 'a government bond with interest and/or redemption payments linked to the cost of living'. In 1974, shortly after the first shock to world economies of substantially higher OPEC oil prices and the onset of higher world inflation, the British government announced two index-linked bond schemes in the National Savings range designed for small savers. Inflation in the UK reached cyclical peaks in late 1975 at around 26 per cent per annum and in early 1980 at around 21 per cent per annum. Perhaps it was inevitable that the introduction of the first index-linked government securities issue in March 1981 signalled the end of the soaring and unpredictable inflation rates of the 1970s and presaged the beginning of lower inflation rates in the 1980s. Indeed, the achievement of a lower rate of inflation was, and remains, a central plank of the policy of the Conservative government elected in 1979 and in power ever since.

In the post-war years, conventional gilt-edged securities had given very poor returns and during the 1970s, the years of high inflation led to negative real rates of return. Expectations of inflation built into gilt yields were on average two or three years out of date. In the 1970s this led to negative real rates of return (Figure 4.1).

The first issue of index-linked gilts was restricted to ownership by pension funds. The logical links with their inflationary liabilities was self-evident. The following March in 1982 all restrictions were removed.

Index-linked stock is characterized by the fact that both the capital repayment and the coupon payments increase in accordance with the Retail Price Index, but with a time lag of eight months in indexation. Thus coupons are known in advance. Note that the Bank of England has rights under the terms of each prospectus in the event that a change in the coverage of the basic calculation of the Index is in the Bank's opinion detrimental to the

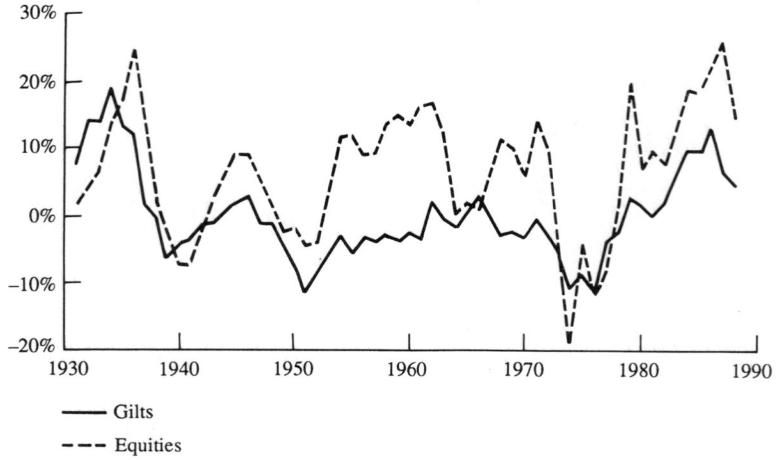

Figure 4.1 *Five-year average real returns*
Source: Kleinwort Benson Gilts Limited

interests of stockholders. Stockholders can be offered the right 'to require Her Majesty's Treasury to redeem their stock in advance of the revised Index becoming effective'. At the end of 1987 there were thirteen index-linked gilts with nominal coupons of either 2 per cent or 2.5 per cent and redemption dates varying from 1988 to 2024. The projected real redemption rates based on a prospective inflation rate of 5 per cent varied from around 2.5 per cent to just over 4.1 per cent. On the same day the yield on the FT-Actuaries All Share Index was also 4.1 per cent.

In our companion volume (*A General Introduction to Institutional Investment*) we devoted one chapter to a consideration of the background of the inflationary environment in the UK and the relevance of different asset classes in inflationary conditions. While not rehearsing the same arguments, there are aspects of index-linked stocks worth restating here.

4.1.1

Yields on index-linked stocks have risen broadly since the first issue in 1981. The initial yield on the 2 per cent Index Linked 1996 stock was 2.6 per cent. It is currently 3.0 per cent. Yields have in fact been quite volatile and this leads to the conclusion that some stocks can only be regarded as safe if held to redemption. This may seem perverse but conventional gilts have, of course, also been very volatile.

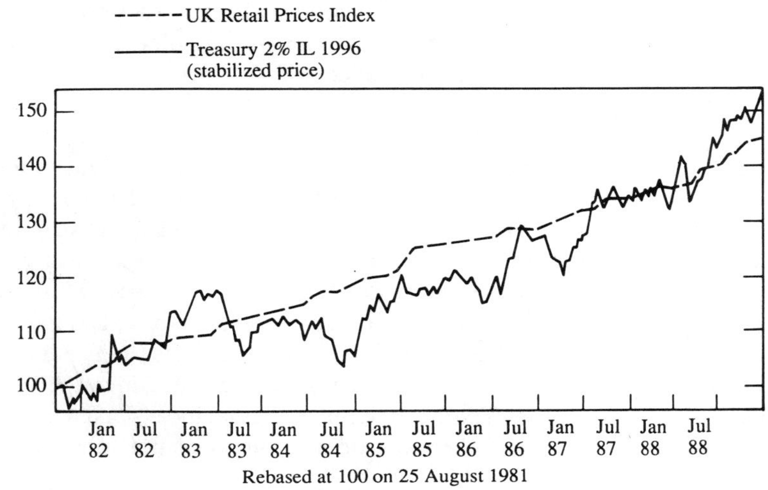

Figure 4.2

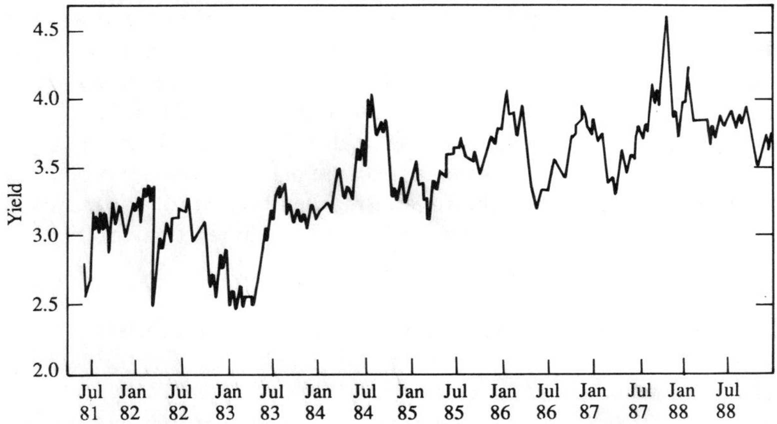

Figure 4.3 *Index-linked real yields*

4.1.2

Following the removal of ownership restrictions, the low coupons clearly make short-dated index-linked stocks attractive to tax payers. This is also perverse, given that their introduction was heavily geared to the needs of non-tax paying pension funds. The proportion of the total return derived from the maturity value as distinct from income makes the stock attractive to investors paying high income taxes who are long-term holders. This is also true of low coupon conventional gilts, of course.

4.1.3
The relative valuations of conventional gilts, index-linked gilts and equities largely depends on assumed prospective levels of inflation and, in the case of equities, growth prospects for dividends. The reverse yield gap between conventional gilts and equities is well established and the reasons known. What is less clear is why index-linked gilts, which provide a risk-free rate of real return, should yield in some cases the same as the yield on the equity market. Considerable attention has been given by portfolio analysts to the nature of the risk premium between the two classes of asset and the ultimate relationship with conventional gilts. There can be no doubt that index-linked gilts are a unique asset category and therefore offer a means of portfolio diversification.

4.1.4
Despite the theory, index-linked gilts were generally unloved by investors because of the superior performance by equities until 1987. It remains to be seen whether the events of Black Monday (19 October 1987) have produced a true watershed in the history of index-linked gilts. Because of the volatility of the market, trading opportunities for fleet-footed operators have abounded. On many occasions, however, conventional gilts and index-linked gilts had substantial price movements in the same direction when theory might have suggested a divergence of movement because of inflationary expectations. It should also be observed that their overall marketability is not good. Only a few market-makers make prices on a consistent basis in reasonable size.

4.1.5
In conclusion, the four principal users of index-linked stock are:

4.1.5.1
The long-term pensions funds prepared to take a passive approach and ready to hold stock to redemption.

4.1.5.2
The high taxpayers who may also wish to hold over the long term.

4.1.5.3
The traders wishing to exploit sentiment by using the volatility of prices to make short-term profits, or to switch between equities and index-linked

stocks as a policy move. In the latter case consideration will be given to assumed real yields on index-linked stocks, break-even inflation rates at different tax rates for comparison with conventional gilts, and the yield on the FT-All Share Index.

4.1.5.4

There are substantial holdings by insurance companies using the stocks to match liabilities (expenses increasing with inflation, index-linked annuities, etc.).

4.2 Variable rate gilts

We have already alluded to the circumstances of the 1970s. During the decade the importance of managing monetary aggregates developed in importance. The growing Public Sector Borrowing Requirement was by and large funded by gilt sales and many institutions were becoming restless about continuing purchases of gilts particularly, as we have already noted, because of the negative real returns they were producing. In order to pursue its monetary policy the authorities realized the need for innovation. One result was the partially-paid stock introduced in 1977. A further step towards tempting institutional buyers into the marketplace, at a time when sterling was very unattractive to overseas buyers, was the variable rate stock issued for the first time also in 1977. Three stocks were issued and all have now been redeemed. In some ways these stocks resembled what we now know as floating rate notes. The rate of interest on the stocks was in all cases defined as 0.5 per cent above the average Treasury bill tender rate over the relevant period. Calculations were cumbersome and the stocks were not popular with the non-bank public at whom they were directed. They were issued with lives of less than five years and were most popular with the members of the banking system.

4.3 Other forms of government debt

The principle forms of funding the PSBR are gilts and Treasury bills. Forms of non-marketable government debt exist and the role of National Savings increased during the early 1980s, but has decreased recently. Between 1980 and 1987 specific targets were set for sales of National Savings instruments as a contribution to the PSBR. Terms on the various 'products' can be varied quite quickly but the government cannot really use National Savings as a mechanism for short-term management of funding policy. The principal instruments are National Savings Certificates, the Save As You Earn Scheme, the Yearly Plan, the Ordinary and Investment National Savings Accounts, Premium Bonds, Income Bonds and Capital Bonds.

The carrot for investors in these schemes varies. In the case of Premium

Bonds it is the small chance of a huge win. In other cases it is the taxation advantage to higher-rate tax payers of a return offered tax free with no further liability. Conversely, non-taxpayers would find the gross rate of interest offered on the Investment Account and Capital Bonds highly attractive compared with savings in a bank or building society which offer a rate after tax with no right to reclaim tax.

Most of these schemes are available only to individuals but corporations may apply for certain of them. Industrial and commercial companies are far more likely to be holders of Certificates of Tax Deposit which were introduced in October 1975 for taxpayers generally. They can be used in the settlement of tax liabilities.

4.4 Government guaranteed stocks

There are a number of stocks which have the British government as guarantor. The issues are not large and in relation to stocks discussed in Chapter 5 are relatively unimportant. There used to be three other classes of stock which were regarded as quasi-government stocks although they do not have a British government guarantee. These are:

- Corporation and County stocks
- Commonwealth Government and Provincial Securities (Table 4.1)

Table 4.1 *Commonwealth – Government*

Name, description
British Guiana (Demerera Railway) 4% Perp Stk
(Demerera Railway) Perm Anns (£1 of Ann)
South Australian 3% Cons Ins Stk 1916 (or after)
Southern Rhodesia 2½ Stk 65/70 (Unassented)
3% Stk 71/73 (Unassented)
3½% Stk 61/66 (Unassented)
3½% Stk 67/69 (Unassented)
4% Stk 72/74 (Unassented)
4½% Insc Stk 58/68 (Unassented)
4½% Stk 87/92 (Assented)
4½% Stk 87/92 (Unassented)
5% Stk 75/80 (Unassented)
6% Stk 76/79 (Unassented)
Jersey Electricity Co Ltd 6% Gtd Stk 2000
8% Gtd Stk 2000

Source: Daily Official List

- Public Boards – the nature of the borrowers and their borrowings has been the subject of much recent change and they are discussed in Chapter 5 which concentrate on borrowers other than the UK government.

4.5 Government borrowing on Euromarkets

In 1985 and 1986 the government raised $2.5 billion and $4 billion respectively by way of a Floating Rate Note. The action was caused by the government's response to pressure on sterling and by their concern at the low level of reserves in relation to imports. In effect, the government raised a war chest comprising billions of dollars which would enable it to defend sterling against certain negative factors in the long term. The most important consideration at the time was the worrying prospect of a large current account deficit in 1987 for the first time since 1979. The idea of the two FRNs was to make intervention in the foreign exchange market a viable alternative to raising interest rates to support the pound. It has to be said that both FRNs preceded an election period – the election eventually took place in June 1987 and there was much talk at the time of the UK joining the European Monetary System (EMS) or of a move towards 'target zones' for currencies. The FRNs raised reserves to a level which would make it easier to abide by any obligations to intervene in the EMS, thus fuelling at the time speculation of an imminent entry. In the event, 1987, which included the re-election of the Conservative Thatcher government, saw a prolonged bout of sterling strength and a dramatic increase in UK Official Reserves through Bank of England intervention. In retrospect it became apparent that during a period when the dollar plunged and had the limelight, the authorities in the UK were maintaining a sterling/Deutschmark rate of three Deutschmarks to the pound.

The two issues demonstrated clearly the authorities' inventiveness in domestic monetary management.

4.6 Taxation of gilt-edged stocks and other bonds

A new basis of taxation was embodied in the 1985 Finance Act. The accrued income scheme took effect on 28 February 1986 and applies to all fixed-interest securities, whether in sterling or foreign currency. Another set of rules relating to capital gains took effect on 2 July 1986 which exempts disposals of most sterling-denominated bonds from capital gains tax completely but non-sterling denominated securities are still included within the capital gains tax net.

The *accrued income scheme* applies to all taxpayers be they individuals, companies or trustees who are resident or ordinarily resident in the UK. It also applies to non-residents if they are trading in the UK through a branch or agency but only in relation to investments in connection with the UK branch or agency. The scheme does not apply to the investment income of exempt bodies or to financial concerns whose profits from sales of securities are charged to tax as income rather than as capital gains. Syndicates at Lloyds, for instance, are taxed on a calendar year cycle and coupons are brought into their profit and loss accounts as received. In a good trading year purchase of low coupon gilts rather than high coupon gilts will have the effect of depressing their profits.

The scheme does not cover ordinary or preference shares convertibles, National Savings Certificates, certificates of deposit or Treasury Bills.

When a transaction takes place, the accrued interest since the previous payment date will be treated as income in the hands of the seller, while the purchaser will receive a credit of equal amount which he can use against the next payment of interest on that stock. The accrued interest cannot be transferred to other stocks. In the case of ex-dividend transactions where the accrued interest is negative (known as rebate interest), the seller receives a credit of the rebate interest, whereas the purchaser is charged to tax on the rebate interest.

The purpose of the legislation was to prevent investors exchanging income payments for capital gains ('bond washing').

The position on *capital gains* is that transactions after 1 July 1986 in gilts and other 'qualifying corporate bonds' have not been subject to capital gains tax irrespective of the length of time since purchase. Losses are not allowable and for many this was a valuable concession to lose. This feature leads to the perverse conclusion that 'non-qualifying' may well be more efficient than 'qualifying' corporate bonds. Preference shares, unquoted debentures of a company not quoted on the Stock Exchange or USM, and non-sterling denominated government bonds do not qualify and thus may still be used to establish tax losses.

Much effort was put into ensuring that the transitional arrangements between the old rules and the new measures were fair. This detail is beyond the scope of this volume.

5

Corporate borrowings

5.1 Introduction

The first four chapters of this volume have concentrated on UK government debt. We turn now to the corporate marketplace and also look at international bond markets. The following figures will assist in putting the market into context. Figure 5.1 shows the wholesale markets regulated by the Bank of England. Some of the instruments in the 'Traditional' markets have already been discussed, especially UK Treasury Bills. Figure 5.2 looks at the principal long-term debt markets both in sterling and internationally. 'Euro' issues are often arranged outside the country where borrowings are required and come in a variety of forms. The largest market is in Eurodollars but markets in Eurosterling, Euroyen and so on are also highly developed.

Broadly speaking our considerations fall into three distinct groups. Borrowings by governments, public or private bodies in their own country (domestic issues); borrowings arranged by foreigners in another country; and borrowings arranged in the 'Eurobond' marketplace.

Within the UK the first category includes government debt and domestic debentures and loan stocks. Bulldogs are an example of the second category, being borrowings by foreigners in the UK market.

Debentures and loan stocks are now seen as part of the Sterling bond market. Despite their historical importance the only substantial borrowers in the sterling fixed-rate bond market during the second half of the 1970s were the British government and UK local authorities. Most British corporate borrowers had, by contrast, deserted this market, and overseas borrowers continued to find it impracticable to raise sterling bonds because of the application of exchange controls. The improving economic climate in the 1980s and the abolition of UK exchange controls in 1979 led to a revival of issues of both fixed-rate sterling bonds by British companies and a reopening of the long-closed bulldog sector of the market, which comprises sterling bond issues in the UK by overseas borrowers, whether sovereign or corporate.

Bank borrowings and shorter-dated instruments are discussed in this

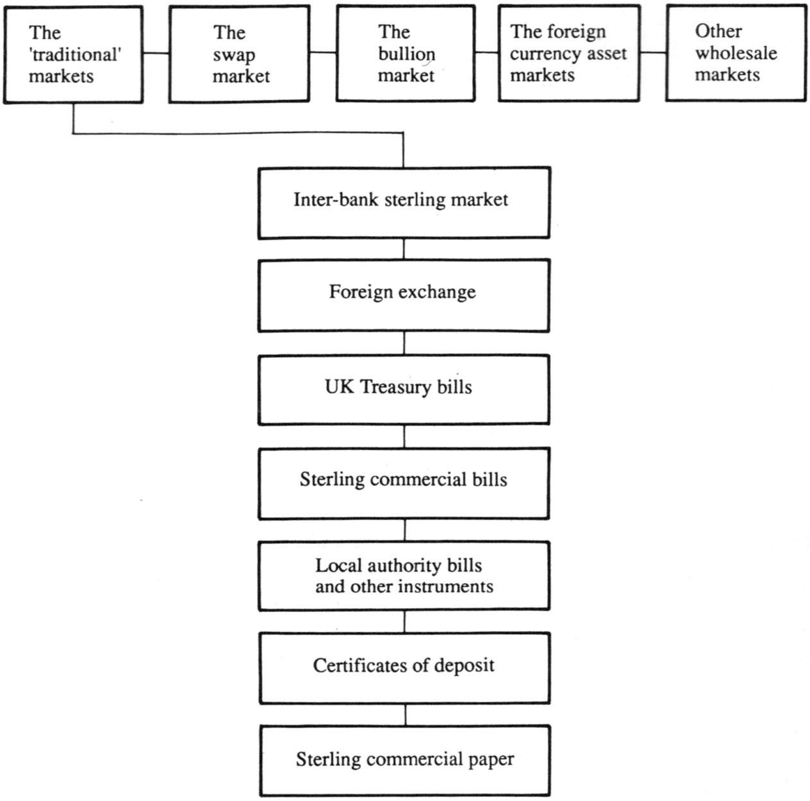

Figure 5.1 *Wholesale markets regulated by the Bank of England*

chapter. Because of their increasing role in wholesale money markets building society borrowings are discussed in Section 5.8.

5.2 Corporation and county stocks, public boards

Before examining further money market instruments in some detail and before looking at corporate debt in the UK we refer to the quasi-Government bodies that used to play a large role in the fixed-interest market but have now, as issuers, either become extinct or have changed role.

5.2.1. LOCAL AUTHORITIES

Until 1971 these issues were frequent (and were in total substantial) when-

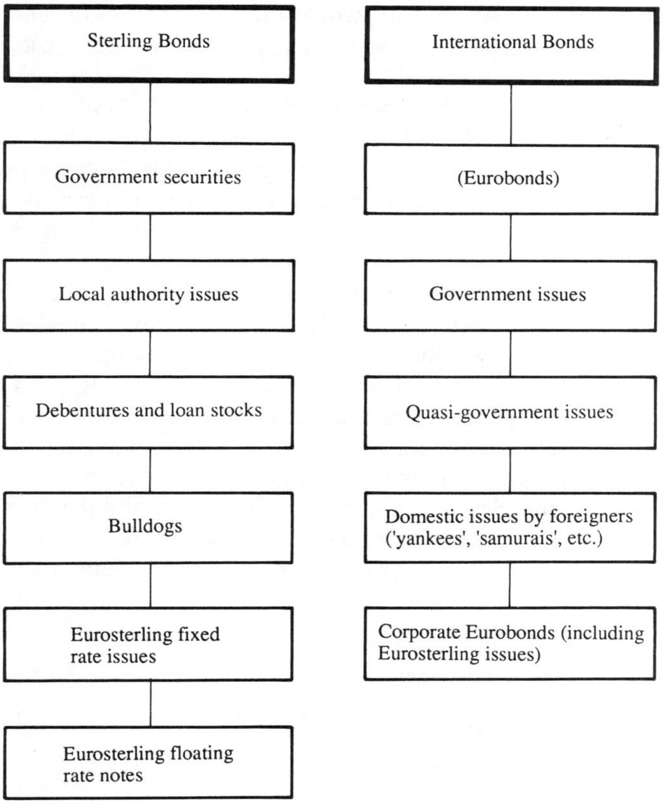

Figure 5.2 *Long-term debt markets*
Note: Theoretically all corporate issues could be fixed rate or floating rate and may be convertible into ordinary or common stock

ever market conditions were favourable. There was normally a queue of borrowers regulated by the Government Broker who allowed applications to come to the market as quickly as he thought the market could absorb the issues. This depended on sentiment and demand as the Government Broker wanted and needed to maintain a healthy market. The corporations do, of course, borrow short-term money and stockmarket issues normally fund short-term debts, but basically the money is needed for capital projects of all sorts – housing, sewerage, roads, etc. Interest and capital are a charge on the authority's rates which can be raised to meet expenditure so that in theory there is no risk of default. Because of the rebellious attitude of one or two small councils to the central government, most institutions would have a list of local authorities to whom they would not lend even in the short term. Most local authorities have protected their good name and would not risk defaulting.

Some of the LCC and GLC issues were as large as £50 million, but, even although transfers were free of stamp duty, their marketability was disappointing compared with British government securities. Because prices are wider there was relatively little trading or switching and they were not usually attractive to the discount market so that they were bought with the intention of retaining as a long-term investment (Table 5.1).

There have been periods when the local authorities have been financed centrally by the government, which has then issued government stocks for this purpose, but currently the local authorities raise money subject to the discipline of the market. Indeed when interest rates were high and the gilt-edged market unreceptive to new issues the local authorities showed flexibility and initiative; an active market in deposits was developed so that short-term money could be 'placed' with local authorities very easily and with the minimum of expense. Several brokers specialize in this and the rates offered vary with the term, overnight, seven days, one month, three months, etc., but are slightly higher than similar rates from the clearing banks or building societies.

Table 5.1 *Corporation and county stocks*

Name, description
Corp of London
$3\frac{1}{2}$% Deb Stk 83/93
Greater London Council $6\frac{3}{4}$% Stk 90/92
Aberdeen (City of) 10.80% Red Stk 20/11
Aberdeen Corp Gas Annuities per 25p
Birmingham Corp $2\frac{1}{2}$% Stk 1926 (or after)
3% Stk 1947 (or after)
3% (1902) 1932 (or after)
$3\frac{1}{2}$% Stk 1946 (or after)
Gas Anns (per £1 of Ann)
Water Anns (per £1 of Ann)
Birmingham District Council $11\frac{1}{2}$% Red Stk 2012
$13\frac{1}{2}$% Stk 1989
Blackburn Corp $3\frac{1}{2}$% Irrd Stk
4% Cons Deb Stk Irrd
Bristol (City of) $11\frac{1}{2}$% Red Stk 2008
Bristol Corp Deb Stk ($3\frac{1}{2}$%)
Croydon Corp $3\frac{1}{2}$% Stk
Glasgow Corp $3\frac{1}{2}$% Irrd Stk
Gas $6\frac{3}{4}$% Ann Stk (Perp)
Gas 9% Ann Stk (Perp)

Table 5.1 — *continued*

Name, description
Glasgow Corp *continued*
Waterworks Anns per £1 of Ann
Waterworks Funded Debt 4%
Waterworks Funded Debt 3½%
Hull Corp 2½% Red Stk 1938 (or after)
3½% Stk (1st Iss)
3½% Stk (2nd Iss)
Islington Corp 11.9% Red Stk 2017
12.65% Red Stk 2007
Kensington & Chelsea (Royal Borough) 11.15% Red Stk 2006
Kirklees Metropolitan Council 11.6% Red Stk 2031
Leeds (City of) 13½% Red Stk 2006
Leeds Corp 2½% Red Stk 1927 (or after)
3% Deb Stk 1927 (or after)
5% Irrd Stk
Lincoln Corp 3% Red Stk 1919 (or after)
Liverpool Corp 2½% Red Stk 1923 (or after)
2¾% Red Stk 1925 (or after)
3% Red Stk 1942 (or after)
3½% Stk
Manchester (City of) 11.5% Red Stk 2007
Manchester Corp 3% Red Cons Stk 1928 (or after)
1891 3% Red Stk 1941 (or after)
4% Cons Irrd Stk
Merton (London Borough of) 11¼ Red Stk 2017
Newcastle-Upon-Tyne (City of) 11¼ Red Stk 2017
Newcastle-Upon-Tyne Corp 3½% Irrd Stk
Norwich Corp 3% Red Stk
Nottingham Corp 3% Stk (Irrd)
Water Anns (of £3.50)
Water Anns (of £1.35)
Gas Anns (of £3.25)
Oldham Corp 4% Deb Stk
Oldham Met Borough Council 11.25% Red Stk 2010
12.40% Red Stk 2022
Reading Corp 3% Stk 1962 (or after)
3½% Stk
3½% Stk 1978 (or after)
Sunderland (Borough of) 11¾% Red Stk 2008
Sunderland Corp (River Wear Comm) 3% Funded Debt Anns
4½% Funded Debt Anns
Swansea (City of) 13¾% Red Stk 2006
Swansea Corp Stk (3½%)
Wigan Corp 3% Red Stk

Table 5.1 — *continued*

Short-dated bonds

Local Authority 97/16% Bds 11/1/89
$9\frac{5}{8}$% Bds 18/1/89
$9\frac{1}{2}$% Bds 25/1/89
$9\frac{1}{4}$% Bds 1/2/89
$9\frac{9}{16}$% Bds 8/2/89
$9\frac{13}{16}$% Bds 15/2/89
$9\frac{13}{16}$% Bds 22/2/89
$9\frac{11}{16}$% Bds 1/3/89
$9\frac{7}{16}$% Bds 15/3/89
$9\frac{3}{16}$% Bds 22/3/89
$9\frac{3}{16}$% Bds 29/3/89
$8\frac{15}{16}$% Bds 19/4/89
$9\frac{1}{16}$% Bds 3/5/89
$9\frac{3}{16}$% Bds 10/5/89
9% Bds 24/5/89
$9\frac{1}{4}$% Bds 21/6/89
$10\frac{5}{16}$% Bds 5/7/89
$10\frac{3}{8}$% Bds 12/7/89
$9\frac{15}{16}$% Bds 26/7/89
$10\frac{15}{16}$% Bds 2/8/89
11% Bds 9/8/89
$11\frac{1}{2}$% Bds 23/8/89
$12\frac{3}{16}$% Bds 6/9/89
$11\frac{3}{8}$% Bds 27/9/89
$12\frac{1}{8}$% Bds 4/10/89
$11\frac{3}{4}$% Bds 11/10/89
$11\frac{7}{16}$% Bds 18/10/89
$11\frac{5}{8}$% Bds 25/10/89
$12\frac{1}{16}$% Bds 22/11/89
$11\frac{1}{2}$% Bds 13/12/89
$9\frac{7}{8}$% Bds 25/7/90
$9\frac{3}{8}$% Bds 15/5/91
$9\frac{1}{4}$% Bds 5/6/91
11% Bds 18/9/91
$9\frac{3}{16}$% Bds 2/12/92

Source: Daily Official List

One class of local authority borrowing deserves special mention. Local authority negotiable bonds are all quoted on the Stock Exchange and are issued for any maturity between one and five years. Since late 1977 some have been issued at a variable rate for periods of three, four and five years. Broadly the coupon varies at six-monthly intervals and is fixed at a margin above the six-month interbank rate. Most issues continue to be at fixed rates. Local authority stock issues are much the same as negotiable bonds, but are usually underwritten when issued on the Stock Exchange and the sums raised by an issue are usually in excess of £10 million. Stock issues are also generally for longer maturities.

One other innovation in recent years has been the drop-lock loan. The borrower (often a local authority), at a time of high interest rates borrows money at some margin over LIBOR (London Inter-Bank Offered Rate) from a syndicate of banks. The interest payable varies according to money market conditions. At some predetermined level if rates fall the loan 'locks' into a traditional bond, the capital for which has been provided by institutional lenders on an agreed basis at the beginning of the syndicate loan. The borrower has the advantage of not being committed to a fixed interest loan at rates he believes to be temporarily too high.

5.2.2 PUBLIC BOARDS

The last group of borrowers are public boards which are entitled by Act of Parliament to borrow on the security of their revenue.

The majority, but not all, of these stocks are transferable free of stamp duty, and most have no capital gains tax concessions, but North of Scotland Hydro-Electric Board was an exception to most rules as its securities have a government guarantee and a capital gains tax concession. The list included such names as:

- Metropolitan Water Board
- Port of London Authority
- Agricultural Mortgage Corporation (Table 5.2)

As there is no government guarantee it is all important for the investor to be certain that the revenues available to the board will pay the interest and that its charges can be raised if necessary. The problems of the Mersey Docks and Harbour Board were a salutary lesson in this respect; changing commercial patterns combined with labour problems led to a financial crisis for the Mersey Docks and Harbour Board which came to a head towards the end of 1970. In the face of a declining trade the board was unable to increase its charges, and without higher charges it could not cover the interest on its loans. A fresh Act of Parliament was introduced to allow the undertaking to be taken over by a new company with a reconstruction by 1974 and until then interest payments were reduced and the quotations suspended. The existence of a public board does not imply a government guarantee and the investor must check the safeguards and financial backing for the security.

5.3 Bank borrowings

Over the past few years the range of instruments appearing on banks' balance sheets has grown and diversified dramatically. At the very short end are

Table 5.2 *UK public boards*

Name, description
Aberdeen Harbour Board Bds Reg (7.5% to 12%)
Agricultural Mortgage Corp PLC $4\frac{1}{2}$% Deb Stk 61/91
5% Deb Stk 59/89
$5\frac{1}{2}$% Deb Stk 93/95
$6\frac{1}{8}$% Deb Stk 92/94
$6\frac{3}{8}$% Deb Stk 85/90
$7\frac{3}{4}$% Deb Stk 91/93
$10\frac{1}{4}$ Deb Stk 92/95
Clyde Port Authority 3% Irrd Stk
4% Irrd Stk
Bds Reg (10% to $14\frac{1}{2}$%) 84/89
Dover Harbour Board $4\frac{3}{4}$% 2nd Red Deb Stk 78/93
Dundee Port of Authority Bds Reg (Various)
Forth Ports Authority $3\frac{3}{4}$% Funded Debt
Great Ouse Water Authority $5\frac{3}{4}$% Red Stk 86/88
Londonderry Port Harbour Comm $3\frac{1}{2}$% Cons Stk
Metropolitan Water Metropolitan Water 3% A Stk 63/2003
3% B Stk 34/2003
Chelsea W.W. $2\frac{3}{4}$% Deb Stk 1897
East London Water Works Co 3% Deb Stk
Grand Junction Water Works Co 3% Deb Stk
Kent Water Works 3% Deb Stk
Lambeth Water Works Co 3% Red Deb Stk
New River Co 3% Deb Stk
Southwark & Vauxhall Water Co 3% Deb Stk
Staines Res Joint Comm 3% Gtd Deb Stk
West Middlesex Water Works Co 3% Deb Stk
London Bridge Anns (of £2.50)
North Devon Water Board 4% Stk 1996 (Red)
Port of London Authority 3% Port of London A Stk 29/99
$3\frac{1}{2}$% Stk 49/99
$6\frac{1}{2}$% Reg Stk 87/90
Port of Tyne Authority Bds Reg (Various)
Scottish Agric Sec Corp Ld $3\frac{1}{2}$% Deb Stk 63/93
$5\frac{1}{2}$% Deb Stk 86/88
$7\frac{1}{4}$% Deb Stk 90/92
$10\frac{1}{4}$% Deb Stk 89/91
13% Deb Stk 97/99
14% Deb Stk 1993
Southampton Harbour Board $6\frac{3}{4}$% Red Stk 85/90
Tees and Hartlepools Port Authority $3\frac{3}{4}$% Red Deb Stk 1990
$5\frac{1}{2}$% Red Deb Stk 94/99

Source: Daily Official List

Treasury bills and money-market deposits. At the long-term end are their corporate bonds. The main other forms of debt are as follows.

5.3.1 STERLING CERTIFICATES OF DEPOSIT

The first certificates of deposit were issued by British banks in 1968 following the American pattern. It is a negotiable instrument in bearer form issued by a bank or other financial institutions to certify that a specified sum has been deposited with the issuing institutions at a stated fixed rate of interest for a specified period of time. The deposit is usually for an amount of over £50,000 and terms vary from twenty-eight days to a maximum of five years. Interest is paid yearly or at the end of the term, at a fixed rate and the price reflects the accrued interest.

5.3.2 FIXED-RATE TIME DEPOSITS

Funds are raised in any currency for amounts usually greater than £50,000 on the basis of a simple loan. The funds are repaid at the end of a specified period that is less than twelve months from the date on which the deposit is made. The loan is not transferable.

5.3.3 VARIABLE-RATE TIME DEPOSITS

Funds are issued in the same manner and under the same restrictions as a fixed-rate time deposit. The only difference is that the rate of interest charged is agreed periodically in relation to a predetermined interest rate reference e.g., LIBOR.

5.3.4 DIRECT BANK LOANS

Banks may choose to lend to institutions over longer periods than one year. A 'bullet' loan assumes borrowing of all the desired funds on day one with full repayment at maturity. The rate of interest is normally determined as a fixed margin over a floating rate such as LIBOR. The minimum size of these loans is usually £1 million. Many insurance companies have used such bullet loans to finance their mortgage lendings. Such lendings must, of course, be on a variable rate basis themselves. If the rate of interest on the 'bullet' loan were fixed in absolute terms the institutions might arrange with an international bank, say, an interest rate 'swap' to convert payments of interest to the bank from fixed to variable amounts. This would thus avoid mismatching assets and liabilities.

5.3.5 SYNDICATED BANK LOANS

Developing from the early direct bank loans from just one bank, syndicated bank loans provide a loan facility to lending institutions such as an insurance company or building society which is actually a series of loans from each member of the syndicate to the borrower. Interest is usually fixed at a margin over LIBOR and the 'lead manager' receives an arrangement fee for setting up the syndicate and underwriting the arrangements. The loans may be bullets (payable on maturity) or established on a revolving credit facility basis. Funds issued in this way are usually a minimum of £20 million or so.

The borrower benefits from diversification and is not exposed to just one lender. The price for this is, of course, the front end fee.

There are further varieties of single bank syndicated bank loans. The bank may wish to organize a *transferable loan facility* which enables it to sell the loan to another institution. The bank may have reached its own limit for lending to, say, insurance companies and might wish to switch to a different form of lending which better suits its profitability criteria.

Another variant is a *multi-currency loan facility* under which funds are borrowed in a foreign currency and swapped into sterling. The deal incorporates a spot and forward exchange rate conversion agreement to remove unwanted exchange rate exposure. The cost of this is reflected in the bank's charges.

The final variant is the use of a *tender panel.* A group of banks have a right to bid for the short-term notes issued, or cash advances made, under the facility on each issue date. The facility is supported by an underwriting to take or provide at a predetermined price any notes or cash advances for which suitable tenders have not been received. They are either underwritten by the lead manager or fully committed by the participants of the tender panel.

5.4 Banks and hire purchase companies

The clearing and merchant banks, the discount houses and the hire purchase companies, along with a number of foreign banks with offices in the UK, all compete in a greater or lesser degree for deposits of varying term from overnight to (usually) just under one year. The degree of their competition depends of course on the demand they are experiencing for loans and is affected by any Bank of England restrictions on the growth of deposits. So far as the institutional investor is concerned this is part of the money market – along with local authority loans and 'yearling' bonds, Treasury bills and the other instruments. Ordinary deposits are not negotiable but most of the other alternatives are, i.e. if the investor finds he wishes his cash back earlier than the due repayment date, he can sell the security.

The resultant market is a very free one – it is not, of course, merely in sterling, but equally freely in Eurodollars (US dollars held by non-US residents) and to a lesser extent in a number of other currencies. The degree of risk for the lender depends on both the term of the loan and the quality of the borrower; although in the past a number of smaller banks (both UK and overseas) have been unable to fulfil their commitments, this only applies to a very small proportion of the monies handled in this way; the investor should always satisfy himself as to the ability of the borrower to repay.

What has been described above is essentially a market for institutional investors.

Individuals may, of course, lend money in a number of ways. Hire purchase companies, or finance houses, or instalment credit companies, as they are variously known, obtain the bulk of their fixed-interest finance by means of deposits for varying terms, the great bulk being for periods of less than one year. These organizations compete vigorously for funds, and usually pay rates of interest related closely to LIBOR. The most common practice is to pay a fixed margin over LIBOR so that the interest may vary quite significantly over the life of the loans. They also borrow on fixed terms for periods up to five years, and occasionally longer. Some also run what amount to regular savings accounts, and provide services closely similar to the savings banks – of course paying considerably higher interest rates in recognition of the greater risks that undoubtedly exist in such organizations.

5.5 Sterling commercial paper

Until 1985 the short-term financing opportunities available in the UK to companies were restricted largely to bills of exchange, syndicated loans, advances and overdrafts. The development of the Euronote and Eurocommercial paper markets in London in the early 1980s stimulated interest in the possibility of making even shorter-term sterling note issues as a new form of sterling money-market instrument. Previously, one-name sterling money-market instruments had been issued only by the Treasury, local authorities, banks, licensed deposit-takers and building societies. Money-market instruments other than such single-name paper carried at least two names, that of the issuer and that of one other good name. The vast bulk of such paper consisted of eligible bank bills – bills drawn by a company and accepted by an eligible bank – which the Bank of England was willing to buy in its money-market operation.

Bill finance was sufficiently attractive to many borrowers to suggest that the scope for a commercial paper market seemed less in sterling than in other currencies. Nevertheless, it was felt that the expressed demand for sterling commercial paper ('SCP') should be encouraged provided that adequate investor protection safeguards could be established. As a consequence the Treasury through its powers in the Banking Act 1979 enabled the issuance of corporate sterling short-term debt subject to certain conditions aimed at providing investor protection. The requirements were:

5.5.1
The issuing company should be listed on the International Stock Exchange and have net assets of £50 million or more.

5.5.2
Issues should have an original maturity of between 7 and 364 days.

5.5.3
Issues should be in minimum denominations of £500,000.

5.5.4
Issues must carry a statement that the issuer or its guaranteeing parent is in compliance with the listing rules and there has been no significant adverse change in its circumstances since information was last published in accordance with such rules.

The first programmes were announced in May 1986 and were all for overseas companies, mainly the overseas financing subsidiaries of UK companies. There was initially some uncertainty concerning the legal position of UK companies issuing such paper without a prospectus, hence the use of overseas financing subsidiaries. It was not until February 1987 that domestic issuers outnumbered overseas issuers for all outstanding programmes. By the end of August 1987, seventy-nine programmes had been notified to the Bank, in nine of which SCP was one option in a wider borrowing programme. The average size of programmes established at this stage was just under £100 million, the smallest being £20 million and the largest £300 million.

Many large companies have not yet made use of the market. For many the market may be too small for them to use in their scale of borrowing requirements. Many would have the availability of cheaper finance in the US and Eurocommercial paper markets.

Short-term domestic finance is available through several routes. *Overdrafts* are normally the most expensive but most flexible form of finance.

Money-market lines are priced at a margin over LIBOR, typically $\frac{1}{16}$ per cent for a major corporate customer. The cost of borrowing through *eligible bills* is determined by the rate at which eligible bills are discounted in the market and the acceptance commission charged by eligible banks. The eligible bill rate is a money-market rate influenced by, and itself influencing, other money-market rates. Commissions vary but a typical commission might be $\frac{1}{16}$ per cent for a major borrower and $\frac{1}{8}$ per cent for a lesser one.

The competition between SCP and eligible bills is the closest but it is difficult at this stage of the SCP market to talk of a typical cost to an issuer. The largest and best issuers might be able to borrow at LIBID (about $\frac{1}{8}$ per cent below LIBOR) while others might have to pay twelve basis points over LIBOR. The range of twenty-five basis points ($\frac{1}{4}$ per cent) may reflect in some cases the presence or absence of a rating for the issuer or its funding programme.

5.6 Floating rate notes

Floating rate notes (FRNs) are longer-term securities with a floating rate of interest which is determined periodically (e.g. three months or six months) during the life of the security. The rate of interest is calculated in accordance with a predetermined reference rate (e.g. LIBOR). FRNs were issued largely in substitution for traditional long-term bank credit. FRNs brought new asset-liquidity to the banking market and form part of the trend towards general securitization of credit markets. Sovereign bodies and banks were first to tap this market and initially the market was predominantly US dollar denominated.

Investors have become aware that FRNs are able to outperform alternative money-market instruments such as certificates of deposit and straight bank deposits. New issues now include a wide variety of banking and financial institutions and some major corporations. During 1985 in particular there was a greater variety of currencies borrowed and transactions were often driven by currency and interest swaps. In 1985 the Halifax Building Society was the first such borrower to come to the market and since then over £1,000 million has been raised by building societies. This accounts for around 25 per cent of the whole sterling FRN market. Oversupply has meant that in the latter half of 1987 the supply of new issues did, in effect, stop with only prime quality names able to issue.

The term of the loans usually lies between five and twenty years though banks in particular have issued irredeemably. The security printed notes are commonly in bearer form. A listing is not obligatory but important if any degree of liquidity is to be achieved. London or Luxembourg is usually chosen and settlement is either through the Euroclear or CEDEL clearing system. For sterling notes the reference rate is either LIBOR or LIMEAN.

A call option allows the *issuer* to repay the bonds at par (usually 100) and in the sterling market call options are exercisable from five years after the date of issue. A put option allows the *investor* to demand early repayment of the bond at par.

Investors need to establish whether FRNs issued by banks are unsubordinated, subordinated or primary capital. If a bank goes into liquidation holders of unsubordinated paper will rank pari passu with other depositors of the bank. Any holders of subordinated paper will rank after ordinary depositors. Primary capital ranks on a par with preference shareholders.

A guide to the main instruments

Floating-rate note

This is a medium to long-term bond (most maturities are from five to fifteen years), evidenced by negiotiable bearer notes in denominations of at least $1,000, and with a coupon consisting of a margin over an appropriate short-term reference rate – usually the London interbank offered rate (LIBOR) for three or six months deposits. The coupon is paid at the end of each interest period and is then adjusted in line with current rates for the next interest period. Like fixed-rate eurobonds, most FRNs are nominally listed on a stock exchange, although the market in them in conducted almost entirely by telephone and telex.

Note issuance facility

A note issuance facility (NIF) is a medium-term loan, which is funded by selling short-term paper, typically of three or six months maturity. A group of underwriting banks guarantees the availability of funds to the borrower by purchasing any unsold notes at each roll-over date, or by providing a stand-by credit. Where the borrower is a bank the paper is usually in the form of short-term certificates of deposit; where the borrower is not a bank it is in promissory notes. Note issuance facility is used here as a generic term. In practice, facilities produced by competing banks are called, variously, revolving underwriting facilities, note purchase facilities, and euronote facilities.

Interest rate swap

A swap exploits differences in the assessment and pricing of risk between the bond and bank lending markets, and shares between two different borrowers the advantages which each might enjoy in one of the markets. For example, an internationally unknown UK company, with a medium credit rating, could only raise fixed-rate funds in the international bond markets, if at all, by paying a very high coupon, although floating-rate bank loans could be obtained more cheaply. An international corporation or bank with 'triple A' credit rating, on the other hand, might expect to pay among the lowest coupons on a fixed-rate bond issue.

By arranging a bank loan at floating interest rates, and swapping interest payments with a borrower with good access to the bond market, a lesser rated borrower can obtain fixed-rate debt at lower cost than had it issued a bond under its own name. The interest benefits are usually shared between the two parties so that the bank pays an interest rate below LIBOR. Interest rate swaps can therefore be a cheaper source of long-term floating-rate funding than issuing FRNs, and bank borrowing in the FRN market has fluctuated with opportunities and cost advantages available in the swap market.

Figure 5.3
Source: *Bank of England Quarterly Bulletin, September 1984*

Within building societies, as the share account depositors 'own' their societies, their claims rank after outside providers of funds including issues of certificates of deposit and FRNs. A guide to the main instruments is given in Figure 5.3.

5.7 Financial engineering

The development of the corporate treasury market and the increased sophistication of the participants has led to the development of financial tools of bewildering complexity. Largely, these have centred on risk management in the money markets and foreign exchanges. Both of these areas have been very volatile. The use of options, forward transactions and financial futures had led to 'financial engineering' of instruments aimed at assisting the corporate treasurer in his work.

The most common instruments and ideas in use are swaps, caps, collars and floors. These terms and others are defined in the Glossary.

5.8 Building society borrowing

5.8.1 INTRODUCTION

Building societies have a curious structure in that their entire capital is on a fixed-interest basis. The assets of the societies comprise about 80 per cent in loans to members secured by first mortgages; 17–20 per cent in liquid assets of a few strictly regulated types – short-dated gilts (56 per cent), cash (24 per cent), local authority securities (2 per cent), bank acceptances (8 per cent) and 1.25 per cent in fixed assets such as land, buildings, etc. Share account depositors provide around 85 per cent of total funds (about 50 per cent of total personal sector assets). Wholesale funds accounted for only 4 per cent of total funds at the end of 1984.

After adjustments for special items and corporation tax, the excess of income over expenditure is transferred to the general reserve. It will be seen that the bulk of the assets is derived from shareholders, that further substantial funds come from depositors, and that although most of the funds are lent on mortgage, a substantial amount is invested, virtually entirely in British government securities or with local authorities. The Building Societies Act 1986 introduced a number of features which will transform radically the role of building societies in the next few years. Provision has been made for building societies to convert from their mutual status to a corporate structure with their members' agreement. A new Building Societies Commission has taken over responsibility for the supervision of societies. This commission has the power to allow advances secured on land in 'British Overseas Territories' and to permit the creation of subsidiaries in other member states of the EEC. The building societies will have new powers to provide new services as follows:

- Money transmission services, including a specific power to guarantee payments.
- Foreign exchange services, which may be provided to individuals only, but all transactions of under £5,000 are deemed to be to individuals.
- Making or receiving of payments as agents.
- Management, as agents, of mortgage investments.
- Management, as agents, of land. This power is available only to societies with the qualifying asset holding.
- Arranging for the provision of services relating to the acquisition or disposal of investments for individuals either on behalf of an investor or the institution providing this service.
- Establishment and management of personal equity plans. This power is available only to societies with the qualifying asset holding and must be exercised through a subsidiary.
- Arranging for the provision of credit to individuals and providing services in connection with loan agreements.
- Establishment and management of unit trust schemes for the provision of pensions. This power must be exercised through a subsidiary.
- Establishment and administration of pension schemes.
- Arranging for the provision of insurance of any description. This service must be provided primarily to individuals.
- Giving advice on insurance of any description.
- Estate agency services. These must be provided through a subsidiary and no employee of a society may act as agent for the subsidiary.
- Surveys and valuations of land.
- Conveyancing services.

5.8.2 FUNDING

The building societies have new powers to raise funds of which up to 40 per cent can be non-retail funds which are defined as transferable instruments, time deposits, corporate investments, trade union investments, friendly society investments and pension fund investments. In the early weeks of 1988 two societies became the first to make use of the new capital raising powers. The capital raised is subordinated debt subject to certain conditions and such loans will be included in their capital adequacy calculations. Such debts are subordinate to that of other creditors including share account holders. The first such loan was raised by Nationwide Anglia Building Society, Britain's third largest society, for a sum of £100 million. The loan was for ten years at a rate of interest sixty-five basis points (0.65 per cent) above LIBOR. It was subscribed fully, principally by overseas investors. Shortly afterwards the Alliance and Leicester, Britain's sixth largest society, raised a further £100 million on slightly finer terms. The order laid before Parliament enabling building societies to issue subordinated loan stock came into effect only days earlier on 12 January 1988.

Subordinated loans are one form of transferable investment. The other instruments available to societies are as follows:

- Certificates of deposit.
- Foreign currency certificates of deposit.
- Fixed-rate time deposits.
- Variable-rate time deposits.
- Bank loans of all sorts (direct, syndicated, transferable, etc.).
- One-year negotiable bonds.
- Sterling floating rate notes.
- Sterling or foreign currency Eurobonds.
- Index-linked bonds.

An additional source of funding in the future might involve securitization of mortgage assets. This would lie outside a society's normal wholesale funding quota. Until the new facilities became available many building societies raised capital by issuing bonds which were negotiable in that the title is transferable by delivery. The bonds might have a listing and be quoted on the Stock Exchange. The bonds have a limited appeal for the investor as interest is paid net of tax. They are of most interest to those investors who can reclaim tax easily and frequently.

Index-linked bonds have been issued on a similar basis to index-linked gilts under which the price is linked to the Retail Price Index. The bonds are issued in accordance with Stock Exchange rules and may have a listing. The transaction is usually organized on a private placement basis with a limited number of institutions. They may be used to on-lend to, say, a housing association, in relation to a specific project. The Halifax Building Society raised £50 million by way of an unquoted issue and the Nationwide Building Society issued a £60 million quoted issue.

The first building society to receive a debt rating was the Abbey National. The two large US rating agencies, Standard & Poor's and Moody's rated its long-term debt AA – minus and Aa – 1 respectively. By comparison Barclays Bank and National Westminster Bank receive the highest rate of AAA from Moody's and Aa–1, the next level down, is the rating that Bank of Scotland receives.

5.8.3 CHANGES IN THE INDUSTRY

The building societies are rapidly changing. Despite the increasing competition their balance sheets are improving. The aggregate reserve ratio at the end of 1986 was 4.23 per cent, the highest figure since 1965. The free reserve ratio, i.e., total reserves less fixed assets as a proportion of total assets less fixed assets was 3.29 per cent at the end of 1986, a full 1 per cent higher than the figure in 1980. At the end of 1986 there were 151 building societies in the UK but the largest sixteen controlled around 87.5 per cent of the total business. The smallest eighty societies controlled only 1 per cent of the total assets of the industry. The largest three societies control around half of the total assets of the industry.

Wholesale funding has undoubtedly changed the face of the industry and its cost pressures. There has been a persistent competitive pressure for retail deposits from National Savings, unit trusts and the government's privatization programme. The level of mortgage demand has risen consistently over recent years but the provision of mortgage funds has become increasingly competitive with UK banks, overseas banks and insurance companies offering both conventional funding and innovative products. Wholesale funding has on average been cheaper than retail deposits by 1–1.5 per cent since societies have had access to the wholesale markets (Table 5.3 and Figure 5.4).

Table 5.3 *Proportionate distribution of retail and wholesale net funding*

Year	*Retail net receipts (£ million)*	*(%)*	*Wholesale net receipts (£ million)*	*(%)*
1980	3816	100	Nil	0
1981	3601	97.25	102	2.75
1982	6466	96.25	252	3.75
1983	6839	80.71	1635	19.29
1984	8572	79.37	2228	20.63
1985	7462	70.70	3093	29.30
1986	6592	51.77	6141	48.23
1987	7487	70.39	3150	29.61
1988	13554	70.88	5569	29.12

Source: Building Society Gazette

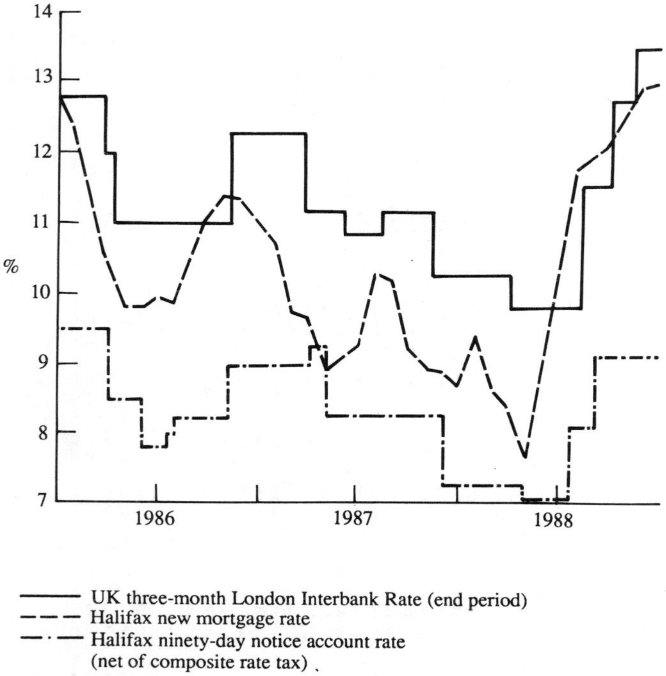

Figure 5.4 *The price of money*
Source: Datastream International

Greenwell Montagu Gilt-Edged
Member of The International Stock Exchange
Member of The Securities Association
10 Lower Thames Street, London EC3R 6AE
Telephone 01-260 0389 Telex 27783 GMGILT G
Facsimile (Groups 3, 2 & 1) 01-220 7113
TOPIC SERVICE: Key '*2050 # TELERATE: 22490
REUTER MONITOR: MGNA - N
KNIGHT-RIDDER: PAGES 182 - 195

FIXED INTEREST STOCKS

Tuesday 3rd January, 1989

TREASURY 9% 2008	
Price 97–20	**9.258**
Long Bulldog Index Yield	**10.48**
Yield Margin	**1.22**

Treasury 13½% 04-08
Price
129–31
Yield
9.687

For Seven Day Settlement Unless Otherwise Indicated

Compound Interest Volatility • •	Amount of Issue out-standing	Corporate Issues		Next xd date	Gross Accrued Interest	Tick Change Since previous day	PRICE	Yield	Redem. Yield	1 Tick Varia-tion in Price	Net yield Cap 0% Inc. @ 35%	Margins since January 1988 – December 1988 Margin over 9 % 2008 except where indicated			Current Margin over 13½ % 04-08
												High	Low	Current	
1.793	100.0	**NAT. WESTMINSTER 12½% Sub Loan Stock** Int. 5 J. 5 J.	5 July 2004		0.17 (+5)	−3	‡ **110–19**	**11.303**	**11.057**	.0039	**6.994**	**1.84**	**1.34**	**1.80**	**1.37**
1.630	100.0	**MIDLAND BANK 14% Sub Loan Stock** Int. 31 M. 30 N.	31 May 2002-7		1.57 (+41)	−3	‡ **117–05**	**11.950**	**11.456**	.0041	**7.090**	**2.21**	**1.59**	**2.20**	**1.77**
1.623	100.0	**BARCLAYS BANK PLC 16% Sub Loan Stock** Int. 15 M. 15 N.	15 Nov. 2002-7		2.45 (+56)	−3	‡ **132–07**	**12.101**	**11.327**	.0036	**6.772**	**2.07**	**1.53**	**2.07**	**1.64**
1.656	100.0	**STAND. CHART. BANK 12⅞% Sub Loan Stock** Int. 31 M. 30 S.	30 Sept 2002-07		3.60 (+102)	−3	‡ **107–19**	**11.966**	**11.737**	.0044	**7.468**	**2.48**	**2.07**	**2.48**	**2.05**
1.774	488.0	**B.A.T. INDUSTRIES 12¼% Loan Stock** Int. 2 J. 2 D.	2 Dec 2003-08		1.31 (+39)	−3	‡ **108–20**	**11.277**	**11.049**	.0041	**7.015**	**1.80**	**1.24**	**1.79**	**1.36**
2.032	50.0	**WATNEY MANN & TRUMAN HLDGS PLC 12⅛% Deb.** Int. 31 M. 30 S.	30 Sept 2008		3.39 (+102)	−3	‡ **114–16**	**10.590**	**10.375**	.0034	**6.556**	**1.40**	**1.07**	**1.12**	**.69**
2.006	100.0	⑦ **T.S.B. 10⅝% Sub Loan Stock** Int. 21 A. 21 O.	21 Oct 2008		2.18 (+75)	−3	‡ **96–12** ▲	**11.025**	**11.073**	.0040	**7.249**	**1.82**	**1.64**	**1.81**	**1.39**
2.061	75.0	**ALLIED-LYONS PLC 11¾% Deb.** Int. 30 J. 31 D.	30 June 2009		0.32 (+10)	−3	‡ **111–08**	**10.562**	**10.411**	.0034	**6.626**	**1.39**	**1.07**	**1.15**	**.72**
2.020	150.0	**BARCLAYS BANK 12% Sub Loan Stock** Int. 15 J. 15 J.	15 July 2010		0.16 (−5)	−3	‡ **108–06xd**	**11.092**	**11.001**	.0036	**7.056**	**1.75**	**1.34**	**1.74**	**1.31**
2.140	100.0	**PEEL HOLDINGS 9⅞% 1st Mort. Deb.** Int. 30 A. 31 O.	30 Apr 2011		1.92 (+71)	−3	‡ **93–08**	**10.590**	**10.665**	.0039	**7.017**	**1.75**	**1.26**	**1.41**	**.98**
1.963	100.0	**BRIT.CWEALTH HLDGS. PLC 10½% Unsec. Loan Stk.** Int. 31 J. 31 J.	31 July 2012		4.69 (+163)	−3	‡ **87–00**	**12.069**	**12.179**	.0046	**8.061**	**2.95**	**1.91**	**2.92**	**2.49**
1.961	104.0	④ **BRIT.CWEALTH HLDGS. PLC 10½%'A' Unsec Loan Stk.** Int. 31 J. 31 J.	31 July 2012		3.19 (+111)	−3	‡ **87–00**	**12.069**	**12.187**	.0046	**8.065**	**2.96**	**2.40**	**2.93**	**2.50**
2.104	200.0	**ENTERPRISE OIL 10¾% Loan Stock** Int. 2 J. 2 D.	2 June 2013		1.15 (+39)	−3	‡ **97–08**	**11.054**	**11.073**	.0038	**7.226**	**2.04**	**1.05**	**1.81**	**1.39**
2.167	150.0	**BRITISH SUGAR 10¾% Deb. Stk.** Int. 2 J. 2 J.	2 July 2013		0.24 (+8)	−3	‡ **101–09**	**10.614**	**10.599**	.0036	**6.876**	**1.79**	**1.26**	**1.34**	**.91**
2.270	65.0	**GREAT PORTLAND ESTATES PLC 9½% 1st Mort. Deb.** Int. 31 M. 30 S.	31 Mar 2016		2.65 (+102)	−3	‡ **91–11**	**10.400**	**10.460**	.0038	**6.880**	**1.48**	**1.07**	**1.20**	**.77**
2.265	50.0	**T.R. INDUSTRIAL & GENERAL 10%** Int. 31 M. 30 S.	31 Mar 2016		2.79 (+102)	−3	‡ **96–12**	**10.376**	**10.397**	.0036	**6.791**	**1.54**	**.95**	**1.14**	**.71**
2.188	20.0	**TR TRUSTEES CORPORATION 10½%** Int. 31 M. 30 N.	31 May 2016		1.18 (+41)	−3	‡ **97–00**	**10.825**	**10.840**	.0037	**7.072**	**1.78**	**1.41**	**1.58**	**1.15**
2.275	100.0	**GLOBE INV. TRUST PLC 10% Deb. Stk.** Int. 31 M. 30 S.	30 Sept 2016		2.79 (+102)	−3	‡ **96–16**	**10.363**	**10.380**	.0036	**6.778**	**1.49**	**1.06**	**1.12**	**.69**
2.079	100.0	**B.O.C. GROUP 12¼% Loan Stock** Int. 2 A. 2 O.	2 Oct 2012-17		3.36 (+100)	−3	‡ **111–09**	**11.008**	**10.902**	.0034	**6.977**	**1.69**	**1.35**	**1.64**	**1.22**
2.256	50.0	**GOVETT STRATEGIC INV. TST. 9⅞% Deb.** Int. 15 A. 15 O.	15 Oct 2017		2.35 (+87)	−3	‡ **93–11**	**10.579**	**10.610**	.0037	**6.951**	**1.72**	**1.24**	**1.35**	**.92**
2.222	80.0	**FIRST DEBENTURE FINANCE PLC 11⅛% Sev.Gtd.Deb.** Int. 2 J. 2 J.	2 Jan 2018		0.24 (+8)	−3	‡ **104–05**	**10.681**	**10.655**	.0034	**6.895**	**1.65**	**1.28**	**1.40**	**.97**
2.210	15.5	**ESTATES & AGENCY 11¼% 1st Mort. Deb.** Int. 30 J. 31 D.	31 Dec 2020		0.31 (+10)	−3	‡ **102–29**	**10.932**	**10.913**	.0034	**7.077**	**1.72**	**1.63**	**1.65**	**1.23**
2.356	70.0	**M.E.P.C. 10¾% 1st Mort. Deb.** Int. 1 J. 1 J.	1 July 2024		0.27 (+9)	−3	‡ **104–14**	**10.293**	**10.280**	.0032	**6.660**	**1.27**	**.95**	**1.02**	**.59**
2.397	400.0	**LAND SECURITIES PLC 10% 1st Mort. Deb.** Int. 31 M. 30 S.	31 Mar 2025		2.79 (+102)	−3	‡ **98–13**	**10.162**	**10.162**	.0033	**6.614**	**1.26**	**.86**	**.90**	**.47**
2.420	200.0	⑤ **LAND SECURITIES PLC 10% 1st Mort. Deb.** Int. 31 J. 31 J.	31 July 2030		0.77 (+91)	−3	‡ **31–09** ▲	**10.140**	**10.132**	.0033	**6.593**	**1.04**	**.82**	**.87**	**.45**
2.228	152.0	⑧ **M.E.P.C. 10½% Unsec. Loan Stk.** Int. 1 A. 1 O.	1 Apr 2032		0.61 (+70)	−3	‡ **25–27** ▲	**10.999**	**10.999**	.0037	**7.163**	**1.75**	**1.59**	**1.74**	**1.31**
		Eurosterling Issues													
1.591	100.0	**WORLD BANK 10⅜%** Int. 18 Feb.	18 Feb 1999		9.28 (+322)	−2	‡ **97–30**	**10.593**	**10.430**	.0050	**7.360**	**.34**	**.04**	**.25** (−)	–
1.818	100.0	**ASDA GROUP PLC 9⅝%**	25 Apr 2002		6.82 (+255)	−1	‡ **87–03**	**11.051**	**11.242**	.0049	**8.006**	**1.99**	**1.24**	**1.98**	**1.56**

All Yields calculated on a semi-annual basis

		Int. 25 Apr.																
1.895	100.0	I.C.I. PLC 10% Int. 15 Apr.	15 Apr 2003		7.36 (+265)	−3	‡	93–06		10.731	10.666	.0044	7.444	1.41	.86	1.41		.98
1.852	75.0	M.E.P.C. 10¼% Int. 15 Apr.	15 Apr 2003		7.55 (+265)	−3	‡	91–02		11.256	11.226	.0046	7.881	1.97	1.48	1.97		1.54
1.917	75.0	M.E.P.C. 9⅞% Int. 15 Apr.	15 Apr 2004		7.27 (+265)	−3	‡	88–11		11.178	11.202	.0046	7.894	1.94	1.48	1.94		1.52
2.004	100.0	I.C.I. PLC 9¾% Int. 15 Apr.	15 Apr 2005		7.18 (+265)	−3	‡	90–19		10.762	10.717	.0043	7.485	1.48	.97	1.46		1.03
2.006	150.0	HANSON TRUST PLC 10% Int. 18 Apr.	18 Apr 2006		7.28 (+262)	−3	‡	89–16		11.173	11.096	.0044	7.744	1.86	1.23	1.84		1.41
2.035	50.0	SCOTTISH & NEWCASTLE 9¾% Int. 25 Apr.	25 Apr 2006		6.91 (+255)	−3	‡	89–09		10.921	10.868	.0043	7.581	1.61	1.24	1.61		1.18
2.013	50.0	JOHN LEWIS 10¼% Int. 6 May	6 May 2006		6.95 (+244)	−3	‡	92–17		11.077	10.933	.0042	7.556	1.67	1.08	1.67		1.25
2.046	50.0	WELLCOME FOUNDATION 9¾% Int. 19 May	19 May 2006		6.26 (+231)	−3	‡	89–30		10.841	10.776	.0042	7.478	1.52	1.12	1.52		1.09
2.169	52.5	BILLINGSGATE CITY SECS. 6⅝% D.D. 1st Mort.Deb. Int. 30 M. 30 N.	30 May 2006 ●		0.74 (+41)	−2	‡	67–17		9.810	10.744	.0053	6.938	2.03	1.23	1.49		1.06
2.011	100.0	TRAFALGAR HOUSE 10⅝% Int. 25 Sept.	25 Sept 2006		3.10 (+105)	−3	‡	94–28		11.199	10.986	.0041	7.397	1.78	1.48	1.73		1.30
2.069	200.0	LAND SECURITIES 9½% Int. 29 Apr.	29 Apr 2007		6.62 (+251)	−3	‡	86–02		11.038	11.018	.0044	7.714	1.76	1.46	1.76		1.33
2.052	50.0	SLOUGH ESTATES 10% Int. 27 May	27 May 2007		6.19 (+223)	−3	‡	89–22		11.150	11.038	.0042	7.634	1.89	1.52	1.78		1.35
2.117	150.0	PRUDENTIAL FINANCE PLC 9⅝% Int. 4 June	4 June 2007		5.63 (+216)	−3	‡	88–01		10.650	10.608	.0042	7.361	1.35	1.06	1.35		.92
2.176	350.0	WORLD BANK 9¼% Int. 20 July	20 July 2007		4.37 (+170)	−3	‡	90–30		10.172	10.102	.0039	6.919	.96	.66	.84		.41
2.024	100.0	① PEARSON PLC 10½% Int. 13 June	13 Jun 2008		2.10 (+207)	−3	‡	90–22		11.578	11.417	.0043	7.699	2.16	1.52	2.16		1.73
2.029	100.0	BRITISH AIRWAYS 10⅞% Int. 15 June	15 Jun 2008		6.19 (+205)	−3	‡	94–00		11.569	11.328	.0041	7.734	2.08	1.55	2.07		1.64
2.145	100.0	② FINLAND 10⅛% Int. 22 June	22 Jun 2008		1.77 (+198)	−3	‡	96–05		10.530	10.339	.0038	6.889	1.21	1.01	1.08		.65
2.059	50.0	③ RANK ORGANISATION PLC 10⅝% Int. 11 July	11 July 2008		2.64 (+179)	−3	‡	44–14		11.259	11.050	.0040	7.416	1.80	1.50	1.79		1.36
2.210	150.0	BLUE CIRCLE INDS. 10¾% Int. 29 Nov.	29 Nov 2013		1.22 (+41)	−3	‡	96–27		11.100	10.828	.0036	7.168	1.70	1.52	1.57		1.14
2.179	150.0	⑥ HALIFAX BUILDING SOC. 11% Int. 17 Jan.	17 Jan 2014		2.54 (+83)	−3	‡	97–13		11.293	11.010	.0037	7.326	1.77	1.66	1.75		1.32
2.264	100.0	TESCO PLC 10½% Int. 22 Nov.	22 Nov 2015		1.40 (+48)	−3	‡	95–20		10.980	10.717	.0036	7.107	1.47	1.38	1.46		1.03
2.213	75.0	⑪ ASSOCIATED BRITISH PORTS 10⅞% Int. 16 Dec.	16 Dec 2015		0.00 (+0)	−3	‡	96–20	▲▲▲	11.255	10.981	.0037	7.231	1.72	1.68	1.72		1.29
2.270	100.0	⑩ LUCAS INDUSTRIES PLC 10⅞% Int. 10 July	10 July 2020		0.00 (+0)	−3	‡	97–10	▲▲	11.175	10.906	.0035	7.165	1.65	1.57	1.65		1.22
0.778	60.0	REDLAND 0%	25 Apr 1992		70.750 §	−4		68–11		0.000	11.888	.0147	8.445	1.16	.31	1.08	†††	–
0.784	100.0	S. PEARSON 0%	7 May 1992		70.942 §	−5		68–00		0.000	11.948	.0147	8.555	1.25	.24	1.14	†††	–
1.755	100.0	McDONALDS 0%	4 June 1996 ●		55.112 §	−2		45–13		0.000	10.955	.0098	8.533	.97	−0.23	.61	†††	–
1.987	300.0	DOW CHEMICALS 0%	30 May 1997		42.059 §	−2		40–10		0.000	11.128	.0098	8.295	1.05	.17	.79	†††	–
		Short Dated Bulldogs																
0.191	16.0	CREDIT NATIONAL 13½% Notes Int. 5 M. 5 N.	5 Nov 1989 #		2.44 (+66)	−2	‡	100–31		13.370	12.125	.0406	7.462	.58	−0.38	.40		–
0.891	28.5	CREDIT NATIONAL 13½% Notes Int. 5 M. 5 N.	5 Nov 1993 #		2.44 (+66)	−3	‡	109–26		12.294	10.817	.0080	6.367	1.88	−0.48	.18	††	–
		Long Dated Bulldogs																
1.780	100.0	EUROPEAN INVESTMENT BANK 9% Loan Stock Int. 16 J. 16 J.	16 July 2001 • #		0.30 (−12)	−1	‡	90–02xd	▲	9.993	10.437	.0049	7.056	1.19	.73	1.18		.75
1.785	75.0	EUROPEAN INVESTMENT BANK 11% Loan Stock Int. 23 M. 23 S.	23 Sept 2002 • #		3.10 (+103)	−3	‡	104–02	▲	10.571	10.429	.0042	6.688	1.18	.72	1.17		.74
1.752	75.0	INTER-AMERICAN BANK 12½% Loan Stock Int. 8 J. 8 J.	8 Jan 2003 •		0.14 (−4)	−3	‡	114–07xd	▲	10.944	10.529	.0039	6.554	1.28	.95	1.27		.84
1.837	200.0	WORLD BANK 11½% Loan Stock Int. 9 M. 9 N.	9 Nov 2003 •		1.76 (+56)	−3	‡	108–10	▲	10.617	10.383	.0039	6.585	1.13	.76	1.13		.70
1.927	100.0	EUROPEAN INVESTMENT BANK 10⅜% Loan Stock Int. 22 M. 22 N.	22 Nov 2004 • #		1.22 (+43)	−3	‡	99–30	▲	10.381	10.378	.0041	6.747	1.13	.74	1.12		.69
1.863	75.0	KINGDOM OF DENMARK 13% Loan Stock Int. 30 J. 31 D.	31 Dec 2005		0.36 (+10)	−3	‡	116–15		11.162	10.846	.0036	6.794	1.71	1.38	1.59		1.16
1.868	30.0	CAISSE NATIONALE AUTOROUTES 16% Loan Stock Int. 15 J. 15 D.	15 Dec 2006 #		1.14 (+26)	−3	‡	143–20		11.140	10.531	.0029	6.301	1.45	1.20	1.27		.84
1.909	50.0	CREDIT FONCIER DE FRANCE 14¾% Loan Stock Int. 31 M. 30 S.	31 Mar 2007 #		3.88 (+96)	−3	‡	134–14	▲	10.972	10.471	.0030	6.364	1.41	1.13	1.21		.78
1.816	25.0	TRANSCANADA PIPELINES 16½% Mort. Bond Int. 1 M. 1 S.	1 Sept 2007		5.92 (+131)	−3	‡	139–03		11.863	11.391	.0031	6.948	2.55	1.94	2.13		1.70
2.029	100.0	NEW ZEALAND 11¼% Loan Stock Int. 4 M. 4 N.	4 May 2008 #		1.88 (+61)	−3	‡	106–04	▲	10.601	10.500	.0036	6.739	1.44	1.16	1.24		.81
1.926	30.0	CIGNA CORPORATION 13% Loan Stock Int. 28 F. 28 A.	28 Aug 2008		4.81 (+135)	−3	‡	113–30		11.410	11.214	.0036	7.114	2.14	1.75	1.96		1.53
2.031	75.0	ELECTRICITE DE FRANCE 12½% Loan Stock Int. 28 F. 28 A.	28 Aug 2008 #	26 Jan	4.42 (+129)	−3	‡	118–19	▲	10.540	10.267	.0032	6.437	1.25	.96	1.01		.58
1.996	50.0	IRELAND 12½% Loan Stock Int. 12 A. 12 O.	12 Oct 2008 • #		2.88 (+84)	−3	‡	115–00	▲	10.870	10.658	.0034	6.736	1.77	1.35	1.40		.97
2.124	100.0	ASIAN DEVELOPMENT BANK 10¼% Loan Stock Int. 24 M. 24 S.	24 Mar 2009 • #		2.86 (+102)	−3	‡	100–15	▲	10.202	10.191	.0037	6.618	1.15	.85	.93		.50

Compound Interest Volatility • •	Amount of Issue out-standing	Corporate Issues		Next xd date	Gross Accrued Interest	Tick Change Since previous day	PRICE	Yield	Redem. Yield	1 Tick Varia-tion in Price	Net yield Cap 0% Inc. @ 35%	Margins since January 1988 – December 1988 Margin over 9 % 2008 except where indicated High	Low	Current	Current Margin over 13½ % 04\08
2.065	50.0	**REPUBLIC OF FINLAND 11½% Loan Stock** Int. 15 A. 15 O.	15 Apr 2009 #		2.74 (+87)	−3	‡ 109–09	10.523	10.387	.0035	6.632	1.39	1.06	1.13	.70
1.970	75.0	**MALAYSIA 10¾% Loan Stock** Int. 31 J. 31 J.	31 July 2009 #		0.62 (−21)	−3	‡ 93–25xd	11.463	11.549	.0042	7.591	3.20	2.01	2.29	1.86
2.188	100.0	(9) **EUROPEAN INVESTMENT BANK 9½% Loan Stock** Int. 9 J. 9 D.	9 Dec 2009 •		0.68 (+26)	−3	‡ 95–01 ▲	9.997	10.069	.0038	6.614	.83	.75	.81	.38
2.073	50.0	**AFRICAN DEVELOPMENT BANK 11⅛% Loan Stock** Int. 4 J. 4 J.	4 Jan 2010 •		0.00 (+0)	−3	‡ 104–11 ▲	10.662	10.603	.0036	6.837	1.54	1.24	1.34	.92
2.039	50.0	**KINGDOM OF SWEDEN 13½% Loan Stock** Int. 22 J. 22 J.	22 Jan 2010 #		0.67 (−18)	−3	‡ 126–08xd ▲	10.693	10.399	.0030	6.471	1.37	1.09	1.14	.71
2.072	60.0	**KINGDOM OF SPAIN 11¾% Loan Stock** Int. 24 M. 24 S.	24 Mar 2010 #		3.28 (+102)	−3	‡ 110–08 ▲	10.658	10.529	.0034	6.721	1.51	1.22	1.27	.84
2.044	100.0	**AUSTRALIA 13½% Loan Stock** Int. 28 J. 28 J.	28 July 2010		0.89 (−24)	−3	‡ 125–19xd ▲	10.749	10.487	.0030	6.546	1.47	1.16	1.23	.80
1.995	75.0	**BANK OF GREECE 10¾% Loan Stock** Int. 6 M. 6 S.	6 Sept 2010 #		3.71 (+126)	−3	‡ 93–18	11.490	11.560	.0042	7.594	2.47	2.14	2.30	1.87
2.208	100.0	**WORLD BANK 9½% Loan Stock** Int. 24 M. 24 S.	24 Sept 2010 • #		2.65 (+102)	−3	‡ 94–20 ▲	10.040	10.106	.0037	6.640	.94	.70	.85	.42
2.122	75.0	**ELECTRICITE DE FRANCE 11¼% SERIAL LOAN STOCK** Int. 17 M. 17 N.	17 May 2009-12 #		1.55 (+48)	−3	‡ 113–06 ▲	10.381	10.230	.0033	6.499	1.24	.90	.97	.54
2.007	40.0	**HYDRO-QUEBEC 15% Loan Stock** Int. 31 M. 30 N.	31 May 2011		1.44 (+35)	−4	‡ 134–30 ▲	11.116	10.820	.0029	6.710	1.70	1.45	1.56	1.13
1.987	30.0	**PROVINCE OF NOVA SCOTIA 16¾% Loan Stock** Int. 30 A. 31 O.	31 Oct 2011		2.98 (+65)	−5	‡ 148–31 ▲	11.244	10.888	.0026	6.673	1.77	1.50	1.63	1.20
2.173	100.0	**KINGDOM OF SWEDEN 11% Loan Stock** Int. 15 J. 15 J.	15 July 2012 #		0.33 (−11)	−3	‡ 105–27xd ▲	10.393	10.336	.0034	6.656	1.35	1.00	1.08	.65
2.233	100.0	**AUSTRALIA 9½% Loan Stock** Int. 14 A. 14 O.	14 Oct 2012 #		2.13 (+82)	−3	‡ 92–28 ▲	10.229	10.302	.0038	6.779	1.38	.98	1.04	.61
2.232	100.0	**CREDIT FONCIER DE FRANCE 10¼% SERIAL LOAN STOCK** Int. 18 F. 18 A.	18 Aug 2011-4 #	17 Jan	3.90 (+139)	−3	‡ 100–16 ▲	10.199	10.180	.0035	6.614	1.25	.86	.92	.49
2.182	50.0	**C.C.C.E. 12¼% Loan Stock** Int. 12 J. 12 J.	12 July 2013 #		0.27 (−8)	−3	‡ 118–07xd ▲	10.362	10.214	.0030	6.472	1.23	.90	.96	.53
2.266	100.0	**KINGDOM OF SWEDEN 9¾% Loan Stock** Int. 15 M. 15 S.	15 Sept 2014 #		2.97 (+111)	−3	‡ 95–08 ▲	10.236	10.273	.0036	6.725	1.33	.96	1.01	.59
2.194	100.0	**NEW ZEALAND 11½% Loan Stock** Int. 25 M. 25 S.	25 Sept 2014 #		3.18 (+101)	−3	‡ 109–08 ▲	10.526	10.449	.0033	6.710	1.43	1.14	1.19	.76
2.288	175.0	**I.A.D.B. 9¾% Loan Stock** Int. 15 M. 15 N.	15 May 2015 •		1.34 (+50)	−3	‡ 95–28 ▲	10.169	10.200	.0036	6.670	1.22	.88	.94	.51
2.170	50.0	**HYDRO-QUEBEC 12¾% Loan Stock** Int. 13 M. 13 S.	13 Sept 2015		3.95 (+113)	−3	‡ 119–07 ▲	10.695	10.573	.0030	6.724	1.57	1.26	1.31	.89
2.231	100.0	**AUSTRALIA 11⅜% Loan Stock** Int. 26 A. 26 O.	26 Oct 2015 #		2.18 (+70)	−3	‡ 109–06 ▲	10.418	10.350	.0032	6.651	1.35	1.01	1.09	.66
2.011	30.0	**REPUBLIC OF ICELAND 14½% Loan Stock** Int. 31 J. 31 J.	31 Jan 2016		0.83 (−21)	−3	‡ 123–27xd	11.708	11.598	.0031	7.378	2.61	1.95	2.34	1.91
2.253	150.0	**REPUBLIC OF PORTUGAL 9% Loan Stock** Int. 20 M. 20 N.	20 May 2016 #		1.11 (+45)	−3	‡ 85–06 ▲	10.565	10.677	.0041	7.081	1.76	1.37	1.42	.99
2.232	60.0	**PROVINCE OF NOVA SCOTIA 11¾% Loan Stock** Int. 18 A. 18 O.	18 Apr 2019		2.51 (+78)	−3	‡ 110–02 ▲	10.676	10.626	.0032	6.842	1.63	1.29	1.37	.94
2.245	50.0	**PROVINCE DE QUEBEC 12¼% Loan Stock** Int. 15 M. 15 S.	15 Mar 2020		3.73 (+111)	−3	‡ 115–11 ▲	10.620	10.559	.0030	6.773	1.57	1.24	1.30	.87
4.273	30.0	**NATIONWIDE B/S 3.875% Index Linked Loan Stock** Int. 30 J. 30 J.	30 July 2021		0.24 (−20)	−6	‡ 99–01xd	Inflation 5%	4.536	.002	4.536	1.01	.69	.85 ††	–
		Base R.P.I. = 378.4 (Nov. 1985)						Inflation 10%	4.389	.002	4.389	.93	.49	.82 ††	–
2.091	35.0	**LETINVEST 9¼%-11¼% Stepped Int.** Int. 3 M. 3 S.	3 Mar 2012 ●		3.29 (+123)	−8	‡ 99–16 ▲	9.799	11.121	.0038	7.262	2.20	1.39	1.86	1.43
2.200	100.0	**NEC LTD. 10⅝% ULS** Int. 31 M. 30 S.	30 Sept 2016 ●		2.79 (+96)	−6	‡ 98–20 ▲	10.773	10.775	.0036	7.015	1.66	.97	1.52	1.09
2.180	20.0	**S.E.C.W.A. 12¼% Loan Stock** Int. 30 J. 31 D.	31 Dec 2018		0.13 (+4)	−8	‡ 112–00 ▲	10.938	10.879	.0032	6.996	1.85	1.14	1.62	1.19
2.226	20.0	**S.E.C.W.A. 12¼% Loan Stock** Int. 30 J. 31 D.	31 Dec 2023		0.13 (+4)	−8	‡ 112–08 ▲	10.913	10.876	.0031	7.014	1.87	1.17	1.62	1.19
4.161	15.0	**HALIFAX 3.875% Index-Linked Loan Stock** Int. 29 A. 29 O.	29 Oct 2020		–	−6	101–00 ▲	Inflation 5%	4.641	.002	4.641	1.07	.58	.96 ††	–
		Base R.P.I. = 376.7 (August 1985)						Inflation 10%	4.620	.002	4.620	1.15	.59	1.06 ††	

1. First Interest payment of £6.5625% due on 13 June, 1989.
2. First Interest payment of £6.3281% due on 22 June 1989.
3. Announced on 8 June, 1988 @ £97.678%. £47.743 paid with balance of £49.935% due on 11 January, 1989. First Interest payment of £7.96875% due on 11 July, 1989.
4. Issued on 1 September, 1988 @ £90.59%. Fully paid.

8. Announced 18 October 1988 @ £99.623%. £30% paid with balance of £69.623% due on 28 February, 1989. First Interest payment of £2.0034% due on 1 April, 1989. Cash Settlement until 28 February, 1989.
9. Announced 30 November 1988 @ £95.586%, Fully Paid. First Interest payment of £4.75% due on 9 June, 1989.

§ Reference Prices.
# Available with Bearer Option.
● Non-Qualifying Bond.
•• Percentage change in price for 25p change in Gross Redemption Yield.
( ) Measured Against 10⅛% 99.

• Stocks paying interest gross.
†† Margin over issue Gilt(s)
††† Margin over Gilt.
‡ Accrued Interest not included in price.

Private circulation only
E & O.E.

6

Debentures and loan stocks

6.1 Introduction

This section describes the nature of that part of a company's corporate capital which is not share capital. Loan capital represents borrowings other than current liabilities. In the event that a company is put into liquidation these borrowings are repayable before any distribution of residual assets to shareholders. The principal is a liability of the company, and the interest is a charge against the company's income and a liability until paid.

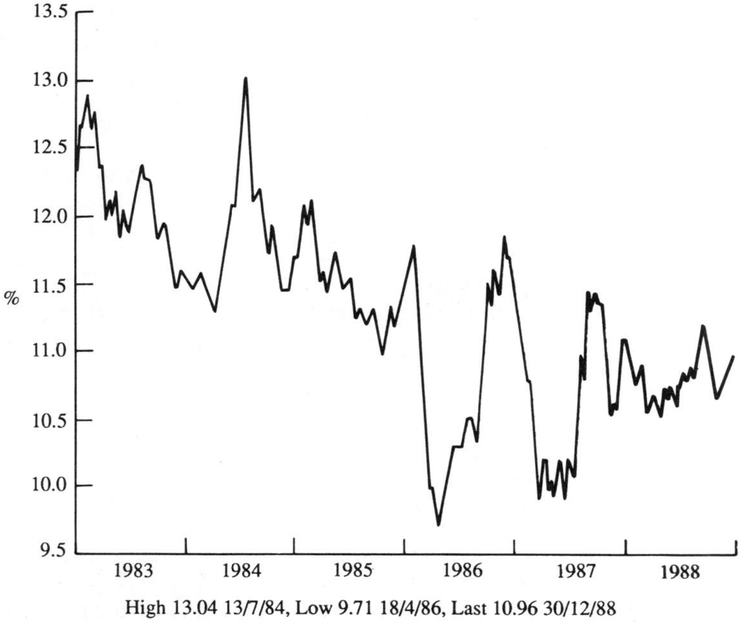

Figure 6.1 *Redemption yields on twenty-five year corporate debentures*
Source: Datastream International

Figure 6.1 shows recent redemption yields on twenty-five year corporate debentures.

The domestic corporate bond market, which had been especially active in the late 1960s and early 1970s did not experience a revival of issuing activity until 1982, prompted by a fall in long-term sterling interest rates from 14 per cent to 12 per cent. The value of new issues has fluctuated since then with no sustained upward trend. The various types of loan capital can be categorized as follows:

6.1.1 DEBENTURES

The legal definition of a debenture includes any acknowledgement of a loan issued by a company under seal. The commonest form of debenture involves a liability to pay a fixed rate of interest on certain dates and to repay the capital sum on a single date. Most debentures are secured by a floating charge on the assets of a company; the debenture holders thus become entitled in certain circumstances (usually when the company is insolvent) to appoint a receiver. The receiver will sell the assets of the company and pay the proceeds to the debenture holders in preference to all other loan creditors.

6.1.2 PERPETUAL DEBENTURES AND IRREDEEMABLE DEBENTURES

These are rare debentures where the company does not undertake to repay the loan, except on liquidation.

6.1.3 MORTGAGE DEBENTURES

Such debentures are principally secured by a fixed charge upon specified property.

6.1.4 UNSECURED LOAN STOCKS

The equivalent of debentures except that they are not secured in any way and, on the liquidation of the company, the holders are treated in the same way as trade creditors. Both mortgage debentures and unsecured loan stocks are common.

6.1.5 BONDS AND NOTES

Usually short-term loans which tend not to be secured.

6.1.6 GUARANTEED LOAN STOCKS

These loans are secured by an outside guarantor, usually by the parent company of a subsidiary.

6.1.7 CONVERTIBLE LOANS

These are normally unsecured and give holders the right to exchange the stock for new ordinary shares at a stated price on stated dates. The rate of interest is normally higher than the dividend yield on the equity but, because of the potential equity participation, not as high as would be necessary for an unconvertible loan stock. Convertible loans are frequently offered in a takeover as they defer dilution of the equity capital until the benefits of the takeover have been established (although earnings per share are generally reported as if conversion had taken place).

6.1.8 VARIABLE INTEREST LOANS

Occasionally any of the above forms of loans may be issued with a rate of interest which is not fixed, but which varies in accordance with a formula commonly linked to the six-month interbank rate. A novel variation of this is a loan for which the coupon rises in steps until it reaches a market level after several years. The borrower eases his cash flow in the early years; the lender is compensated by a higher than average yield to redemption at outset, this yield being calculated by a variation of the usual compound interest formula.

6.1.9 EURODOLLAR BORROWINGS

The growth of the Eurodollar market has enabled many UK companies to borrow dollar loans through a fairly liquid and well-established market. Interest payments may be fixed or related to money market rates.

From the investor's point of view the advantage of loan capital, apart from the high yield, is that it tends to be more secure, both as to income and repayment of capital, than shares. The interest is payable whether or not the company has made profits, and loan creditors rank for repayment before shareholders. For the company, interest on loan stocks is deductible from profits before taxation and repayment terms are fixed regardless of any depreciation in money values. The company is obliged (failing any renegotiations) to meet payments of interest and the repayment of capital regardless of its trading position. The Companies Act 1948 (now consolidated with other Companies Acts in the Companies Act 1985) allows a company to buy back in its own loan stock.

6.2 General description

It must first be emphasized that all these stocks are simply ways of organizing the borrowing of money, from groups of individuals and institutions, by companies.

As with all loans, the interest, its timing, and the terms and date of repayment must be specified and the most important task of the lender's investment manager is ensuring that there is sufficient protection should something go wrong. Otherwise, provided the comparison between the terms of the loan and those available in alternatives is satisfactory, there are no problems in lending money to companies.

The best arrangement is to lend to a company which does not have difficulty – all the precautions propounded below will then be unnecessary – and that really means a company which makes such ample profits in relation to its debt that the difficulty does not occur. In other words, the best security of all in company borrowers is a supply of profit or cash flow; nothing can ever change this and the potential lender, in considering opportunities on differing terms, must never neglect this point.

Having said this, it is unfortunately true that profit prospects change, and some of the best companies may let the lender down – hence the precautions we are about to discuss. In that case the lender must fall back on the assets, on which he will have obtained certain rights. Sadly, the best assets usually turn up in the best companies! A doubtful company, in financial straits, rarely seems to have really valuable assets. Property turns out to be run-down factories in depressed industrial areas; stocks consist of half-finished and wholly worthless articles, and so on. However, one should be aware that, usually, office and shop property is more readily marketable and thus more valuable than factories; special purpose factories are less valuable than all-purpose ones; and plant and machinery has value only if it will make profits for someone. Equally, when one comes to that comprehensive item 'stocks and work in progress', a bullion dealer's stock of gold has a precise and immediate value, while a washing-machine manufacturer's stock of partly-made machines has almost none if he goes out of business.

In other words, a lender first looks at the profits and then at the assets; in both cases stability is vital while growth is useful. Volatility is never of value to lenders.

Thinking of Sovereign debt for a moment, the dangers of lending to governments using oil reserves as security for loans is a clear example of 'profit volatility' caused by volatile prices.

These stocks are thus the formal expression of the debt of a company, excluding that part which is essentially short term such as bank overdrafts or bills. They may be quoted on a recognized stock exchange, and most of the larger ones in fact are. In general, there are four forms, mortgages and mortgage debentures, debentures, unsecured loan stocks and Eurosterling loans.

Mortgages and mortgage debentures are debts which are primarily secured on specific items of property. The former is simply a loan secured on a single asset and secured by a mortgage deed; the latter is a type of security, whether quoted or unquoted, secured by a fixed charge normally on more than one of the company's assets. If the borrowers fail to meet the terms of the loan, the lenders can take over the property and dispose of it in some way to get their money back. This is known as a 'fixed charge'; the property is said to be charged to the lenders in security and the right to take it over is called the right of foreclosure.

The second category is *debentures*. This term is much vaguer than 'mortgage'. Usually, it means that the borrower gives as security for repayment a 'floating charge' on some or all of his assets. In this case the lenders can still enter into possession if the borrower does not meet the terms of the agreement, but until this happens the borrower can, within certain broad rules, switch around and change the form of the assets under the charge. If he defaults the floating charge becomes a fixed charge on the assets that happen to be in the bracket at the moment of default, and then things go on just as in a mortgage. It is worth noting that the term debenture is, however, a rather loose one and although the usual meaning is that given above, the expression 'unsecured debenture' is perfectly valid, as a wider interpretation of the word and is simply a deed executed by a company in acknowledgement of a debt.

The third type of long-term borrowing is the *unsecured loan stock*. This is a much less protected operation from the point of view of the lender. If the borrower does not meet his obligations, the lender can sue for his money, but he is certainly in no stronger position than any other unsecured creditor of the company (he will be worse off than some! – see below) and if there are not enough assets to pay everyone off he will get no more than the proportion of the remaining assets that his loan bore to the total debt of the company.

Eurosterling issues are part of the Eurobond market. In time Eurosterling issues may well become as popular or even more popular than traditional loan stock. They are easier to issue and there is no reason why Eurosterling issues should not have good covenants. The remainder of this chapter explores more fully the UK domestic debenture and loan stock market.

There are a number of variations of the first three categories above of which three require a little more explanation. The first is the *subordinated debenture*. This means, as might be guessed, that the rights of the debenture holders are in some way subordinated to those of some other group, e.g. a bank's borrowings would be subordinated to the rights of the depositors. Another, chiefly of historical interest nowadays, is the '*income debenture*'. This is a bit of a misnomer as it cannot be treated as a true debenture at all. The interest in such a debenture is only payable in any year if the company has that much income (defined usually as pre-tax profits) and, of course, if anything goes wrong there is no income right away. Debt of this sort is difficult to value, and by its very name, open to doubt. The third category is the *convertible debenture or loan stock*. This is debt which carries a right of conversion into some other form of investment – usually ordinary stock. The treatment of these stocks is somewhat complex, involving the addition of the conversion characteristic on the normal debt form.

In evaluating the various types of borrowing, there are two principal questions to be answered. The first concerns the nature of the rights attaching to the stock; these vary from case to case, and as in any case no two companies are identical, each stock has to be considered on its merits. The second concerns the price to be paid and the resulting yield to the lender who may in fact be purchasing the rights from another lender.

6.3 Trust deeds

In all debenture stocks and in the great majority of quoted unsecured loan stocks a trustee is appointed to act for the lenders to take charge of the security for the loan, to ensure that the borrower fulfils his obligations in respect of the loan and to take action in the event of a default or similar occasion in order to protect the rights of the lenders. The nature of the trust, the rights of the beneficiaries (the lenders) and all other relevant matters will be set out in a trust deed. For most borrowings this deed forms the basis of the entire transaction throughout its life.

The development of the trust deed has been an important factor in widening the scope for different types of loan stock which are suitable both for the company and the investor. Formerly, loan stocks were issued by deed poll. The deed set out the conditions of the issue and was a separate agreement between each stockholder and the company. Any variation of the conditions required the separate consent of each stockholder, a cumbersome process when applied to large and complex companies and their asset structures. Under a trust deed the appointed trustee is given discretion to allow transactions in the assets up to specified limits. The body of stockholders is only approached on broader matters. The rules covering all these aspects are set out in the trust deed. There are two situations worth mentioning where the trust deed will be absent. The first is where property is mortgaged directly to a single body or group and the rights accruing are not expected to be transferred. In this case, the mortgage deed itself sets out the lenders' rights. Where there is a trust deed the mortgage deed places the property in the trustee's hands. The disadvantage is that if the rights are to be transferred a new mortgage deed must be drafted and the previous one endorsed at considerable expense. In effect, the loan is repaid and then reborrowed. Under a trust deed the lenders are a class and transfer of rights can take place by a simple deed of transfer. Even a single investor may still require a trustee. However, where the amount is small or there is no likelihood of transfer, the mortgage deed is all that is needed – the most obvious situation is where an individual buys a house on mortgage.

The trust deed is also absent in the case of some unsecured loan stocks. Obviously in an unsecured loan there are no assets to be charged and the trustee is really acting as a representative of the lenders. A trust deed, therefore, is not an essential from the transferability aspect. In a few cases, therefore, the company makes a formal declaration of indebtedness and recognizes the transferees of the original lenders as having the same rights (as creditors) as if they had themselves been original lenders. The disadvantage of this method from the point of view of the lenders is that they have no formal representative to regard their interests and the wording of the declaration is less precise than that of a formal trust deed.

Returning now to the normal type of quoted debt, with a trust deed, it must first be emphasized that the status and quality of the trustee is of great importance. For preference a corporate body should take this role simply for reasons of continuity. The trustee should obviously have no financial connection with the borrower nor be in any position which could lead to a conflict of interest. It is very important that lenders should be satisfied with their trustee from the start. It is both difficult and costly to appoint a new or additional trustee.

In order to consider the trustee's position and other relevant security matters in greater detail, the simplest method is to set out an example of the chief conditions of a debenture trust deed.

6.3.1 THE SECURITY FOR THE DEBT

This will recite the properties charged in the case of a mortgage or, where the charge is 'floating', state what is covered – usually the whole of the undertaking, property and assets of the borrowing company together with those of some or all of its UK subsidiaries. It is not unusual for a fixed charge to be supported by a floating charge on the remainder of the assets. Subsidiaries must be brought in as above otherwise the charge only affects the shareholding owned by the borrowing company. As the subsidiaries may not be a party to the borrowing it is usual to obtain from them a floating charge securing a guarantee of the fulfilment of the debtor's obligations. It is usual also to require that any change in the charging subsidiaries requires the consent of the trustee. A range of restrictions on the issuing of capital in subsidiaries to outsiders is also necessary. Without this an issue of preference shares, redeemable or not, may lead to a 'siphoning' of profit or assets. The expression 'charging group' frequently arises in this context. Because more and more companies have adopted group structure a debenture stock issued by the parent company with a floating charge only on its own assets was unsatisfactory when the main assets were in the hands of the operating subsidiaries. In effect the charge applied only to the shares of the subsidiaries as pointed out above so, in modern trust deeds, the debenture is secured on the assets of a 'charging group' of companies, usually comprising the parent and its main subsidiaries. Those subsidiaries whose assets are unsuitable, such as overseas companies, can be excluded. The assets and profits of the charging group can then be employed in the application of all the rules of the trust deed.

6.3.2 PAYMENT OF INTEREST

The deed will state the amount and due dates of payment and specify any initial part payment to be made to the first due date.

6.3.3 REDEMPTION

The date of repayment is given and if there is an option to redeem earlier this will state the possible dates and the notice required, usually three months. If a sinking fund is to operate, the dates and amounts to be applied will be stated. Usually the borrower also has the power to buy stock in the market and surrender it on the required dates so that he is not committed too heavily to buying at specific moments. Some sinking funds require that the stock must be drawn by lot at the due date. If this is mandatory then, of course, the borrower must not buy in advance. It is usual, however, for drawings to remain simply as an alternative in case it is not possible to buy the required stock in the market.

6.3.4 FURTHER BORROWINGS (FURTHER ISSUES OF THE SAME STOCK OR OF BORROWINGS RANKING EQUALLY OR IN PRIORITY)

This is one of the most important subjects covered in any trust deed. Usually the company reserves the right to make further issues of the same stock, provided the trustee gives his consent and there are sufficient assets to ensure that the asset and income cover (see 6.3.4.2) do not fall below some specific minimum. Where a fixed charge is concerned the assets affected are not available as security for further borrowing except in so far as a subordinate floating charge may include them. A similar restriction is made regarding any other borrowing which ranks *pari passu* which means it ranks with equal priority both for interest and capital in the event of liquidation. It is also usual that no borrowing can be made on terms which give that lender priority over the lenders under the deed. The usual restrictions on further borrowings might be as follows:

6.3.4.1

The aggregate of all the principal borrowed including all pari passu borrowings and any earlier borrowings shall not exceed two-thirds of the share capital and reserves (defined to exclude intangible assets and amounts set aside for taxes).

6.3.4.2
The annual average of profits and losses over, say, the past three years must be sufficient to cover the interest cost of all these borrowings at least four times.

6.3.4.3
No further stock or loan other than bank borrowings can be raised with a maturity date earlier than the stock to which this deed applies.

6.3.4.4
If there is a sinking fund, it must be increased proportionately if there is any further issue.

6.3.5
There is usually a power to raise a prior ranking debt but only with the consent of the trustee and only for the purpose of acquiring further assets. Thus the asset and income cover as required above remain unimpaired. A further provision may be that the total of such borrowings does not exceed 10 or 15 per cent of the share capital and reserves. Existing prior borrowings are acknowledged and remain unaffected at their present level.

6.3.6
There is also a range of restrictions on further lower-ranking borrowings so that the company cannot overborrow. A stringent restriction of this nature would limit all company borrowings to one-and-one-half times shareholders capital and reserves (less tax and intangibles).

6.3.7
In addition the trustee is given powers to supervise transactions in the assets of the company. A typical clause would read, 'The company may not, except with the consent of the trustee, sell, transfer, lend or otherwise dispose of the whole or any part of its undertaking or, except in the normal course of trading, its assets whether by a single transaction or a series of transactions, nor may the company make any significant alterations in the nature of the business.' This is known as a 'Tickler' clause after a company which took advantage of the absence of such a restriction to change greatly the nature of its business and assets and thus affected the security behind its borrowings. This clause usually is subject to various provisos so as not to hamper the development of the business.

6.3.8
The borrowing company is forbidden to redeem or pay off any share capital of its own or of any subsidiaries within the charge.

6.3.9
There is usually a provision for the debenture stockholders to modify their rights by an extraordinary resolution of stockholders but, naturally, they cannot make the terms more stringent without the consent of the company which is not very likely to be forthcoming once the issue is made.

6.3.10
There are various provisions to indemnify the trustee against various acts. However, the trustee cannot be indemnified against the stockholders for negligence or criminal acts.

6.3.11
There will be a variety of minor provisions specifying, for example, that each stockholder will have a certificate, that stock may be transferred in units of, say, £1, that the company will recognize valid transfers and issue a fresh certificate, and that when the transferee's name is entered in the company's register he will be, thereafter, treated in all respects as if he were the original owner of the stock. They will also cover the mechanics of interest and principal payments in various eventualities and the processes arising from the death or bankruptcy of a stockholder.

Having seen the nature of the restrictions surrounding a borrowing of this nature, it remains to discuss the courses of action open to the trustee should the company fail to fulfil its obligations. In fact the chief remedies will also appear in the trust deed. Usually, the right of foreclosure is applied and a receiver is appointed. He takes charge of the company and applies the monies coming to hand to discharge the obligations in their order of priority. He may, in fact, be appointed receiver 'and manager'. In other words he will endeavour to keep the company going so as to preserve the value of the goodwill interest in the business. If it is possible he will ensure that the debts in respect of which he has been appointed are paid off and if after that the business is continuing he will hand over to the shareholders once more. If, as is far more common, the company is no longer viable he will hand the remainder to the liquidator who winds up the company. Where there is a fixed charge, however, the trustee may directly enter into possession, on default, without appointing a receiver and simply sell these assets to pay off the debts. The receiver will only be needed if recourse has to be had to the other assets of the company in order to obtain repayment in full, i.e. the appointment of a receiver relates to a floating charge and not to a fixed one.

Obviously the foregoing discussion will not apply (wholly) to unsecured loan stocks. First, there will be no security, merely a recital that the company has borrowed certain sums and will repay at a specific time. No right of foreclosure exists but, of course, the trustee or the borrowers may in the event of default make an application to the court for the company to be wound up. If the court agrees the official receiver takes over acting as professional liquidator until a meeting of creditors has taken place. After this the process goes forward in accordance with the rules of court, all debts being paid off out of the assets, if available. If the assets are inadequate the creditors share proportionately.

One group of creditors have priority over all others whether holding security or not. These are the employees of the company in respect of unpaid wages. This category of creditor is protected by the Companies Acts and any debenture holder must keep their priority in mind in considering representations for and against liquidation of the company. Again, this has relevance only to floating charges. A fixed charge has priority over these claims in respect of the asset charged.

6.4 Pricing

The pricing of debentures and loan stocks requires a comparison with each other and with alternative investments. The yield on the stock may be calculated in accordance with compound interest formula bearing in mind two particular factors. First, as with gilts, account must be taken of optional redemption dates and thus assumptions concerning the general level of interest rates will be necessary. Secondly, if a stock operates a sinking fund which operates by purchase in the market at par or below by drawings the yield calculation is complicated further. New issues in the UK rarely have sinking funds nowadays. As long as interest rates are *higher than the coupon* of the stock, there is a *free market* in it, and the sinking fund is *not designed to redeem* the whole stock before the final date, and provided the holder of the stock *does not wish to sell* then his return will be calculated as usual. If, however, interest rates fall below the effective coupon rate the stock will instead be drawn and there is nothing the holder can do. His return will be reduced by the need to reinvest for the balance of the life of stock at a lower rate. Clearly both of these adjustments, one in assuming the redemption date if there is a spread and the other if a sinking fund may operate, are subjective. It is not unreasonable to assume the worst possible outcome.

Let us assume that a return has been calculated. The next step in deciding whether this is adequate is to consider the marketability of the stock. Lack of liquidity demands a premium. If an investor is effectively locked into a stock until redemption he will adjust his required return accordingly.

In comparing yields it is customary and convenient to use as a yardstick the appropriate government debt instruments. In the UK a suitable gilt or possibly a combination of two or three of a similar term are often used. The yield of the loan stock may then be pitched by reference to the yield of this parcel of gilts on a certain day. It may be thought sufficient to offer a yield premium of 0.75 per cent per annum (seventy-five 'basis points') and this fixed margin will determine the price of the stock at outset. The differential reflects not only security, gilts, for instance, being regarded as risk-free, but also marketability.

Further considerations of security include the calculation of income cover and capital cover and other matters are deferred to Sections 10.12 and 10.13.

In the general consideration of holding debentures and similar stocks two final points arise. First, in a new issue of a debenture for cash it is reasonable to include the cash raised less the issue costs, as part of the cover for the debenture. It is perfectly true that in the immediate future, directly after these monies have been invested by the company, they will be worth less than the original cash. Nevertheless it must be assumed, if the company is efficient and makes decisions for the ultimate benefit of the ordinary shareholders, that the investment will give a higher return to the company than the cost of the debenture and, ipso facto, in cash terms will be worth more than the original subscription.

Second, consideration of a debenture purchase by an investor should always be part of a decision to invest in a company as a whole. A company's capital may consist of debt plus equity or equity alone.

The difference between the two cases is that in the first some investors are given a priority over others in return for a sacrifice of potential. A highly geared equity may be ungeared by an investor by taking up sufficient debt along with his equity interest to restore his position to that of investing in an ungeared company. It is, therefore, perhaps an oversimplification to look at a company's debt by itself. It is still primarily a part of the company and the first consideration for the investor must always be the position and status of the company. Once any part of a company's finances raises doubts, all parts raise doubts. It must, therefore, be emphasized that the mechanics of debt investment which we have been discussing are always subordinate to the general question of whether the investor is prepared to invest in the company at all. Although the treatment of individual asset classes requires separation into different categories the final decision should require consideration of the whole company. This is not a universal view, however, and some investors would not think along these lines for a well-secured high yielding debenture standing below par.

Finally, it is customary practice for institutional investors to examine offers of such stocks by analysing them on a standardized form. This has the merit of ensuring that all the subjects requiring consideration are covered and the practice is to be commended as simplifying and reducing the decision-making problem to a more practical size. The following sets out the chief detail of such a form (Figure 6.2). A certain amount of modification

Name of Company:
Offer of £ of Loan stock/Debenture stock 19

New Issue/Quoted since
Capital structure:

	ordinary	
	preference	Not necessary
	loan	if statistical
	debentures	data available
Amount of issue:	If new, method of issue:	
Broker:	Issuing house:	
Trustee:	Special features:	
Quoted:	If quoted already, recent price: range:	

Redemption terms (and sinking fund, if any):

Interest and dates:

Nature of security:	Borrowing powers	
Yield	At net price after expenses	
	Gross	Net
Flat:		
Redemption:		
Index yields:		

Priority percentages on income and capital:

Existing holdings in company:

Figure 6.2 *Debentures and loan stocks*

Market prices of other company securities:

Index comparisons:

Business of company:

Profit history and forecast:

Summary of prospects:

If new issue, purpose:

Decision range: dear at:
cheap at:

If underwriting offer

Commission offer:

Period on risk:

Special features (e.g. commitment subject to consents):

Market opinion:

Effect of underwriting on level of investment in company (if in excess of 5% of total quoted capital further analysis required):

Amount of underwriting received from this source this year:

last year:

Profitability:

Figure 6.2 — *continued*

may be carried out to relate to the investor's individual circumstances. In particular, the speed of decision making required in current conditions may not give time to be too bureaucratic.

It will be seen that many of these questions may require a fuller treatment than would be possible in the space available. The form is only a model and special requirements in fact vary from case to case. The net yields should of course be calculated at the marginal rates of tax applicable to the investor. Index comparisons should be used with discretion to indicate whether the company's capital tends historically to be valued in excess of or below the average for relevant quoted securities as a group. On the matter of underwriting even in the most secure case it is important to consider the effect on investment policy if the whole of one's commitment has to be taken up. The relevance of the source of an underwriting offer is that the institutional manager must consider at all times whether his underwriting profits are sufficiently favourable to justify the risks of investment distortion. Each source of such offers should be able to justify any individual offer as part of a profitable investment activity for the ultimate underwriter.

While the style of form should be of more general use it should be noted that 'immediate' acceptance is usually required of Eurosterling issues. Thus completion of forms is an impossible luxury. The institutional bond manager needs to carry a mental checklist of questions ready for such issues and, of course, the issuing houses (there are often several for one issue) will have prepared a sales brief for the fund manager to digest.

7

Preference shares

7.1 Introduction

In many ways the preference share is an anachronism in modern investment conditions. When the joint stock company with limited liability to shareholders was first evolved and was given a statutory existence the attitude to such companies did not permit debt other than on an extremely short-term basis. Furthermore, there was no taxation of profits until they became income in the hands of an individual. It was natural in these circumstances for some of the stockholders to be more cautious than others in a particular venture and thus to seek 'preference' in their entitlement to profits at the expense of the, no doubt questionable, prospect of the unlimited wealth combined with a lower priority for immediate gain. The company of shareholders could have no objection because there was no tax penalty and both the cautious and the adventurous could combine to provide the assets needed to develop the business.

Over the 200 years since the idea of limited liability became a practicality there have been many varieties in company capital structures and, equally, many of those regarded as successful (because they raised money!) have become unsatisfactory either because of legislation and taxation, or because companies and shareholders have changed. Before governments took a serious interest in companies and their structures the tendency was to devise schemes which appeared ideal for the particular company, but sometimes with an eye to the way in which its promoters believed it would develop.

In the UK during the first half of this century the change from government of foreign policy to government of economic and social policy has meant standardization of company capital structure, a growth in the concept of the company as an entity apart from its shareholders, and a polarization of debt capital and equity capital. In this situation the preference share has become, as we have said above, an anachronism. It is not under any interpretation of law and practice a form of debt. It is emphatically capital. Yet its return from the company is limited absolutely so that it is not equity. Nevertheless, company legislation consists primarily of a series of restrictions and definitions of debt and capital that tend to the interpretation of these words as debt and equity where equity essentially implies residue of wealth after the satisfaction of debt.

It must be appreciated that in order to evaluate preference stocks they are not debt yet not equity. They have in old companies many forms and indeed in recent years have on occasions been the vehicle of astute schemes to relieve the burdens of taxation. Each must be treated on its merits because comparisons are usually unsatisfactory and a knowledge of the limitations of these stocks must always be at hand in their valuation.

A preference share then is, in the eyes of the law, a part of the capital of a company and therefore as much at risk as any other part of that capital. Nevertheless, the holder of this part of the capital is treated in different company situations in a manner as different from holders of the remainder as if his relationship were both weaker and more distant than the expression 'preference' implies. The origins of preference shares as has been said above lie in the early days of joint stock companies at a time when the debt of such organizations was very small and their security poor. In such situations investors in the company seeking some stability of income in conditions of risk and insecurity were prepared to give up the possibility of growth in income, combined with the risk of reduction, in return for a priority to some level of income out of the company's profits.

7.2 General description

Their form has not changed much over the years. Usually, the shareholder is entitled to a certain level of income, provided enough profits are available, before the other shareholders get anything. The exact conditions will be written in the company's Articles of Association, and the following are fairly standard conditions to be looked for.

7.2.1
The preference shareholders will receive a *dividend* of x per cent of their capital, which will be paid out of the profits available in a given year for shareholders before any other shareholder receives any part of these profits.

7.2.2
In any year in which no dividend is paid on the preference shares the right to this dividend is carried forward to future years, and until their arrears are paid the ordinary shareholders may not receive any distribution of profits. This clause makes the preference share *cumulative*. If the Articles do not

specify whether a preference share is cumulative or not the courts will presume that it is cumulative. It is usual that this right to arrears cannot be waived without the consent of the preference holders obtained at a separate class meeting.

7.2.3

The holders of the preference shares usually have no *vote* in ordinary circumstances but have full voting rights if their dividends are unpaid. Some such shares have full voting rights at all times but this is unusual. Also unusual is a situation where, if the preference dividend is unpaid, the preference shareholders receive sufficient votes to give them control of the company. This type of share receives a high market valuation because of the negotiating strength it gives its holders. It is, however, nowadays rarely seen.

7.2.4

In a *winding-up* the preference shareholders rank equally with ordinary shareholders up to the nominal amount of their capital and then have no further rights. This will be the presumption of the law unless the Articles specify otherwise. It is, however, nowadays customary for preference shareholders to be given rights in a winding-up in priority to the other shareholders and not merely for the nominal worth of their shares but, in addition, for the average excess of the market price over the nominal value in the six months prior to the winding-up. As some preference shares are issued with very high coupon rates this latter right may well be important, particularly as such shares will be issued at prices much above the nominal value. For example, a 15 per cent £1 preference share would naturally, when comparable yields are about 7.5 per cent, be issued at around 200p, so a winding-up without this provision could be rather harsh as shareholders would only get back 100p. This type of proviso is known as a 'Spens' clause after the investment manager who devised it.

Sometimes instead of a Spens clause a fixed premium is payable on a winding-up and other variants are occasionally seen.

7.2.5

The Articles will normally provide that no *capital issue* may be made giving a priority for dividends, or capital in a winding-up, over the existing preference issue. If a prior issue exists there must be a proviso that it cannot be increased. Similarly, where pari passu issues are concerned, it is normal that they will only be permitted provided the cover for capital and income is in excess of some specified level. The capital cover will be based on the latest balance sheet, and the income cover on profits for the last three or five years.

7.2.6
It is usual to provide that the *borrowing powers* of the company can be altered only with the permission of the preference shareholders voting separately. Normally an extraordinary resolution is required. Otherwise, a company might borrow very large sums, say for a very risky project, so that the preference holders' cover is greatly diluted if things go wrong, while if things go well they benefit only to the extent of getting some improved cover and the ordinary shareholders get all the benefits. Such clauses on borrowing powers must be designed to cover all subsidiary borrowings and indeed subsidiary preference issues to which, of course, the provisos under 7.2.5 will also apply.

7.2.7
Repayment of the preference issues, other than in a winding-up, should only be possible with the consent of the preference shareholders obtained by extraordinary resolutions in a separate meeting. Repayment should also be defined specifically to include arrears of dividend in all events, i.e. whether or not a winding-up is involved.

7.2.8
Whether or not the voting rights of the preference holders are subject to non-payment of dividends it is highly desirable that the proportion of the *capital vote* that they possess cannot be eroded by, say, scrip issues of ordinary shares. Evidently, if preference holders have more than 25 per cent of the votes they can effectively prevent any alteration in the Articles and therefore in their rights. If a series of scrip issues of ordinary shares takes place these rights may be reduced rapidly and if the preference vote is only available in special circumstances, such as non-payment of dividends, this erosion may well pass unnoticed unless the Articles provide otherwise. A satisfactory clause will ensure that in every free issue of voting ordinary shares the preference vote is automatically increased in proportion. Every other issue of voting stock for payment has either to be offered in proportion to the preference holders or their permission must be granted by a separate meeting of preference voters who would be very unwise not to insist on a quid pro quo. The value of a vote is, of course, volatile, and it is not easy to put a price on any particular situation. However, there are one or two cases where it will be substantial and these are worth detailing more specifically.

Case 1 A company has a capital consisting of 250,000 ordinary shares of £1 and 100,000 preference shares of £1 all carrying votes, but the preference will vote only if their dividends are unpaid. The company runs into severe difficulties and the preference dividend is not paid. The company has substantial assets but the ordinary shareholders wish to employ them on a risky venture which involves a change in the Memorandum. The preference shareholders can prevent such a change in objects because a 75 per cent vote in favour is required, and can insist that the ordinary shareholders receive nothing until at least their arrears are paid off (since any other course of action would be a breach of the Memorandum). If the preference holder only had 50,000 votes in the same circumstances they could not prevent such changes, nor indeed could they prevent the Articles being amended to allow the ordinary shareholders dividends, unless the 'separate meeting' clause had been imposed. It will be seen that the preference shareholders have a very strong position and can ensure that their rights are maintained, simply because they have the vital 25 per cent of votes.

Case 2 A company (A) has a capital consisting of 300,000 ordinary shares, standing at £5 each and 80,000 preference shares standing at 90p each (both at current market prices) and all shares have full voting rights. Two other companies (B) and (C) decide independently that they would like to take over company (A). Company (B) approaches a major shareholder of (A) and buys from him 160,000 shares. Company (C) can then only hope to win control by buying not merely the remaining ordinary shares, but also the preference shares. In practical terms, therefore, the preference shares are at this moment worth just as much as the ordinary shares. This example is obviously somewhat strained – the votes are worth this provided they give control – if control is not obtained the preference shares go back to being voting preference shares having less than 25 per cent voting power. The bidders (B) and (C) will therefore temper their desire for preference shares by the fear of losing. Nevertheless the company's market capitalization, instead of being £1,572,000:

300,000 at £5 each	=£1,500,000
80,000 at 90p each	=£ 72,000

might well, assuming (B) and (C) both value (A) at, say, £2 million, rise to £2,000,000 like this:

300,000 at £6 each	=£1,800,000
80,000 at 250p each	=£ 200,000

The preference vote is (provided control is won) a cheap way to gain extra votes, even if the price is greatly in excess of that ruling when control is not sought, since the price of the ordinary share vote is already so high. Situations such as this occur rarely but do show just how important voting rights can be if circumstances favour the preference shareholder and although these examples are exaggerated, they indicate the type of difficulty that can arise.

7.3 Varieties of preference share

We consider next the more unusual varieties of preference and their particular features.

7.3.1
The first of these is the *redeemable preference share*. Normally no part of a company's capital may be repaid except by permission of the courts and the wish of the different classes of shareholder but some preference shares are issued with an express right to repayment after a specific period of years. Such a repayment, provided it is written into the Articles at the time of issue, may be carried out without a court order although it is an effective reduction of the company's capital. The law on companies is very restrictive on this question because of the legislature's fear that companies might use this practice to evade liabilities to creditors. In the case of redeemable preference shares the repayment may only take place either out of accumulated profits of the company, principally the revenue reserves, or out of the proceeds of a new issue. The comments in 7.2.2 above will apply, of course, and it is usual to require that repayment must include all arrears, and that if repayment is delayed the ordinary shareholders cannot receive anything until repayment has taken place. In other respects the same protective provisions as for normal preference shares will apply.

Another curiosity of redeemable preference shares in the UK is that they must be issued for cash or in replacement of another issue. The normal preference share may not be issued as a capitalization issue out of accumulated profits. The reason for this is tax avoidance. In the former case there would be an opportunity to translate withheld dividends (i.e. the accumulated profits) into capital gains and thus the effective tax liability to a shareholder would be reduced substantially. The case for such a restriction is now reduced following the 1988 Finance Act which has changed radically the relationship between income tax and capital gains.

7.3.2
The next variant to be discussed is the *participating preference share*. In this case, the preference shareholder gets his x per cent each year but is also entitled, usually after the ordinary shareholders have had a y per cent distribution, to a further share in the profits. Thus a company might have an 8 per cent participating preference issue on the following basis. After the preference shareholders have received 8 per cent on their capital in any one year the ordinary shareholders receive the remainder of the distributable profits up to a maximum of £1,000,000. Thereafter the remaining distributable profits will be allocated to preference and ordinary shareholders in the proportions

of their respective nominal capitals. There would need to be a protective clause in the Articles to prevent the ordinary capital being increased by scrip issues! Obviously there are a number of other ways of having participation and it is usual for such participation to apply also in the event of a winding-up.

7.3.3

The third important variety is the *convertible preference issue*. This simply permits, at some specific time, a change from preference share to ordinary share. They used not to be very common. It is the case that following a resurgence of venture capital investment in the 1980s in the UK much use has been found for the preference share in its various forms, including the convertible variant, in capital structures.

7.4 Pricing

In discussing the rights of preference shareholders it must always be remembered that since these shares are part of the capital the directors of a company may at any time decide there are no distributable profits and pay no preference dividend. The shareholder's only redress comes from his rights under the Articles. He is not a creditor, and only if there is a breach of the Articles or of company law can he seek the protection of the courts.

There is no need to give an analysis form for preference issues. The one proposed for debenture issues will serve adequately provided adjustment is made for the cover requirements and tax charge (see Chapter 10).

Preference issues are expensive as a means of raising capital for companies and as a result the flow of new preference issues to the market is limited except in its new form for venture capitalists. Nevertheless, when a company reaches the limit of its borrowing powers and does not wish to raise monies from its ordinary shareholders the preference issue is an excellent way of increasing the borrowers powers. Provided these extra powers are then used to the full the cost of raising the capital is in total not so much in excess of the cost of pure debt as appears at first sight since it will be the combined cost of the preference issue and the fresh borrowings that can be borne 'on its back'. Where new preference issues are made it is worth enquiring as to these points and examining the features of the issue on the assumption that the company will seek to raise capital in the cheapest way possible. Cheapness, of course, should mean the production of a better return for the ordinary shareholders than alternative courses of action.

There are two rather uncommon company situations beyond that just mentioned where the issue of preference capital may be necessary. The first occurs where a company has little in the way of chargeable assets. An obvious example is a mineral exploration company. If it is desired to give some of the shareholders a degree of prior sharing in the profits of the company a preference issue is the natural way of doing so. Indeed this was, as pointed out at the beginning of the chapter, the origin of the preference share. This is one reason for recent popularity amongst venture capitalists. The other situation is that of a company whose profits are almost entirely received as franked income. In this case preference capital is no longer dearer than loan capital, once the company's unfranked income has been used up, as the interest paid on a loan will not now receive relief at the full corporation tax rate. The only relief is in respect of the ACT on the franked income received which can be carried as the tax deducted on the interest payments. This, however, is the same as the relief available on preference dividends, so that a preference share with a dividend rate equal to the interest rate (net of basic tax) on a debenture will cost, pound for pound of capital, the same as that debenture so far as the ordinary shareholder is concerned. This, of course, is very different from the 'normal' situation outlined in the general description above.

7.5 Other investments

So far in Chapters 3 to 7 inclusive the discussion has concerned itself with investments quoted on a recognized stock exchange. There are, however, many alternatives which are not so quoted. To begin with, most of the varieties described earlier may be found in similar unquoted forms. For example, in the UK there is a substantial body of unquoted government and quasi-government debt in the form of Treasury bills, tax reserve certificates, local authority bills and loans. National Savings is another form of central government debt and includes Certificates, Income Bonds, Capital Bonds and Premium Bonds. Furthermore, there are in existence some 1,000,000 companies in the UK alone of which only a few thousand have any part of their capital or debt structure quoted. Yet every one must have some capital at least. Obviously all forms of unquoted debt are less marketable than the comparable quoted forms. In some cases, such as government debt, the difference is marginal. In others it can be of the greatest importance.

There are, however, some forms of unquoted investment which have no strictly comparable quoted form. These may take the form of savings accounts with statutory controlled bodies such as building societies, trustee savings banks in the UK, and the savings and loans associations in the US. The latter may, nevertheless, have part of their capital quoted on a stock exchange. Alternatively, they may take a less rigid form, such as the classes of investment associated with property, either debt in the form of a mortgage with individuals (where statute and case law in most countries tends to protect the borrower rather than the investor) or direct ownership, known in England as freehold, where the ownership is absolute, and leasehold where ownership is limited to a specific period and is subject to some restrictions. Similarly, it is possible to invest in movable objects such as paintings or antique silver or immature wines and spirits. Although in the case of silver it is certainly possible to make some quantitative calculations of worth by weight, not necessarily of much relevance, in most of the others it is not. We shall not concern ourselves in any degree with investments where such calculations have little meaning nor to any great extent with those where the investor must also provide an entrepreneurial function.

8

International bonds

8.1 Overseas borrowers – UK securities

In this section we examine debt raised by overseas institutions in the UK. It includes the Commonwealth government stocks referred to in Section 4.4 but as part of the globalization of markets that has taken place in the last few years a great number of new borrowers have used London to raise money. The market is known colloquially as the bulldog market. Generally, they are loans raised by non-UK residents, often overseas governments, in sterling-denominated bonds at a yield in excess of that obtainable on UK government stock. The bonds traded in the fixed-interest market are the responsibility of the issuer and are not in any way guaranteed by the UK government. The London market is reasonably liquid and good quality, large issues trade easily in £1 million lots. London has access to many potential investors and is thus very attractive to overseas borrowers whose domestic market is limited, or who may wish to diversify the currencies in which their liabilities are expressed (Table 8.1).

Table 8.1 *Amounts raised by sterling Eurobond issues by UK borrowers £ millions*

	1980	*1981*	*1982*	*1983*	*1984*	*1985*	*1986*	*1987*
Banks	12	–	–	75	–	–	60	450
Building societies	–	–	–	–	–	–	460	630
Other	40	–	85	70	345	522	1,267	2,644
Total	52	–	85	145	345	522	1,787	3,619
of which equity-related	–	–	–	–	*155*	*35*	*228*	*1,911*
UK borrowing as percentage of all issues	15	–	18	17	21	26	54	45

Source: Bank of England Quarterly Bulletin, February 1988

The most usual measure of a bulldog price is to compare it against a gilt of appropriate maturity. More highly-developed models have been made especially using the concept of a hypothetical 'composite gilt', i.e. one with the same coupon and term to maturity as the bulldog itself. During 1987 there was a spate of issues of debentures in the UK domestic market on very attractive yield differentials compared with gilts and the bulldog market became relatively quiet. There have been few new issues since the middle of 1986 and the total amount of bonds in issue has fallen to around £3,000 million. Some early issues have already been redeemed including New Zealand 14.25 per cent 1987 and World Bank 14 per cent 1987. Lists of issues are shown at the end of this chapter.

The performance of bulldogs as any other non-gilt sterling bond tends to lag that of gilts and opportunities to switch between gilts and bulldogs often occur when yields are either at extremes of high or low. 1987 appears to have been a watershed in the history of bulldogs. Most were issued in the period 1982–84 but in 1987 the World Bank which had used the bulldog market on several occasions for its long-term debt raised finance in the Eurosterling market. The dearth of new issues in the bulldog market was not an isolated phenomenon. All other long-term sterling markets were affected, probably because of the level of UK interest rates relative to other countries, especially the US. While the bulldog market is more stable and less vulnerable to changing market conditions, entry into the Eurosterling market is easier and quicker.

Most bulldogs have now been entered into the CGO settlement system. The remaining seventeen bulldog issues together with all major corporate domestic fixed interest stocks are settled on a seven day settlement basis.

There are three broad groups of borrowers, namely, Supranational banks, Sovereign borrowers and Corporate borrowers.

All of the Supranational bank issues are Category 1 issues which implies good liquidity. Of the five issues the European Investment Bank and the International Bank for Reconstruction and Development are the two best credits. Supranational banks have been traditional providers of project finance for underdeveloped regions or countries. They use commercial criteria in their lending policy and over the years have been able to add to their reserves. They are owned jointly by their member governments and all operate within constraints imposed either by statute, or by the covenant of their bank issues, or by their own internal policy guidelines. Whatever the reason the overall effect is to impose relatively conservative financial management. Sovereign issues in the list include, for convenience, the debt of publicly-owned companies and regional authorities. It is the largest sector in the bulldog market accounting for some two-thirds of the total. These issues are the successors to the Commonwealth Government and Provincial securi-

Table 8.2 *Current differences between domestic bonds and sterling Eurobonds*

	Domestic sector	*Eurobonds*
Type of instrument	Usually registered	Usually bearer but some issuers have an option to be registered
Security/covenants	Often secured and/or with detailed restrictive covenants	Usually unsecured but with a negative pledge
Tax	Coupons paid net of UK income tax	Coupons paid gross
Investors payments	Semi-annual	Annual
Listing	Invariably London	Usually London or Luxembourg
Method of placing	Placed with investors at a fixed price on a particular day	Placed over a period at varying prices
Secondary trading	Through the London Stock Exchange starting the day after issue	Immediate over-the-counter trading organized by issuing banks with settlement by means of book entry transfer using one of the standard Euromarket clearing systems.
Issuing houses	Mainly stockbrokers and British merchant banks	British and overseas banks
Investors	Mainly domestic	Both domestic and overseas

Source: Bank of England Quarterly Bulletin, February 1988

ties of the past although, of course, issuers are not all members of the Commonwealth. The yield margin over gilts, called the spread, at the end of 1987 varied from around ninety basis points (£0.9 per annum) in the case of the Swedish and Finnish issues to around 200 basis points for Iceland, 250 basis points for Trinidad and Tobago and over 700 basis points for the Mexican issue. By contrast, the World Bank issues were around 65 basis points above gilts.

The six corporate bulldog issues are the least liquid of the bulldog issues; the spread over gilts varies from 150 basis points to 240 basis points. It is an area of the market that has fallen into disfavour.

The traditional benchmark of Treasury 13.5 per cent 2004/08 has become anomalous. It became increasingly necessary to introduce a new benchmark more appropriate to the longer bulldog issues. 9 per cent Treasury 2008 is now the most commonly used benchmark gilt.

Finally, we list some of the salient technical features of bulldogs. *Prices* are quoted net of accrued interest. *Interest payments* are on a semi-annual basis. Interest accrues on a 365 day basis. All bulldogs are *listed* in London. Issues can be either *Registered* or *Bearer* and if the latter they can be delivered via Euroclear or CEDEL. In all cases the governing law is English except that some details of the trans-Canada pipeline issue are subject to Canadian law. In two issues the investor has the right to early redemption. Two issues have a sinking fund provision. Credit ratings are by reference to Moodys, and Standards and Poors (Table 8.2).

8.2 Overseas bond markets

8.2.1 INTRODUCTION

The international bond markets include, of course, all UK government and corporate bonds but in this section we describe principally overseas domestic government borrowings and the Euromarkets. The international bond market includes fixed and floating rate securities and such securities may be referred to in practice variously as bonds, notes and debentures. A *Eurobond issue* is an international bond issue underwritten by an international syndicate of banks and sold principally, and at times exclusively, in countries other than the country of the currency in which it is denominated. Eurobonds are always available in bearer form thus preserving anonymity of ownership. Another class of international bond issue sold largely outside the country of the borrower is called, generally, a *foreign bond.* It is usually underwritten by a syndicate of banks composed primarily from one country, distributed on a similar basis to domestic issues in that country, and denominated in the currency of that country. Bulldogs are the UK foreign bond instruments.

Bonds issued in *domestic markets* by domestic borrowers are normally referred to as domestic bonds. These securities are often designed for local investors and are not always suitable for foreign investors. Regulations may restrict access to the domestic markets, the securities may be available only in registered (not bearer) form and, in particular, withholding tax may be deducted at source from interest payments. Double taxation agreements may make certain domestic bonds attractive. UK debentures and loan stocks are, of course, part of the UK domestic market.

Eurobonds are normally so arranged that interest is paid free of withholding or other taxes.

Foreign bonds are normally so arranged that interest is paid free of withholding taxes although tax may have to be deducted from interest payments to investors resident in the country of issue.

Domestic bonds will be subject to deductions of withholding taxes from interest paid if the country in which they are issued imposes such a tax on bond interest. Non-resident recipients of interest on domestic bonds will often be able to claim reductions or refunds of such withholding taxes if they are residents of a country which has a double taxation treaty with the country of issue.

The bond markets in the US, Germany and Japan are now described briefly in tabular form. These have increased in importance to UK investors recently. One reason for this is the increasing sophistication of investors particularly in their use of mathematical techniques. For instance, 'synthetic gilts' can be manufactured from a forward foreign exchange deal and an overseas bond. The development of bonds with unusual currency features lies beyond the scope of this volume but the reader should be aware of their existence.

8.2.2 UNITED STATES DOLLAR MARKETS

8.2.2.1 International bonds (US): Eurodollar bonds

- Accounts for 60 per cent of overall Euromarket.
- Highly innovative marketplace:
  - Deferred purchase bonds
  - Bonds with warrants
  - Partly-paid issues
  - Currency-linked convertibles
  - Convertible floating rate notes
  - Fixed to fixed convertibles.
- Regulatory environment – no central authority ultimately responsible for regulating flows to the market.
- Listing – usually on London or Luxembourg Stock Exchanges.
- Not registered with Securities and Exchange Commission (SEC) and not available to US citizens and residents.
- Not available in UK other than to persons whose ordinary business is to buy or sell shares or debentures, *unless* a prospectus is filed with the Registrar of Companies.
- Borrowers:
  - Sovereign governments and their agencies
  - Supranational institutions
  - Banks
  - Private sector corporations.
- Maturity dates – average of between five and ten years.
- Size – often in excess of US$100 million.
- Coupons – paid annually.
- Interest accrues on a thirty-day per month, 360 day per annum basis.
- Secondary market – transactions conducted by banks and securities companies on an over-the-counter basis.
- Spread – 0.5 per cent in active conditions – marketability on new issues is significantly better than on old.

8.2.2.2 International bonds (US): foreign bonds

- Nomenclature – called the Yankee market.
- Declining importance relative to the overall international bond market.
- Regulatory environment – issues must be registered under the Securities Act of 1933 and (if listed) the Securities Exchange Act of 1934. Must be registered with the SEC and meet its disclosure requirements and financial reporting standards.
- Bonds are usually rated by at least one of the two major agencies.
- Listing – virtually all Yankee bonds have been listed on the New York Stock Exchange.
- Interest is paid semi-annually.
- Borrowers:
  - Governments
  - International institutions
  - Government-owned or guaranteed bodies
  - Municipalities.
- Maturity dates – up to twenty-five years.
- Size – average amounts over US$100 million.
- Secondary market – mainly through brokers and investment banks operating as market-makers.

8.2.2.3 US domestic bonds

- Largest market in the world in terms of gross funds raised.
- Borrowers:
  - US government
  - Government agencies
  - Government sponsored enterprises
  - Private, commercial, industrial and financial enterprises.
- Types of issue:
  - US Treasury notes and bonds
  - US agency issues
  - Corporate bonds.
- Secondary market:
  - the most liquid in the world
  - Domestic corporates listed on the New York Stock Exchange
  - Fine spreads (as little as $\frac{1}{16}$ per cent)

8.2.3 DEUTSCHMARK MARKETS

8.2.3.1 Deutschmark international bonds: Eurobonds and foreign bonds

- Foreign bonds intended for placement in the German domestic market.
- Eurobonds aim for broader international distributions.
- Foreign bond issue syndicate consists only of German banks.
- Eurobond issue may include banks from outside Germany.
- All bonds subject to the same issuing and trading restrictions.
- All DM international bond markets subject to regulations by the Central Capital Market Sub-Committee.
- Borrowers include governments, public corporations and municipalities, multinational and national private corporations. Principal foreign issuers have been the World Bank, EEC organizations and agencies and regional development banks.
- Suppliers of funds include non-resident institutional investors including central banks, insurance companies, pension funds, investment trusts, trust companies and public agencies.
- Maturity dates tend to lie between five and twelve years.
- Size is usually for DM international bonds of the order of DM50–250 million.
- DM international bonds normally have denominations of DM1,000, DM5,000 and DM10,000.
- Transactions in public issues can be transacted either through a German stock exchange or directly between banks which maintain an over-the-counter market in that specific issue.

8.2.3.2 German domestic bonds

- Market dominated by banks specializing in long-term lending to the housing sector, public authorities and small and medium-sized enterprises, including agriculture. Three general types of bonds are issued – mortgage bonds, municipal bonds and general purpose bearer bonds.
- Access to the market is controlled by the Central Capital Market Committee.
- Main investors are the German deposit banks and the non-financial sector, mainly private individuals.
- Secondary market transactions either through a stock exchange or in over-the-counter trading between banks.
- Schuldscheindarlehen are not legally bonds but are issued by, and placed with, same categories of borrowers and investors as in the DM bond markets. Technically it is a loan evidenced by issue of a promissory letter.
- Government bonds are issued by the Federal Republic itself, the Federal states and Federal institutions. As a direct issuer of bonds this group is smaller than the bank sector.

8.2.4 YEN MARKETS

8.2.4.1 International bonds: Eurobonds

- All issues subject to approval by Japanese Ministry of Finance.
- Main borrowers are supranational organizations and sovereign borrowers meeting certain criteria.
- No Japanese regulations affecting the investor in a Euroyen bond issue.
- Maturities range between seven and ten years.
- Size around 20 billion yen.
- Limited secondary trading market.

8.2.4.2 International bonds (Japan): foreign bonds

- Foreign yen bond, Samurai bond, is a domestic bond issued in Tokyo by a foreign borrower.
- Available in bearer or registered form.
- Anonymity still preserved despite role of Ministry of Finance.
- Total volume of issues is restricted.
- Qualified issuers are international organizations of which Japan is a member or with which Japan has close relations. Public sector issues dominate the market.
- Maturities tend to be around ten or twelve years.
- Amounts can vary from as little as 5 billion yen to 100 billion yen.
- Secondary market is mainly over-the-counter.

8.2.4.3 Japanese domestic bonds

- Second largest domestic bond market after the US.
- Main issues are the government, government guaranteed agencies, municipalities, banks and corporations.
- Main classes of security are government bonds, government agency and government guaranteed bonds, municipal bonds, bank debentures and corporate bonds.
- Foreign residents may purchase freely any domestic yen bonds.
- Bearer or registered form.
- 95 per cent of secondary trades are made over-the-counter.
- Government issues have maturities between two and twenty years. Others are in the seven to ten years range, with corporate bonds slightly longer on occasions.

Greenwell Montagu Gilt-Edged
Member of The International Stock Exchange
Member of The Securities Association
10 Lower Thames Street, London EC3R 6AE
Telephone 01-260 0389 Telex 27783 GMGILT G
Facsimile (Groups 3, 2 & 1) 01-220 7113

EURO-STERLING BONDS

Tuesday 3rd January, 1989
For Seven Day Settlement

Volatility	Amount Out-standing	STOCK	Interest and Redemption Date	Gross Accrued Interest	Tick Change Since Previous Day	Clean Price in 32 Ticks	AIBD Yield	Flat Yield	Redem. Yield	4 Tick Variation in Price	Margins Since July 1987 Semi Annual Margin Against 10H92 High	Low	Current
0.651	50.0	**KREDITBANK 10⅝%**	26 Jan 1992	10.15 (+344)	−8	**96−28**	**11.897**	**10.968**	**11.554**	0.049	**0.91**	**−0.98**	**0.73**
0.656	50.0	**AMRO 10⅜%**	28 Jan 1992	9.86 (+342)	−8	**97−28**	**11.225**	**10.600**	**10.926**	0.049	**0.86**	**−0.36**	**0.10**
0.662	75.0	**ALGEMENE BANK 10½%**	11 Feb 1992	9.60 (+329)	−8	**97−20**	**11.438**	**10.755**	**11.118**	0.048	**0.84**	**−0.18**	**0.29**
0.675	85.0	**TRUSTHOUSE FORTE 10¼%**	10 Mar 1992	8.54 (+300)	−12	**95−16**	**12.009**	**10.733**	**11.679**	0.048	**1.30**	**0.08**	**0.85**
0.686	50.0	**DAI-ICHI KANGYO 9¾%**	25 Mar 1992	7.72 (+285)	−12	**94−08**	**11.976**	**10.345**	**11.649**	0.048	**1.17**	**0,30**	**0.82**
0.698	60.0	**ECSC 9⅜%**	6 Apr 1992	7.14 (+274)	−12	**95−20**	**11.019**	**9.804**	**10.734**	0.047	**0.60**	**−0.53**	**−0.09**
0.717	36.0	**AETNA LIFE 9¼%**	14 May 1992	6.06 (+236)	−12	**94−08**	**11.369**	**9.814**	**11.073**	0.046	**0.96**	**−0.84**	**0.25**
0.726	75.0	**MORGAN GUARANTY 9%**	27 May 1992	5.57 (+223)	−8	**93−20**	**11.331**	**9.613**	**11.034**	0.046	**1.36**	**−0.36**	**0.21**
0.732	50.0	**NIPPON CREDIT 9⅛%**	15 Jun 1992	5.20 (+205)	−8	**92−12**	**11.914**	**9.878**	**11.582**	0.046	**1.27**	**0.25**	**0.76**
0.755	50.0	**AMRO 9⅛%**	28 Jul 1992	4.11 (+162)	−12	**93−20**	**11.363**	**9.746**	**11.065**	0.044	**0.90**	**−0.75**	**0.24**
0.769	50.0	**FORD CREDIT FUNDING 9½%**	1 Sept 1992	3.40 (+129)	−12	**94−08**	**11.478**	**10.080**	**11.159**	0.043	**0.66**	**0.06**	**0.33**
0.794	75.0	**CREDIT LYONNAIS 10½%**	4 Nov 1992	1.92 (+66)	−12	**98−20**	**10.933**	**10.646**	**10.641**	0.040	**0.49**	**−0.41**	**−0.18**
0.814	50.0	**FORD CREDIT 9⅝%**	15 Dec 1992	0.67 (+25)	−12	**93−24**	**11.687**	**10.267**	**11.361**	0.041	**0.75**	**0.01**	**0.54**
											Semi-Annual Margin Against 10 93		
0.814	60.0	**J. SAINSBURY 10⅞%**	7 Jan 1993	0.09 (+3)	−8	**98−00**	**11.526**	**11.097**	**11.204**	0.039	**0.82**	**−0.13**	**0.73**
0.837	200.0	**SEARS 10¼%**	12 Feb 1993	9.34 (+328)	−8	**95−24**	**11.599**	**10.705**	**11.267**	0.039	**0.80**	**0.18**	**0.79**
0.850	75.0	**B.N.P. 9⅝%**	25 Feb 1993	8.42 (+315)	−8	**94−16**	**11.350**	**10.185**	**11.032**	0.039	**0.58**	**0.21**	**0.56**
0.859	150.0	**BRITISH TELECOM 9½%**	11 Mar 1993	7.89 (+299)	−8	**94−24**	**11.119**	**10.026**	**10.833**	0.038	**0.36**	**−0.31**	**0.36**
0.861	150.0	**MARKS & SPENCER 9¾%**	15 Mar 1993	7.99 (+295)	−8	**96−24**	**10.732**	**10.078**	**10.468**	0.037	**0.29**	**−0.18**	**−0.01**
0.853	50.0	**WOOLWICH 10¼%**	18 Mar 1993	8.31 (+292)	−8	**95−16**	**11.640**	**10.733**	**11.329**	0.038	**0.86**	**0.31**	**0.85**

0.861	75.0	**I.C.I. 9¾%**	22 Mar 1993	7.80 (+288)	−8	**95−08**	**11.203**	**10.236**	**10.916**	0.038	**0.47**	**0.12**	**0.44**
0.863	75.0	**NATIONWIDE 10⅛%**	3 Apr 1993	7.79 (+277)	−8	**95−12**	**11.537**	**10.616**	**11.213**	0.038	**0.88**	**0.02**	**0.74**
0.871	250.0	**BARCLAYS BANK FINANCE JERSEY 9½%**	6 Apr 1993	7.23 (+274)	−8	**94−12**	**11.210**	**10.066**	**10.915**	0.038	**0.66**	**0.32**	**0.44**
0.869	60.0	**III 10%**	9 Apr 1993	7.53 (+271)	−8	**95−16**	**11.362**	**10.471**	**11.036**	0.038	**0.78**	**−0.28**	**0.56**
0.872	100.0	**B.P. CAPITAL B.V. 9¾%**	9 Apr 1993	7.34 (+271)	−8	**94−28**	**11.305**	**10.277**	**10.981**	0.038	**0.52**	**0.12**	**0.51**
0.875	80.0	**DENMARK 9½%**	13 Apr 1993	7.05 (+267)	−8	**94−16**	**11.162**	**10.053**	**10.868**	0.038	**0.60**	**0.15**	**0.39**
0.877	100.0	**SWEDEN 9⅜%**	14 Apr 1993	6.93 (+266)	−8	**94−12**	**11.072**	**9.934**	**10.783**	0.038	**0.32**	**−0.02**	**0.31**
0.873	50.0	**FORD CREDIT FUNDING 9⅝%**	14 Apr 1993	7.11 (+266)	−8	**94−12**	**11.330**	**10.199**	**11.029**	0.038	**0.75**	**0.43**	**0.55**
0.871	75.0	**NATIONAL & PROVINCIAL 10%**	18 Apr 1993	7.28 (+262)	−8	**94−28**	**11.553**	**10.540**	**11.235**	0.038	**0.77**	**0.38**	**0.76**
0.879	50.0	**S.E.K. 9½%**	21 Apr 1993	6.83 (+259)	−8	**94−12**	**11.193**	**10.066**	**10.900**	0.038	**0.48**	**0.10**	**0.42**
0.872	100.0	**HALIFAX 10%**	22 Apr 1993	7.17 (+258)	−8	**94−20**	**11.629**	**10.568**	**11.313**	0.038	**0.91**	**0.29**	**0.84**
0.880	100.0	(1) **I.B.J. 9⅝%**	28 Apr 1993	6.76 (+253)	−8	**94−20**	**11.235**	**10.172**	**10.941**	0.037	**0.54**	**0.12**	**0.46**
0.881	100.0	**NEW ZEALAND 9½%**	28 Apr 1993	6.65 (+252)	−8	**93−24**	**11.385**	**10.133**	**11.082**	0.038	**0.67**	**0.33**	**0.61**
0.885	50.0	**NIPPON CREDIT 9¼%**	1 May 1993	6.40 (+249)	−8	**92−20**	**11.481**	**9.987**	**11.157**	0.038	**0.85**	**−0.30**	**0.68**
0.895	100.0	**EXPORTFINANS 9⅛%**	19 May 1993	5.86 (+231)	−8	**93−04**	**11.169**	**9.799**	**10.880**	0.037	**0.58**	**0.29**	**0.40**
0.901	100.0	**AUSTRIA 9%**	26 May 1993	5.57 (+223)	−8	**93−04**	**11.038**	**9.664**	**10.755**	0.037	**0.36**	**0.06**	**0.28**
0.897	50.0	**LEEDS PERMANENT 9¼%**	28 May 1993	5.70 (+222)	−8	**92−20**	**11.446**	**9.987**	**11.144**	0.038	**0.98**	**0.12**	**0.67**
0.897	120.0	**NATIONAL MUTUAL 10%**	15 Jun 1993	5.69 (+205)	−8	**94−28**	**11.500**	**10.540**	**11.190**	0.037	**0.80**	**0.41**	**0.71**
0.910	50.0	**BANQUE INDOSUEZ 9⅝%**	6 Jul 1993	4.92 (+184)	−8	**93−24**	**11.443**	**10.267**	**11.138**	0.037	**0.67**	**0.17**	**0.66**
~~0.917~~	~~100.0~~	~~**BRITISH TELECOM 9¼%**~~	~~6 Jul 1993~~	~~4.73 (+184)~~	~~8~~	~~**93−20**~~	~~**11.093**~~	~~**9.880**~~	~~**10.806**~~	~~0.036~~	~~**0.42**~~	~~**0.13**~~	~~**0.33**~~
0.925	100.0	**JAPAN DEVELOPMENT BANK 9¼%**	26 Jul 1993	4.21 (+164)	−8	**93−16**	**11.113**	**9.893**	**10.828**	0.036	**1.27**	**0.16**	**0.35**
0.924	100.0	**HALIFAX 9⅝%**	5 Aug 1993	4.14 (+155)	−8	**93−20**	**11.456**	**10.280**	**11.144**	0.036	**0.87**	**−0.07**	**0.67**
0.926	75.0	**TAYLOR WOODROW 11½%**	6 Oct 1993	3.00 (+94)	−8	**98−20**	**11.860**	**11.660**	**11.526**	0.034	**1.11**	**0.75**	**1.05**
0.953	60.0	**FORD CREDIT FUNDING 10¾%**	10 Nov 1993	1.79 (+60)	−8	**98−08**	**11.217**	**10.941**	**10.912**	0.033	**0.61**	**0.33**	**0.44**
0.949	100.0	(3) **H.M.C. MORTGAGE 11⅛%**	17 Nov 1993	1.64 (+53)	−8	**98−20**	**11.489**	**11.280**	**11.171**	0.033	**0.86**	**0.46**	**0.70**
0.977	60.0	**GMAC 9¾%**	21 Dec 1993	0.51 (+19)	−8	**93−20**	**11.504**	**10.414**	**11.189**	0.034	**0.71**	**−0.12**	**0.71**
											Semi-Annual Margin Against 10 94		
0.974	50.0	**CREDIT LYONNAIS 10¾%**	6 Jan 1994	0.12 (+4)	−8	**98−16**	**11.156**	**10.914**	**10.854**	0.033	**0.68**	**−0.20**	**0.42**
0.992	50.0	**CREDITANSTALT 10½%**	4 Feb 1994	9.80 (+336)	−8	**98−04**	**10.993**	**10.701**	**10.694**	0.032	**0.95**	**0.08**	**0.26**
1.004	30.0	**SNCF 11¼%**	28 Mar 1994	8.81 (+282)	−8	**100−20**	**11.059**	**11.180**	**10.778**	0.031	**0.45**	**−0.18**	**0.34**
1.040	50.0	**I.I.I. 9⅜%**	28 Apr 1994	6.56 (+252)	−8	**92−20**	**11.271**	**10.121**	**10.974**	0.032	**0.75**	**0.17**	**0.54**
1.049	100.0	**BP AMERICA INC. 9½%**	23 May 1994	5.99 (+227)	−8	**93−12**	**11.176**	**10.174**	**10.887**	0.032	**0.56**	**0.20**	**0.45**
1.060	75.0	**DENMARK 11⅞%**	13 Sept 1994	3.86 (+117)	−8	**102−12**	**11.252**	**11.600**	**10.949**	0.029	**0.75**	**−0.24**	**0.51**

Volatility	Amount Out-standing	STOCK	Interest and Redemption Date	Gross Accrued Interest	Tick Change Since Previous Day	Clean Price in 32 Ticks	AIBD Yield	Flat Yield	Redem. Yield	4 Tick Variation in Price	Margins Since July 1987 Semi Annual Margin Against 10H92 High	Low	Current
1.123	250.0	**EIB 9½%**	17 Nov 1994	1.40 (+53)	−8	**94−16**	**10.802**	**10.053**	**10.520**	0.029	**0.60**	**−0.20**	**0.08**
1.109	50.0	**WORLD BANK 11%**	14 Dec 1994	0.79 (+26)	−8	**100−28**	**10.784**	**10.905**	**10.506**	0.028	**0.33**	**−0.53**	**0.07**
											Semi-Annual Margin Against 10Q95		
1.107	75.0	**EIB 11½%**	9 Jan 1995	0.03 (+1)	−8	**102−04**	**10.997**	**11.261**	**10.704**	0.028	**0.65**	**−0.15**	**0.28**
1.142	60.0	**SWEDEN 11¼%**	28 Mar 1995	8.81 (+282)	−8	**101−04**	**10.968**	**11.125**	**10.690**	0.027	**0.47**	**−0.18**	**0.26**
1.174	100.0	**NEW ZEALAND 9⅝%**	9 Apr 1995	7.25 (+271)	−8	**93−24**	**11.040**	**10.267**	**10.744**	0.028	**1.00**	**0.05**	**0.32**
1.181	50.0	**CREDITANSTALT 9¾%**	27 Apr 1995	6.85 (+253)	−8	**95−16**	**10.746**	**10.209**	**10.476**	0.028	**0.71**	**0.01**	**0.05**
1.162	100.0	**WORLD BANK 11¼%**	15 May 1995	7.34 (+235)	−8	**101−20**	**10.853**	**11.070**	**10.575**	0.026	**0.52**	**−0.26**	**0.15**
1.165	75.0	**IADB 11⅜%**	29 May 1995	6.98 (+221)	−8	**101−28**	**10.920**	**11.166**	**10.636**	0.026	**0.70**	**−0.05**	**0.21**
1.202	75.0	**SNCF 9⅛%**	2 June 1995	5.53 (+218)	−8	**91−00**	**11.141**	**10.027**	**10.846**	0.029	**0.49**	**0.35**	**0.42**
1.200	75.0	**ICI 11¼%**	20 Sep 1995	3.44 (+110)	−8	**99−24**	**11.277**	**11.278**	**10.974**	0.026	**0.84**	**−0.10**	**0.55**
1.262	50.0	**EIB 10½%**	30 Jan 1996	9.92 (+340)	−8	**98−16**	**10.809**	**10.660**	**10.524**	0.025	**0.46**	**−0.42**	**0.10**
1.344	100.0	**SWEDEN 8¾%**	29 May 1996	5.37 (+221)	−8	**89−20**	**10.841**	**9.763**	**10.560**	0.026	**0.41**	**−0.47**	**0.13**
											Semi-Annual Margin Against 10H97		
1.400	100.0	(2) **EIB 10%**	3 Feb 1997	1.86 (+67)	−4	**95−24**	**10.729**	**10.444**	**10.488**	0.023	**0.42**	**0.11**	**0.14**
1.401	70.0	**CNT 10%**	27 Feb 1997	8.69 (+313)	−4	**95−28**	**10.776**	**10.430**	**10.490**	0.023	**0.45**	**−0.24**	**0.14**
1.382	100.0	**HALIFAX 10⅜%**	3 Mar 1997	8.85 (+307)	−4	**95−12**	**11.258**	**10.878**	**10.962**	0.024	**1.07**	**0.47**	**0.62**
1.397	100.0	**AUSTRALIA 10¼%**	5 Mar 1997	8.68 (+305)	−4	**97−12**	**10.736**	**10.526**	**10.461**	0.023	**1.02**	**−0.16**	**0.12**
1.400	100.0	**FINLAND 10⅛%**	5 Mar 1997	8.58 (+305)	−8	**96−20**	**10.754**	**10.479**	**10.478**	0.023	**0.52**	**−0.24**	**0.13**
1.428	100.0	**SWEDEN 9½%**	15 Apr 1997	6.99 (+265)	−4	**93−00**	**10.805**	**10.215**	**10.529**	0.024	**0.73**	**0.07**	**0.18**
1.420	100.0	**BRITISH AIRWAYS 9½%**	6 May 1997	6.44 (+244)	−8	**89−20**	**11.479**	**10.600**	**11.170**	0.025	**0.90**	**−0.08**	**0.82**
1.450	50.0	**ASIAN DEV. BANK 9½%**	1 Jul 1997	4.99 (+189)	−4	**92−12**	**10.901**	**10.284**	**10.621**	0.023	**0.72**	**−0.02**	**0.27**
1.469	250.0	**BARCLAYS BANK 10¼%**	10 Dec 1997	0.85 (+30)	−8	**95−12**	**11.085**	**10.747**	**10.787**	0.022	**0.92**	**0.40**	**0.44**
1.488	100.0	**BRITISH AIRWAYS 10%**	2 Mar 1998	8.56 (+308)	−8	**92−00**	**11.444**	**10.870**	**11.138**	0.023	**0.86**	**0.46**	**0.79**
1.486	150.0	**LLOYDS BANK 10¼%**	11 Mar 1998	8.51 (+299)	−4	**93−20**	**11.392**	**10.948**	**11.089**	0.022	**0.96**	**0.69**	**0.74**
1.479	125.0	**ROYAL BANK OF SCOTLAND 10⅝%**	24 Mar 1998	8.44 (+286)	−4	**95−16**	**11.423**	**11.126**	**11.118**	0.022	**1.00**	**0.70**	**0.77**
1.488	50.0	**LEEDS 10½%**	21 Apr 1998	7.55 (+259)	−4	**94−08**	**11.520**	**11.141**	**11.208**	0.022	**1.12**	**0.81**	**0.86**
1.558	50.0	(4) **McDONALDS 10⅜%**	7 Dec 1998	0.95 (+33)	−8	**95−16**	**11.140**	**10.864**	**10.844**	0.021	**0.57**	**0.22**	**0.50**
1.522	100.0	**LLOYDS BANK 11⅜% SERIAL**	14 Dec 1994-98	0.82 (+26)	−8	**99−12**	**11.502**	**11.447**	**11.164**	0.021	**1.08**	**0.78**	**0.82**

Private Circulation Only
E. & O.E.

1. First Interest payment of £9.6517% due on 28 April, 1989.
2. First Interest payment of £12.5% due 3 February, 1990.
3. First Interest payment of £11.125% due on 17 November, 1989.
4. First Interest payment of £10.375% due on 7 December, 1989

9

Methods of issue of debt securities and market practice

9.1
This chapter looks at the main methods of issue of gilt-edged and other securities (the primary market) and then examines the secondary market dealings in various types of asset. Some of the methods of issue for gilt-edged securities have now become somewhat academic as the government's financial position has changed and now there is a substantial public sector debt repayment (PSDR). These are, nevertheless, included for completeness and because, at least on the basis of historical precedent, PSDRs are often short-lived. The chapter concludes with sections on taxation.

Primary issues

9.2 GILTS

There are four main mechanisms which are used by the government to issue gilt-edged securities. These are by offer for sale at a fixed price, by tender, by tap (or taplet) and by auction. In addition, short-dated paper (e.g. three-month Treasury bills) is issued in a separate market.

9.3 Offer for sale at a fixed price

This method of issue requires the determination of a fixed price, the publication of a prospectus and the allowance of sufficient time for investors to send their applications in (usually three business days). It is a suitable method in stable market conditions, but has drawbacks when price movements of 1 per cent in a day are by no means uncommon. If the market price falls between the announcement of the issue and the deadline for applications, then the issue would have few applications, but if the market rose there could be substantial excess demand. Indeed in 1979, the demand for one partly-paid stock was so great that there was total chaos as investors tried to lodge applications, and this became known as the 'Battle of Watling Street'. Between 1979 and 1988 other methods of issue have usually been preferred.

9.4 Offer by tender

The tender system avoids the problems of substantial price changes between the announcement of an issue and the closing of applications. The tender may, or may not, state a minimum tender price, and can be on a fully-paid or partly-paid basis. Each investor states a tender price, and the Bank of England then determines a strike price which is common to all successful investors, irrespective of the tender price. Successful investors are those tendering at, or above, the strike price, but the amount allocated may depend on the tender price. The Bank has complete latitude in determining the strike price and can allocate stock in full or in part, and does not have to issue all the stock on offer if it so chooses. When stock is not fully subscribed, it can be taken into the Bank of England's portfolio or allocated to a number of official government or Bank funds. It can then be offered to the market using the tap system.

This gives the Bank considerable flexibility in meeting the needs of the market and in ensuring a highly liquid gilt market.

9.5 Taps and taplets

A tap is the announcement of the availability of a certain amount and type of stock. It can be partly or, much more likely, fully paid, and the initial price is usually announced. Taplets are usually of smaller amounts which are passed on by the Bank of England to the market-makers depending on prevailing market conditions. A tap can occur because of the failure of a tender issue.

Immediately after an issue, the price of official supplies of stock through a tap is not normally cut below the issue price, as this would discourage investors from applying for future issues and would cause immediate losses for investors at this issue.

Sometimes, there is little alternative to cutting the tap price where there has been a general fall in market prices. Conversely the ability to sell the tap at higher than the issue level will require a general rise in market levels. The Bank of England therefore needs to use considerable skill in operating tap stocks, and to play on investor psychology. They may not supply stocks at levels required by the market-makers and may try to increase tap prices day by day. However, tap stocks are not only sold in rising market conditions. Investors usually need an incentive to purchase a tap stock or switch from existing stocks, and hence tap stocks are generally cheaper than other stocks of similar maturity and coupon. Information about the sales of tap stocks can be important since the relative cheapness of a tap stock can be expected to disappear once the tap ceases. However, the cheapness does not necessarily immediately cease when the tap is officially declared to be finished, and there may still be some holdings retained by government funds, or some selling by those who purchased in anticipation of the exhaustion of the tap.

Taplets are small tap issues, often of £100 million or £200 million nominal stock, which are indistinguishable from an existing issue. Taplets are a much more flexible form of funding for the government without some of the problems of the larger taps. Prices can be easily moved to reflect the prevailing market conditions, with much lower market impact than taps.

9.6 Issue by auction

As the changes were made in the structure of the gilt market in the run-up to Big Bang in October 1986, with a substantial increase in the number of market-makers (previously called jobbers), there were expectations that the methods of issue for gilts would move towards the auction system, which is the only method used for funding in the US.

The Bank of England has tried three experiments with auctions. The first was in May 1987, and the auction system was accompanied by dealings in the stock on a 'when issued' basis. This eased the problem of the bidding price, and investors were required to pay for stock at the price which they bid. The lowest price at which 8 per cent Treasury 1992 was allocated was at £98$\frac{1}{4}$ and the highest was at £98$\frac{3}{4}$. About 90 per cent of the allocated bids were from Gilt-Edged Market-Makers (GEMMs), bidding on their own account and for their customers and bids were for two and a quarter times the stock available. The results of the first auction was thought to be sufficiently encouraging to justify a second auction in September 1987.

In September 1987, the gilt market was unsettled, and the second auction of £800 million of 9 per cent Treasury 2008 'A' on a partly-paid basis was less successful than the first. Bids were received for only one and a half times the available stock (compared with a typical multiple of two and a half times in the US). In January 1988 the final auction took place of £1,000 million of 8$\frac{3}{4}$ per cent Treasury 1979 'C', which was relatively unsuccessful. Bids were just 1.07 times the stock on offer, with £1.60 between the highest and lowest accepted bids. (This compares with a spread of £0.80 in September and £0.50 in the first issue.)

Despite the somewhat disappointing results of these auctions, the system will continue to be used by the Bank of England and was, for example, again used in August 1988. There are a number of reasons why the experiment was not as successful as was hoped:

1 The Bank of England was not prepared to sell stock only by auction, so the role of auctions in funding was likely to be limited. A mixture of the traditional methods of issue and the type of auction used, may have created uncertainty in the gilt market.
2 Other methods of issue give the Bank considerable flexibility in funding, but the auction system needs to be announced well in advance, with the possibility that the auction may occur in poor market conditions. Funding may then not occur at an optimum time.
3 There is no real evidence that auctions are a cheaper and more efficient method of issue. Although the Bank has sold all the stock on offer at each occasion, this has not necessarily been at the maximum possible price and it has been at the expense of market stability.
4 There was no great need for the experiment to be successful. The government finances has greatly improved and any funding necessary could be expected to be easily funded whatever form the issue takes. Hence there is no strong argument in favour of a regular series of auctions compared with some past years when the borrowing requirement was large.
5 The Bank has generally tried to issue stock on a rising market, and in a way to maintain investor confidence. The auction method makes it more difficult to achieve this aim.
6 In the US the primary dealers are obliged to bid for all the stock, and the bids are bound to be accepted so that the auction is completed. In the UK neither condition applies so the event is more half-hearted. Table 9.1 shows the key differences between the UK and US auction systems.

The auction system can also be used for debt repayment and in January 1989 was used to purchase £500 million of two short-dated stocks, Exchequer 10 per cent 1989 and Exchequer 11 per cent 1989. This was the only reverse auction in the 1988/89 financial year, but further reverse auctions may take place in the 1989/90 financial year.

9.7 Treasury bill issue

Treasury bills are a short term way of funding government debt and their method of issue has been discussed in Section 2.7.

NON-GILTS

9.8 Certificates of deposit

Certificates of deposit (CD) are in effect negotiable bank deposits. They are issued by the bank which is receiving the cash, and they promise to pay the

Table 9.1 *The UK and US auction systems*

Name of system	*New UK system* *Auction*	*Current US system* *Auction*
Method of allotment	Stock allotted at price bid	Stock allotted at yield bid
Market-makers' bid	Price	Yield
Non-competitive bids	Up to £100,000 at average price	Up to US$1,000,000 at average yield
Types of issues sold	Short-, medium-, long-; current-coupon issues	2,3,4,5,7,10,30 years at present, current coupons
Approximate announcement date	Several weeks in advance	Regularly scheduled throughout the year
Final details announced	A minimum of one week in advance	6–8 days in advance
When-issued trading	Yes	Yes
Size	£1–1¼ billion	Up to US$10 billion
Settlement	Same-day payment for bids of more than £100,000; next-day payment for bids of up to £100,000; next-day delivery	4–10 days

Table 9.1 — *continued*

Restrictions on bidders	None	Only market-makers may bid
Market-makers required to bid	No	Yes
Partly-paid issues	Yes	No
Entire amount allotted	Not necessarily	Yes
Restrictions on take-up by individual market-makers	The Bank may limit individual bidders to 25% of an issue	No
Other long-term funding in addition to auctions	Yes	No
Issues reopened	The Bank may issue additional tranches by tap or auction 28 days or more after auction	Possible in successive regularly scheduled auctions
Bids submitted (local time)	10:00 a.m. GMT	1:00 p.m. EST

EST Eastern Standard Time
GMT Greenwich Mean Time
Source: Salomon Brothers International Limited

person bringing the certificate to them at the end of the agreed lending period, the capital amount stated on the certificate plus interest at the rate quoted.

A CD is a bearer document which gives the investor a flexible way of holding cash. By contrast, if money is lent to a bank as a fixed deposit, it is not normally possible to obtain the money at an earlier date if the lender's circumstances change. CDs are issued by banks and the leading building societies. The rate on a CD is slightly lower (often $\frac{1}{8}$ per cent) than on a similar bank or building society deposit, and the marketability of the CD will depend on the name of the bank or building society concerned. Clearing bank CDs tend to be somewhat more marketable than other banks or building societies but there is an active secondary market except very near to maturity.

CDs are created by giving an order to the bank by telephone, often via a money-broker, and if dealt before noon are for settlement by 3 p.m. the same day. Dealings after noon are usually for settlement the following day but most of the business is done before noon each day.

9.9 Bills

There are various types of commerical bill, but the general concept is that investors purchase a bill which is a promise to receive a sum of money on a certain day from a specified party. The form of primary issue of a commercial or financial bill is simple and is in effect a promissory note allied to some transaction. Bills of various sorts have been used to finance trade at least for the last 200 years. The payment of certain bills (eligible bills) is guaranteed by a bank, and eligible for discount at the Bank of England. The Bank of England operates extensively in the bill market, but investors such as pension funds and insurance companies do not usually hold their short-term liquidity in bills.

9.10 Sterling commercial paper

In 1986 a sterling commercial paper market became available as a source of short-term finance for corporate borrowers. It was designed to be a cheap alternative method of raising short-term sterling (and in some cases dollar) funds, using a flexible, easy-to-use instrument. It complements the already successful US commercial paper market and rapidly-expanding Eurocommercial paper market.

The sterling commercial paper market was initially handicapped by the fact that the Companies Act 1985 did not permit sales of paper by a document (with certain exceptions for professional investors) but the Financial

Services Act 1986 removed this restriction. Paper is issued using a brief information memorandum with dealing banks making direct arrangements with investors by telephone. Programmes are usually flexible with rights to issue paper with maturities between seven and 364 days. Notes are bearer documents and are issued at a discount. They are negotiable but not quoted.

Although sterling commercial paper may be a cheap and flexible way for companies to borrow, investors need to assess whether the return is adequate having regard to the credit risks undertaken in comparison with other forms of lending. In general, neither insurance companies nor pension funds have found the rates sufficiently attractive to date, but this may change in the future.

The rates of borrowing have tended to range between LIBIR (London Interbank Bid Rate) and up to $\frac{1}{8}$ per cent above LIBOR (London Interbank Offer Rate). At the lower of these two rates a pension fund or insurance company could deposit with a prime bank and such investors may not consider the differential adequate at even LIBOR plus $\frac{1}{8}$ per cent. The main indications are that the banks have somewhat under one-third of the paper in issue at any time, with commercial and industrial investors having over one-half. Overseas investors are believed to be insignificant in this market at present.

The size of the sterling commercial paper market is still relatively small, and during 1987, the sterling commercial paper outstanding at any time reached £2000 million. At the end of 1988 the total paper outstanding was £3126 million. Over 120 companies had announced and initiated programmes. Initially companies have mostly tended to issue paper of under two months to maturity but there are signs that the term to maturity at issue is tending to increase.

9.11 Euroborrowings

There is a wide range of Euroborrowings. For example, a Eurodollar issue by, say, a UK company means that the company borrows US dollars not held by a US resident in exchange for a security. The security is traded outside the US. The Euromarkets are very large, and the Eurobond market, in terms of both the gross amount raised and the trading turnover, is the third largest bond market in the world.

The form of issue of a Euroborrowing depends on its nature. It can take the form of Euronote facilites, which are similar to sterling commercial paper to Eurobond issues similar to domestic bonds. Primary issue is generally to a syndicate of banks who sell on to their clients. Securities are usually issued for terms of up to ten years, but long-dated issues, such as in the UK gilt market, are uncommon in the Euromarkets.

Borrowers wishing to issue sterling-denominated securities have recently favoured Eurobonds and not the UK domestic market (see Section 9.12). This is because of lower costs, greater flexibility and broader appeal to overseas investors. Although initial costs to issuers on Eurobonds are nominally higher than on domestic issues, they have in practice been comparable because of the intense competition for Eurobond business. Issues can be made more quickly in the Eurobond market, which enables borrowers to take advantage of interest rate opportunities in more volatile markets. They can also easily swop the proceeds of an issue into floating rate finance. In the domestic market, issues are usually secured on assets or subject to restrictive covenants. This is not a feature of Eurobonds, where investors rely on the name of the borrower on a secured basis without offering similar security to existing holders of Eurobonds. Eurobonds are bearer stocks which give investors anonymity, and they have the further advantage that interest is paid gross without tax deduction.

9.12 UK debentures, loan stocks and bulldogs

These types of security could be issued by means of an offer for sale, tender, or placing, but in recent years, are usually issued by means of a placing.

The issuing bank or banks usually agree to subscribe, or procure subscribers for the stock to be issued, and then attempt to place the security with institutions. Part of the placing is usually subject to recall from the institutions should the market demand for the stock prove to be substantial. A commission is paid on the stock subject to recall.

Securities are not usually issued at a fixed price, but by calculation of the stock's redemption yield by reference to a specified percentage margin over the redemption yield on a certain fixed interest security (usually 9 per cent Treasury 2008), often at 3 p.m. on the day or day following the placing. The placing document specifies how the price is calculated from the yield.

Issue is generally by means of a renounceable allotment letter, which enables a reasonable secondary market to operate for at least a few weeks after dealing. After this time most debentures and loan stocks are tightly held and not easily marketable in size. Some debenture/loan stocks retain a reasonable level of marketability as do bulldogs, which are mainly larger issues than debentures and loan stocks.

9.13 Overseas domestic debt

There is a wide range of methods of issue of overseas domestic debt, depending on local market practice and whether issue is in registered or in bearer form. Investors need to look at the market practices in each country and check that each issue is permitted to non-residents as well as examining for any fiscal and legal constraints.

In many countries issues of no more than ten years to maturity are considered as the norm in contrast to issues in the UK where some longer maturities are available. The UK may move towards the overseas practice as the UK government repays some of its debts.

9.14 Futures

Financial futures are available for fixed-interest securities in certain markets. Financial futures are traded on recognized exchanges by authorized members either acting on their own behalf as principals or on behalf of their clients. A contract to buy or sell a financial future is guaranteed by a clearing house, and the price is agreed between buyer and seller. Futures are effectively created by willing buyers and sellers, and the number in issue can be determined from the 'open interest'. If an investor buys a future, he can easily cancel his exposure at some stage by an equal and opposite transaction. 'Open interest' is the number of contracts which are still outstanding and which have not been matched by equal and opposite transactions.

Those that operate in the financial futures market have to deposit margins to ensure that they are able to honour the commitments which they have undertaken. The amount of the margin will depend on market conditions and is usually continuously reviewed.

When a futures contract reaches delivery, the contract is usually fulfilled by the delivery of an existing security and not by the creation of additional securities.

Secondary markets

9.15 Gilts

Since the deregulation of the securities market in the UK on 27 October 1986, the gilt-edged market has operated with a system of Gilt-Edged Market-Makers (GEMMs) and Inter-Dealer Brokers (IDBs).

The original idea was to operate from October 1986 with thirty GEMMs, but only twenty-nine started and the number had dropped to twenty-two by early 1989. The GEMMs are expected to make a continuous two-way market.

The dealing size and positions which a GEMM can have will depend on its capital base and within limits which are agreed with the Bank of England. A GEMM acts as a principal with investors. The liquidity of the market is improved by four main aspects:

9.15.1 IDBS (INTER-DEALER BROKERS)

The four IDBs (originally six) only deal between the GEMMs and enable GEMMs to execute trades between each other without disclosing their identity.

9.15.2 BANK OF ENGLAND ACCESS

GEMMs have direct access to the Bank of England and the government broker. The Bank's dealing department may be prepared to supply or purchase stock in size larger than can normally be accommodated in the market, and can also smooth out market fluctuations. They have, in addition, a vital communications role in disseminating information to GEMMs.

9.15.3 LENDING

GEMMs can lend and borrow stock through approved money brokers, and GEMMs have secured borrowing facilities from the Bank of England.

9.15.4 THE FUTURES MARKET

The gilt futures market is highly liquid and this enables not only GEMMs to offset their positions using futures, but also for arbitrage to take place between the cash markets (i.e. the gilt market with physical stocks) and the futures market.

9.16

Institutional investors can deal with a GEMM on a principal basis or they can go to a broker/dealer and pay a commission for the broker/dealer to find the most advantageous dealing price. The commission can be as low as $\frac{1}{64}$ per cent for a large institution to much higher percentages with a substantial minimum for private investors. This is similar to the role previously carried out by a stockbroker (prior to 27 October 1986), but the broker/dealer is able to act as principal if he can deal at a price better than that available from any market-maker.

9.17

Most of the dealing by institutions is done directly with market-makers without the payment of any commission. Unlike equity dealing where an institutional investor is able to see on a screen two-way prices and the size available from each market-maker, this system of guaranteed dealing prices is not available for gilts. Instead the institution telephones a number of GEMMs to request dealing prices and sizes, and then agrees to deal at the most advantageous price. Prices can change while this process is going on, and a rough adjustment in general price changes can be achieved by watching the movement in the gilt future.

9.18

All gilt stocks are dealt in on a clean price basis, to which accrued interest has to be added or subtracted. Stocks within about five weeks and two days of the next dividend date are treated as ex-dividend without entitlement to the next dividend. In this period the accrued interest will be negative. For stocks of over five years to maturity, there is a three week period prior to the ex-dividend date when stocks can be dealt in either cum-dividend or ex-dividend form (actually special ex-dividend). This facility was more important prior to the 1986 tax changes, but investors are now, in effect, taxed on accrued income as opposed to actual income, and do not therefore have a strong incentive to avoid actual dividend payments.

In normal market conditions prices quoted by GEMMs usually hold for lots up to £5 million and for typical conventional stocks are usually four tick spreads. Larger lots generally have a slightly wider differential between the buying and selling quotes. This differential and the dealing size will vary according to the marketability of the stock. A tick is a $\frac{1}{32}$ and gilt prices are conventionally shown (in clean form) per £100 nominal as the figure followed in decimal style format by the number of $\frac{1}{32}$s. For example a price of 102.12 means £102 $\frac{12}{32}$.

9.19

In index-linked securities the stock is also shown as a clean price to which accrued interest is either added or subtracted, but the standard dealing size for quoted prices is normally only £1 million to £2$\frac{1}{2}$ million with a six or eight tick spread (i.e. $\frac{6}{32}$ or $\frac{8}{32}$).

9.20 Stocklending

GEMMs may make a two-way market in a stock but may not have sufficient stock to deliver this to the buyer for settlement the following day. Until delivery takes place the GEMM does not receive any payment. In order to overcome this problem, the GEMM borrows stock to make delivery to the buyer. This makes for greater efficiency in the running of the gilt market and improves its liquidity.

The GEMM borrows stock using one of the ten authorized Stock Exchange money brokers, and the cost of borrowing to the GEMM is around $\frac{3}{4}$ per cent per annum. This cost is small in comparison with money market rates for cash and hence the GEMM has a strong incentive to borrow in order to make delivery to the buyer. The GEMM can terminate the stock borrowing at any time and the fee of $\frac{3}{4}$ per cent per annum works on a daily basis. Hence, they need to borrow only for the time necessary and those lending have no guarantee of the length of time that they will receive the stocklending fee. The amount received by someone lending stock will usually be $\frac{1}{2}$ per cent per annum with the difference going to the broker for arranging the lending.

Confidentiality of both market-makers' positions and lenders' portfolios is vital and this is done by the use of an intermediary (i.e. the ten brokers), and the ten brokers are further insulated from other parts of their own organizations by 'Chinese Walls'. Although in theory it is possible to borrow stock from anyone, without using a broker, the established mechanism is the only practical way to do so with no adverse tax or administrative complications.

9.21 Short-term market

There is a highly active market in London for short-term paper of one sort or another. This can range from Treasury bills with a maturity usually of three months, certificates of deposit usually issued by banks or building societies, to sterling commercial paper issued by companies and commercial bills. Instruments such as Treasury bills are dealt on a discount rate, rather than interest rate basis but, for example, certificates of deposit are dealt in on an interest rate basis. The investors obviously need to work out the underlying interest rates to enable a comparison of the various types of investment. This type of asset will normally be dealt in for same day settlement, provided that dealing is done by noon. Some dealing takes place in the afternoon for settlement the following day but the bulk of the trades are conducted in the morning.

9.22 Bulldogs, debentures and loan stocks

Some fixed-interest securities are not issued by the British government but are nevertheless dealt in the same way as such stocks. Stocks which do not fall within this category which are traded in London are usually dealt on a Stock Exchange account settlement basis. Investors still have the option of dealing directly with a market-maker for bulldogs, debentures or loan stocks, or they may approach an agency broker to action the transaction for the payment of a commission. The bulldog market is generally more fluid than that for most UK debentures or loan stocks, unless such stocks have been recently issued or are large issues. Hence, purchases and sales of debentures and loan stocks will often result in sizable spreads (for example 1 per cent) between the buying and selling prices, and even then the size may be limited to £25,000 or £50,000 nominal of such stock. The bulldog market is usually in larger size (around £1 million nominal) and with smaller spreads. The spreads are often eight ticks (i.e. $\frac{1}{4}$ per cent). Larger transactions, especially for debentures and loans, will need to be on the basis of negotiation, and this usually means that the agency broker will need to approach some of his clients to see if they wish to either sell or buy.

The domestic company debenture and loan stock market has been in long-term decline, although there have been some periods when interest rates have been relatively low when there have been a number of issues. Companies have switched to other more flexible forms of finance rather than pay the cost of a potentially high coupon on fixed-interest stock for a long period. Recent issues have tended to be from financial companies, particularly property companies which can use their portfolios of property for security and actually require long-term finance. Some issues have stepped coupons (i.e. coupons which increase periodically in much the same way as the rental income from the underlying properties is expected to rise). This market may increase in importance as the amount of government debt decreases.

The bulldog market for overseas borrowers issuing long-term sterling debt is smaller than the debenture market at £3.5 billion of nominal stock, but has the advantage of far fewer stocks – just over 100. In each of the four years 1982–85, there were new issues of at least £600 million, but since June 1986, issues have virtually disappeared. Big Bang for the bulldog market took place in July 1986, and it was hoped that this would substantially increase liquidity for this sector. Initially around fifteen firms were expected to act as market-makers, but there are now effectively only four firms with the bulk of this business. The contraction in market-making capacity has taken place at a time of lower sterling interest rates which would normally act as an incentive for issuers to borrow. Existing issues tend to be fairly tightly held by the institutions, and borrowers have the choice to use the bulldog or Eurosterling markets if they wish to issue sterling paper, or overseas markets if they issue in other currencies. Borrowers have chosen other routes, particularly since UK interest rates have been high compared with those of other major currencies. It is difficult to know whether the bulldog market will return to a high level of activity or be in demise.

9.23 Financial futures

The financial futures markets usually operate on the open outcry basis and usually provide a highly liquid market. There is no difference between a primary and a secondary future since each transaction relates to a 'new' contract between a buyer and a seller.

9.24 Tax

Reference was made in Section 3.3 to the new basis of taxation embodied in the 1985 Finance Act. The accrued income scheme took effect on 28 February 1986 and applies to all fixed-interest securities, whether in sterling or foreign currency. Another set of rules relating to capital gains took effect on 2 July 1986 which exempts disposals of most sterling-denominated bonds from capital gains tax completely but non-sterling denominated securities are still included within the capital gains tax net.

The *accrued income scheme* applies to all taxpayers be they individuals, companies or trustees who are resident or ordinarily resident in the UK. It also applies to non-residents if they are trading in the UK through a branch or agency but only in relation to investments in connection with the UK branch or agency. The scheme does not apply to the investment income of exempt bodies or to financial concerns whose profits from sales of securities are charged to tax as income rather than as capital gains. Syndicates at Lloyds, for instance, are taxed on a calendar year cycle and coupons are brought into their profit and loss accounts as received. In a good trading year purchase of low coupon gilts rather than high coupon gilts will have the effect of depressing their profits.

The scheme does not cover ordinary or preference shares, convertibles, National Savings Certificates, certificates of deposit or Treasury bills.

When a transaction takes place, the accrued interest since the previous payment date will be treated as income in the hands of the seller, while the purchaser will receive a credit of equal amount which he can use against the next payment of interest on that stock. The accrued interest cannot be transferred to other stocks. In the case of ex-dividend transactions where the accrued interest is negative (known as rebate interest), the seller receives a credit of the rebate interest, whereas the purchaser is charged to tax on the rebate interest.

The purpose of the legislation was to prevent investors exchanging income payments for capital gains ('bond washing').

The position on *capital gains* is that transactions after 1 July 1986 in gilts and other 'qualifying corporate bonds' have not been subject to capital gains tax irrespective of the length of time since purchase. Losses are not allowable and for many this was a valuable concession to lose. This feature leads to the perverse conclusion that 'non-qualifying' may well be more efficient than 'qualifying' corporate bonds. Preference shares, unquoted debentures of a company not quoted on the Stock Exchange or USM, and non-sterling denominated government bonds do not qualify and thus may still be used to establish tax losses.

9.25

The attractions of each type of investment to each investor will depend on many factors including his objectives, cash flow requirements and tax position. The approximate tax positions for the main types of investor for fixed interest assets are set out in Table 9.2.

Table 9.2

Type	*Tax rate on income or accrued income (%)*	*Tax rate on realized capital gains (%)*
Pension funds	0	0
Life insurance company (no pensions or annuity business)	35	0
Life insurance company (with pensions and annuity business)	10–20 (Note 1)	0 (Note 2)
General insurance company	35	35
Building society	35	35
Bank	35	35
TSBs	35	35
Discount house	35	35
Limited company	35	0
Individual (higher rate tax)	40	0
Individual (basic rate tax)	25	0

Notes:

1 The rate depends upon the business mix between ordinary life business, general annuity and pensions. It is usually between 10 per cent and 20 per cent of total income.

2 Again the rate will depend on the business mix but is often sufficiently close to zero that it can be ignored.

3 Where rates of zero are shown above, this assumes that the investors are not treated as traders by the Inland Revenue.

9.26

The impact of these investors on the UK gilt market is shown in Table 9.3.

Table 9.3

Type	*Short dated (0–7 years)*	*Medium dated (7–15 years)*	*Long dated (over 15 years)*	*Index linked*
Pension funds	Small	Large	Large	Medium
Life assurance company	Small	Large	Large	Medium
General insurance company	Medium	Medium	Small	Small
Building society	Medium	Small	Small	Small
Bank	Medium	Medium	Small	Small
Discount house	Small	Small	Negligible	Small
Limited company	Small	Negligible	Negligible	Small
Individual	Large	Medium	Medium	Small

Notes:

1 Small: holdings of less than £2 billion
Medium: holdings of between £2 billion and £10 billion
Large: holdings of over £15 billion

2 Small, medium and large figures are obtained from the latest available figures as published in *'Financial Statistics'* from the Central Statistical Office, or estimated where data was not available.

3 Additional statistics for gilt-edged investors are given in Tables 9.5 and 9.6.

9.27

The impact of investors on certain other fixed interest securities is shown in Table 9.4.

Table 9.4

	CDs	*Bills*	*UK debentures/ loan stocks*	*Overseas government securities*
Pension funds	Small	Small	Small	Small
Life assurance company	Small	Small	Medium	Medium
General insurance company	Small	Small	Small	Medium
Building society	Medium	Negligible	Negligible	Negligible
Banks	Large	Medium	Small	Medium
Discount house	Medium	Medium	Negligible	Small
Limited company	Medium	Negligible	Small	Small
Individuals	Negligible	Negligible	Small	Small

Notes:

1 Small: holdings of less than £2 billion
Medium: holdings of between £2 billion and £10 billion
Large: holdings of over £15 billion

2 Small, medium and large figures are obtained from the latest available figures as published in *Financial Statistics* from the Central Statistical Office, or estimated where data was not available.

3 Additional statistics for non-gilt investors are given in Table 9.7.

Table 9.5 *Short gilts – client profile*

	Value		Bargains		Av. bargain size		Average commission rate		Share of commission revenue	
	1988 (%)	*1987 (%)*	**1988 (%)**	*1987 (%)*	**1988 (£000)**	*1987 (£000)*	**1988 (%)**	*1987 (%)*	**1988 (%)**	*1987 (%)*
A Individuals	**1.7**	1.6	**21.7**	23.4	**51.1**	37.7	**0.116**	0.198	**32.3**	26.0
B Via agents	**0.3**	0.4	**15.8**	13.6	**11.8**	16.2	**0.411**	0.401	**19.2**	13.2
C Banks as agents	**3.9**	1.6	**31.4**	30.0	**84.9**	29.6	**0.012**	0.185	**27.9**	24.5
Sub total	**5.9**	3.6	**68.9**	67.0	**57.2**	29.7	**0.030**	0.215	**79.4**	63.7
D. Prof. fund mgers	**4.3**	5.9	**7.9**	10.3	**364.5**	311.2	**0.008**	0.022	**5.8**	10.7
E Banks	**13.2**	9.7	**5.2**	5.3	**1,704.4**	978.9	**0.001**	0.004	**1.5**	2.9
F Major institutions	**4.5**	10.6	**3.4**	4.0	**878.8**	1,430.5	**0.001**	0.005	**0.9**	4.2
G Other institutions	**26.3**	41.2	**6.0**	6.7	**2,949.5**	3,323.2	**0.003**	0.003	**11.2**	9.6
Sub total	**48.3**	67.4	**22.5**	26.3	**1,446.6**	1,384.3	**0.002**	0.005	**19.4**	27.4
H Authorized dealers	**13.5**	0.2	**4.3**	0.2	**2,127.8**	537.9	**0.000**	0.000	**0.0**	0.0
I In-house	**0.2**	10.5	**0.6**	4.1	**201.3**	1,381.8	**0.041**	0.000	**1.2**	0.0
J,K Overseas sector	**32.1**	18.3	**3.7**	2.4	**5,853.0**	4,305.9	**0.000**	0.016	**0.0**	8.9
Sub total	**45.8**	29.0	**8.6**	6.7	**3,519.5**	2,565.0	**0.000**	0.015	**1.2**	8.9
Total	**100.0**	100.0	**100.0**	100.0	**738.0**	541.6	**0.005**	0.012	**100.0**	100.0

Source: The International Stock Exchange

Table 9.6 *Medium and long gilts – client profile*

	Value		*Bargains*		*Av. bargain size*		*Av. commission rate*		*Share of commission revenue*	
	1988 (%)	*1987 (%)*	***1988 (%)***	*1987 (%)*	***1988 (£000)***	*1987 (£000)*	***1988 (%)***	*1987 (%)*	***1988 (%)***	*1987 (%)*
A Individuals	**0.3**	0.2	**16.8**	13.0	**15.3**	13.6	**0.025**	0.318	**29.8**	15.8
B Via agents	**0.1**	0.1	**17.4**	9.3	**7.2**	10.3	**0.621**	0.391	**21.5**	10.5
C Banks as agents	**5.4**	4.3	**24.8**	25.8	**196.8**	161.9	**0.006**	0.019	**23.4**	21.5
Sub total	**5.8**	4.6	**59.0**	48.1	**89.0**	92.1	**0.015**	0.039	**74.7**	47.8
D Prof. fund mgers	**12.4**	17.4	**10.7**	11.8	**1,015.0**	1,442.2	**0.002**	0.004	**5.9**	17.1
E Banks	**15.1**	20.0	**3.9**	10.9	**3,376.7**	1,779.3	**0.000**	0.003	**1.4**	13.9
F Major institutions	**22.2**	18.6	**9.2**	11.4	**2,128.2**	1,580.1	**0.000**	0.001	**0.9**	6.6
G Other institutions	**13.1**	11.2	**3.3**	5.0	**3,511.9**	2,146.7	**0.003**	0.003	**10.8**	8.1
Sub total	**62.8**	67.2	**27.1**	39.1	**2,029.2**	1,667.3	**0.001**	0.003	**19.0**	45.7
H Authorized dealers	**17.4**	0.5	**7.3**	0.5	**2,095.3**	878.2	**0.000**	0.000	**0.0**	0.0
I In-house	**1.8**	3.2	**1.0**	3.4	**1,571.5**	934.6	**0.000**	0.002	**0.1**	1.3
J,K Overseas sector	**12.2**	24.5	**5.6**	8.9	**1,935.7**	2,653.5	**0.000**	0.001	**6.2**	5.2
Sub total	**31.4**	28.2	**13.9**	12.8	**1,987.1**	2,086.1	**0.000**	0.001	**6.3**	6.5
Total	**100.0**	100.0	**100.0**	100.0	**1,006.5**	969.8	**0.004**	0.004	**100.0**	100.0

Source: The International Stock Exchange

Table 9.7 *Turnover by security groups – other fixed interest*

	Irish government	*UK local authorities*	*Overseas government*	*Corporate bonds*	*Bargains*	*Business days*
1964		81.9	65.2	121.5	166,930	87
1965		331.2	201.3	479.7	580,558	255
1966		694.4	138.4	584.8	652,450	254
1967		1,202.5	190.4	787.4	664,757	252
1968		731.3	148.5	943.6	817,535	257
1969		839.4	140.9	1,238.0	808,086	257
1970		1,310.3	136.1	1,158.6	737,868	255
1971		1,521.1	218.3	1,679.5	834,953	253
1972		1,345.2	220.3	2,008.5	809,324	254
1973	299.0	1,117.3	179.9	1,682.8	595,286	253
1974	1,882.5	2,585.5	150.2	1,256.4	548,315	255
1975	3,962.8	3,501.1	223.2	1,558.5	572,875	254
1976	4,460.2	4,264.8	196.8	1,424.5	531,289	255
1977	9,197.1	5,365.2	486.8	2,357.7	670,189	252
1978	9,671.4	4,246.7	274.0	1,683.5	607,806	252
1979	9,523.8	4,378.5	216.6	1,763.3	464,302	253
1980	7,994.3	3,819.6	225.4	1,751.0	480,772	254
1981	6,620.3	3,814.8	315.5	1,473.6	394,340	252
1982	11,535.7	4,115.5	854.4	2,435.8	428,175	253
1983	11,614.1	4,656.1	1,366.8	3,063.3	411,912	252
1984	12,685.8	4,437.1	2,064.1	3,690.4	380,181	253
1985	16,098.5	1,480.0	2,021.7	3,790.9	384,303	253
1986	25,030.8	380.8	7,349.8	7,877.6	412,675	253
1987	23,643.9	190.2	22,712.1	15,851.9	431,450	253
1988	28,664.9	170.0	6,287.1	15,742.9	396,735	253

Source: The International Stock Exchange

10

Arithmetic basis

This chapter sets out the mathematical concepts used in the evaluation of debt securities.

10.1 Symbols

The following symbols are used in this chapter:

- a = accrued interest
- $a_{\overline{n}|}$ = annuity of one per period payable at the end of each period for n periods
- C = call on a stock
- d = discount rate
- D = number of days
- f = flat yield
- g = coupon rate
- h = duration
- $2i$ = gross redemption yield (Y)
- J = inflation rate
- n = number of complete years
- P = total price of stock, including accrued interest
- q = time between settlement date and next interest payment, measured as a proportion of a half year
- Q = quoted price (or clean price)
- R = real return
- t = tax rate on income
- w = volatility
- Y = gross redemption yield (annual rate)

10.2 Clean price, total price and accrued interest

Since 28 February 1986 UK stocks have been dealt in on a clean price basis. The total price to be paid is the clean price plus or minus accrued interest

$(P=Q+a)$. If there are more than six months to the next dividend payment then the accrued interest is negative and the total price paid is less than the clean price. This situation occurs shortly after a stock has gone ex-dividend. Where there are less than six months to the next dividend payment, the accrued interest is calculated as the number of days between the last dividend payment and the date of settlement of the transaction multiplied by the coupon and divided by 365. The calculations are modified where the accrued interest is negative by taking the number of days between the settlement of the transaction and the date of the dividend payment which has been missed because of the stock going ex-dividend.

The method of calculating accrued interest in not the same in each market. For example, for some securities a 360 day year is assumed with equal amounts of accrued interest each calendar month. This is shown in Table 10.1.

Table 10.1 *Accrued interest calculation rules*

	Coupon frequency	*Accrued interest basis**
UK gilts	Semi-annual	Actual/182½
UK debentures	Semi-annual	7 day Basis/182½
Eurosterlings	Annual	30/360
US Treasuries	Semi-Annual	Actual/Actual
Eurobonds	Annual	30/360

*Basis is numerator/denominator. '30' means using 30 day months and 182.5 is half of 365. 7 day basis assumes 7 day settlement.
Source: Kleinwort Benson Limited (modified)

10.3 Flat Yield

This is the coupon on the stock divided by the clean price

$$f=\frac{g}{P-a}$$

The net flat yield at a rate of tax t on income is

$$f=\frac{g(1-t)}{P-a(1-t)}$$

This is not the same as multiplying the gross flat yield by $(1-t)$.

10.4 Gross redemption yield

Gilt-edged yields are calculated on a half-yearly basis. For a stock with n years life, paying a coupon of g per cent per annum and with price P, the total gross redemption yield is 2i and is calculated by solving:

$$P = \tfrac{1}{2} g a_{\overline{2n}|} + 100v^{2n}$$

or P = Value of interest payments + value of final redemption amount

If 2n is not integral, and there is a period q between the settlement date and the next dividend date, so that the total time to maturity is 2n + q then:

$$P = \frac{g}{2}v^q + v^q\left(\frac{g}{2}a_{\overline{2n}|} + 100v^{2n}\right)$$

In order to calculate the net redemption yield, it is necessary to take into account the gross accrued income paid at the time of purchase of the security. The investor is liable to pay income tax on the accrued interest included on a sale of a security and receives a tax credit against the accrued interest paid when a stock is purchased. The accrued interest is deemed for tax purposes to be paid on the next dividend date. If the stock is purchased at time q before the next dividend date the net redemption yield is calculated by solving:

$$P = atv^q + \frac{g}{2}(1-t)v^q + v^q\left(\frac{g}{2}(1-t)a_{\overline{2n}|} + 100v^{2n}\right)$$

If the clean price Q is used and P = Q + a:

$$Q = \frac{g}{2}(1-t)v^q(1 + a_{\overline{2n}|}) + 100v^{2n+q} - a(1 - tv^q)$$

No tax rate on capital gains has been included since there is now no capital gains tax on sales of gilt-edged stock and certain qualifying bonds.

With a partly-paid stock, the outstanding calls form part of the left-hand side of the equation and are put in present value terms. Hence if there are calls C_1 and C_2 due in time m_1 and m_2 from the current settlement date, then gross redemption yield is calculated from:

$$P + C_1v^{m_1} + C_2v^{m_2} = \frac{g}{2}v^q + v^q\left(\frac{g}{2}a_{\overline{2n}|} + 100v^{2n}\right)$$

This formula may need further modification if, as is usual, the first interest payment is not g/2.

10.5 Shape of return

Redemption yield is one measure of the overall effects from capital and income combined, but it does not give any information on the shape of the return. Two stocks with the same redemption yield may provide very different combinations of income and capital proceeds. For example, if there are two stocks with the same maturity date and same redemption yield, but one has a coupon of 3 per cent while the other has a coupon of 15 per cent, the 15 per cent stock will pay out more of its return sooner than the 3 per cent stock because the income level is much higher on the 15 per cent stock. This means that if the income on the 15 per cent stock is not needed to pay liabilities and is reinvested, the investor in the 15 per cent stock is more vulnerable to reinvestment rates than the holder of the 3 per cent stock. This means that the accumulated return to maturity if the income is reinvested in gilt-edged securities up to maturity may differ substantially between the two stocks even though the redemption rates are the same. An investment in a stock will realize the stated redemption yield to maturity only if the periodic dividends can always be invested at the redemption yield. Hence, if a stock is selected because it provides the highest redemption yield, it is no guarantee that it will produce the highest accumulated sum at maturity. The vulnerability of stocks to reinvestment rates can be calculated by looking at accumulated sums at maturity on different reinvestment rate assumptions. Where stocks have a spread of redemption dates, e.g. Treasury $11\frac{3}{4}$ per cent 2003/07, the government has the option to choose the date which minimizes its funding cost. The option therefore works against the investor. It is customary to assume that if the stock is priced below par then the longest maturity date is assumed, but the shortest maturity date if the stock is priced above par.

10.6 Yield curves

The yield curve is a graph of gross redemption yield on the y axis measured against term to maturity on the x axis. There are a large number of methods of calculation, but the central approach is to provide a measure of the consensus market redemption yield against which individual stocks can be assessed.

The yield curve is a smooth curve based on the actual data for individual stocks. When its use commenced in the 1960s, it was possible to draw curves which fitted the total gilt market well, since the coupon range was small. As the coupon range increased the yield curve based on all stocks became less useful, since the creation of higher coupon stocks for longer maturity stocks caused the yield curve to rise faster than the general rise in yields. This led to the use of three-dimensional models for the gilt market based on redemption yield, term to maturity and coupon, but also to the use of yield curves with a restricted coupon range. Yield curves can be constructed using data for stocks in say the 10 per cent to 12 per cent range where there are a large number of issues.

Yield curves can have a variety of shapes. A positively sloping yield curve is where longer stocks give a higher redemption yield than shorter stocks. If the differential between rates on short-dated stocks and long-dated stocks increases, the yield curve is said to steepen. In recent years, the yield curve has often had a hump in it reflecting, amongst other things, the government's funding in the medium-dated areas, and often has been negatively sloping. Yield curves are shown diagramatically in Figures 1.1 to 1.5, page 4 *et seq*.

The shape of a yield curve reflects investors' expectations, and a variety of other factors. The interpretation of the reasons for a particular shape may not be straightforward. For example, a negatively sloping yield curve could be due to investors expecting interest rates to decline and therefore buying longer-dated stocks to take greater advantage in the form of an increase in capital value of the expected move. It could, however, be giving no message about future long-term interest rate expectations but reflect an economic situation where it is necessary to employ high short-term interest rates, perhaps to defend sterling. An analysis of the yield curve should also take into account that different types of investor tend to dominate each maturity sector, and hence the yields and the yield curve shape may also be influenced by the taxation position of the various types of investor.

The fitting of a yield curve to the data for actual stocks will be carried out by computer using standard curve-fitting techniques. This may mean that the scales on the y and x axes are not linear.

10.7 Par yield curves

These curves are obtained by assuming that the price of a stock is a function of the coupon, rate of interest and term to maturity, and then finding the values for the coupon to make the price equal to 100. The curve is then fitted to the data for the coupons.

Par yield curves have their advocates and they have been used by the Bank of England to assist in the pricing of gilt issues. However, they have two major problems:

1. If interest rates are high, most of the gilts in issue are priced below par, but the par yield will result in a coupon higher than those in issue.
2. Par yield curves do not necessarily provide a method of measuring general movements in yields.

10.8 Volatility

Volatility is a measure of a stock's change in price for a change in redemption yield.

Mathematically it is:

$$w = -\frac{1}{P} \times \frac{dP}{dy}$$

where P is the price and y is the gross redemption yield. Although not strictly accurate, volatility may be shown as the change in price for a 1 per cent change in gross redemption yield.

Another measure of volatility is the Geometric Term Index (GTI) which is the percentage change in price for a one tenth change in yield either side of the gross redemption yield.

$$GTI = 100 \times \frac{\text{Price to yield } (0.9i\%) - \text{Price to yield } (1.1i\%)}{P}$$

The GTI for irredeemable stocks is constant at twenty. Two stocks with the same GTI can be expected in the short term to have the same proportionate change in price for the same change in yield, but this does not mean that this will continue for a period of time. This is broadly because the GTI can be the same for stocks of widely differing coupon and time to maturity. As with the conventional volatility measure the GTI for some long-dated stocks can be greater than for irredeemable stocks. This occurs because GTI varies inversely with coupon and occurs when the long-dated stock has a price well below par.

10.9 Duration

Duration (h) is a measure of the weighted average life of the stock where each interest payment and the redemption proceeds is weighted by its average term.

$$h = \frac{\frac{g}{2}(v + 2v^2 + \ldots + 2nv^{2n}) + 2nv^{2n} \times 100}{\frac{g}{2}(v + v^2 + \ldots + v^{2n}) + v^{2n} \times 100}$$

h in this case is in half years.

It can also be shown that $h = 100w\,(1 + i)$

i.e. Duration in years $= 100 \times \text{volatility} \times \left[1 + \frac{\text{Redemption yield \%}}{200}\right]$

10.10 Dedication and immunization

Dedication is a process whereby the cash flows of the fixed interest portfolio are matched as closely as possible with the expected cash flows from the liabilities. Dedication is a precise form of asset/liability matching.

Immunization is a process which aims to reduce the reinvestment risk when income receipts are received. If interest rates fall after a bond is purchased, the price will rise, but the income receipts can be reinvested only at a lower rate of interest. Conversely if interest rates rise then the capital value of the bond falls but the income receipts can be reinvested to earn a higher redemption yield. Immunization aims to exactly offset the effects of those two items so that the capital change in the bond by an interest rate change is equivalent to the effect of rolling up income at a revised rate. Immunization results in a known rate of return on the portfolio (or stock) for a defined period. For a single stock the defined period is equal to the duration of the stock.

Immunization is a less precise form of asset/liability matching which may be achieved by equating the duration of the assets to that of the liabilities. The asset and liability flows may not be closely aligned in time, but the matching of interest rate sensitivities can be expected to make their relative values change in a generally predictable way.

10.11 Price model analysis

Many price models have been formulated for the gilt market. Some have been constructed by stockbrokers while others have been devised by investment managers and analysts. A number of models have been detailed in the *Journal of the Institute of Actuaries* and the *Transactions of the Faculty of Actuaries*, such as in *JIA*, **104** (1977) by K. S. Feldman or by R. S. Clarkson in *TFA*, **36** (1978), and *JIA*, **106** (1979).

The price models can vary substantially in their construction and their use. Feldman, for example, used a linear model with different discounting functions for capital and for income whereas Clarkson used a curvilinear model based on the flat yield $\frac{g}{p}$ and the proportionate change in price to redemption 1/P. The price models can be used to produce values for prices or yields of stocks, to compare this with the actual values, and then to see how the differences vary over time. It is possible that similar indications of cheapness or dearness will be given even if the models themselves are different. Models can be used to assist in pricing of new issues such as the Burman and White Bank of England model. This model is described in detail in the December 1972 issue of the *Bank of England Quarterly Bulletin* and was the first model to tackle the 'coupon effect' in a rigorous manner. Models can also be used for predictive purposes to assess the possible effects of future market conditions.

Other stocks

10.12 Income cover for loans

Income cover is the number of times that the loan interest is covered by the pre-tax trading profits after allowance for depreciation. For example if the pre-tax profits are £10 million and there are no charges in priority to the loan interest of £1 million, the interest is covered ten times by the profits, so profits would have to fall to below one-tenth before the loan interest is uncovered. Another way of expressing this is to use a priority percentage for the loan interest which specifies the priority for the use of profits. In this case the priority percentage would be 0–10 per cent.

As a separate example, let us assume that the pre-tax trading profits are £10 million and that there is debenture interest of £1 million and loan interest of £1 million. Debenture interest is paid in priority to loan stock interest; hence the income cover is ten and the priority percentage is 0–10 per cent. The loan stock cover must not be calculated in isolation, but must include debenture loan interest paid in priority to it. Hence, the interest on the loan is £1 million, the interest in priority to it is £1 million, making a total of £2 million. The trading profits available are £10 million and hence the income cover is five, with the loan stock priority percentage 10–20 per cent. When looking at the debenture priority percentage and income cover, it is not apparent that there is subordinate debt. The subordinate debt is still important since a debenture with a high income cover with no subordinate debt is clearly preferable to another (in a company of similar status) with similar income cover with extensive subordinate debt.

An analysis of the income cover should take into account long-term commitments of any form, whether prior to, or subsidiary to, the debt particularly where failure to pay could jeopardize the profit-earning ability of the company. The analysis should calculate cover in recent years and not just in the last year, and generally should be at least 4 times.

10.13 Capital cover for loans

Capital cover enables investors to assess their potential for repayment should the company fail. Investments should not be undertaken with any thought that capital cover should be relied upon; the important issue is to seek out investments in secure companies where the risk of corporate failure is low. Hence the analysis of the company should include trading prospects and wider aspects than those just relating to the cover for the relevant fixed interest security.

In order to calculate capital cover, the tangible assets (e.g. property, plant etc.) should be added to the current assets less the current liabilities. All short-term liabilities such as an overdraft should be treated as current liabilities even if it would not have priority over a debenture on any winding-up. Goodwill is excluded completely. Capital cover is therefore:

$$\frac{\text{Tangible assets plus current assets less current liabilities}}{\text{Amount of loan plus any priority loans or debentures}}$$

As an example of the calculations, consider the following simplified balance sheet:

		£m		£m
Ordinary share capital		60	Property	50
Reserves		55	Plant and equipment	50
Debenture		10	Stocks	30
Loan stock		15	Debtors	40
Current liabilities	–creditors	35	Cash	10
	–overdraft	35	Goodwill	40
	–tax	10		
		220		220

The tangible assets are $50+50+30=130$
The current assets less current liabilities $=40+10-35-35-10$
$=-30$

Cover for the debenture $=\dfrac{130-30}{10}=10$

Cover for the loan stock $=\dfrac{130-30}{10+15}=4$

Priority percentages for capital can be established in a similar way as for the income:

i.e. Priority percentage for capital for the debenture = 0–10%
Priority percentage for the loan stock = 10–25%

Normally investors would seek capital cover of at least $2\frac{1}{2}$ times and would also wish to check that if short-term liabilities are large in relation to long-term debt that there are adequate liquid assets to avoid cash flow problems. For mortgage debentures with capital cover on specific properties, a lower capital cover of around 1.5 (for good quality offices) is appropriate. Income cover in this case needs to be at least one, based on current property rents.

10.14 Income and capital cover for preference shares

The method of calculation of the cover of these shares is basically the same as for debentures and loan stock with a few minor modifications:

1. Since cover is an indication of margin in the event of problems, it is necessary to assume that the company's borrowing powers are exercised to the maximum permitted by the Articles.
2. It is necessary to ascertain whether the preference shares are repaid in priority to the ordinary shares in a winding-up. If they rank pari passu the capital cover is rather meaningless.
3. The preference dividend is paid net and thus should be grossed up.

10.15 Certificates of deposit (CD)

These are marketable securities and if sold in the secondary market the dealing is done using the interest rate which will apply to a buyer for the remainder of the term to maturity. The purchase consideration is then worked out from the interest rate and the days left to maturity.

If a CD is issued for D_1 days to maturity, with a coupon rate of I_1 per cent the maturity proceeds will be $£100\left(1+\frac{D_1}{365}\times\frac{I_1}{100}\right)$ per £100 of original investment.

If a purchase occurs at $D\varepsilon$ days to maturity and the interest rate at which the purchaser agrees to buy is $I\varepsilon$ the purchase price will be found from:

$$P_\varepsilon\left(1+\frac{D_\varepsilon}{365}\times\frac{I_\varepsilon}{100}\right)=100\left(1+\frac{D_1}{365}\times\frac{I_1}{100}\right)$$

$$P_\varepsilon=\left(\frac{36{,}500+D_1I_1}{36{,}500+D_\varepsilon I_\varepsilon}\right)\times 100$$

10.16 Treasury bills

Treasury bills are dealt in using a simple rate of discount. If d is the current rate of discount, the price (P) of a ninety-one day Treasury bill will be:

$$P=100\left(1-\frac{91d}{365}\right)$$

$$d=\frac{365}{91}(100-P)$$

or as a percentage $d\%=\dfrac{36{,}500}{91}(100-P)$

If sold at D_ε days prior to maturity at a discount rate of d_ε the price (P) will be:

$$P = 100\left(1 - \frac{D_\varepsilon d_\varepsilon}{365}\right)$$

It should be borne in mind that the discount rate is lower than the equivalent interest rate if this had been used rather than a discount rate. If the discount rate on a ninety-one day bill was 10 per cent, the price would be 97.507, and the simple interest rate (y) needed to take 97.507 to 100 in ninety-one days is:

$$97.507\left(1 + \frac{91y}{365}\right) = 100$$

$$y = 10.26\%$$

10.17 Sterling commercial paper

This is issued at a discount on an interest rate basis. If the paper is issued for D_1 days at an interest rate of I_1% the price at issue (P_1) will be:

$$P_1\left(1 + \frac{D_1}{365} \times \frac{I_1}{100}\right) = 100$$

$$P_1 = \left(\frac{36{,}500}{36{,}500 + D_1 I_1}\right)100$$

The price at days D_ε before maturity, when quoted rates are I_ε% will similarly be:

$$P_\varepsilon = \left(\frac{36{,}500}{36{,}500 + D_\varepsilon I_\varepsilon}\right) \times 100$$

10.18 Index-linked stocks

Index-linked stocks have been issued in the UK, Ireland and Canada, and more recently in the US, and have their income and redemption proceeds linked to an index. In the UK, this is to the Retail Price Index (RPI). Since it is necessary to calculate accrued interest up to the next interest payment and since there is a delay in the actual calculation of the RPI for a particular month, the RPI in the calculation for UK gilts is lagged by eight months. For example, Treasury 2 per cent 2006, issued on 8 July, 1981, will be redeemed on 19 July 2006, and the redemption proceeds will be:

$$100 \times \frac{\text{RPI in November 2005}}{\text{RPI in November 1980}}$$

Similarly, the half-yearly income payment in July 1992 will be based on the RPI in November 1991 and be calculated as:

$$\tfrac{1}{2} \times 2\% \times \frac{\text{RPI in November 1991}}{\text{RPI in November 1980}}$$

The shape of the return differs substantially from a conventional fixed-interest stock in that there is low immediate income and the expectation of substantial capital gain (compared with a higher immediate income and capital changes limited to a movement towards the nominal redemption value for the conventional stock). Since the income is much lower than for a conventional stock, investors in index-linked gilts are less affected by future investment conditions for the reinvestment of income if they are calculating ultimate rolled up redemption values.

The income and the redemption amounts depend on the RPI eight months prior to the receipt of the income or the date of redemption. Hence, in order to calculate the expected returns on the stock in monetary terms, it is necessary to forecast future levels of inflation. This can either be done using a constant inflation rate throughout the life of the stock or alternatively, a complex set of inflation rates individually forecast for each year can be formulated. Either way, the effect will be to define in monetary terms the cash flows expected in each year until redemption and these amounts can be subject to conventional analysis and a redemption yield calculated. The redemption yields can be compared with conventional stocks.

An index-linked stock can be compared to a conventional stock to ascertain the constant rate of inflation which would equate the redemption yield on the index-linked stock and on the conventional stock. This is known as the break-even rate of inflation. If for example the redemption yield on Treasury $9\frac{3}{4}$ per cent 2002 is 10 per cent and the break-even rate of inflation for Treasury $2\frac{1}{2}$ per cent index-linked 2001 is 6 per cent, the index-linked stock will be generally preferred if the investor believes that inflation will exceed 6 per cent between now and 2001, but he will also need to take account of other factors, e.g. the different shape of the two returns – one with a high income and low redemption value (the conventional stock) and the low income and high redemption value of the index-linked stock. These calculations need to be made using after-tax rates (i.e. net rates) for taxed investors.

Gilt lists for index-linked stocks do not generally show a redemption yield for a stated constant inflation rate but rather a real rate of return for a given inflation rate. If Y is the monetary gross redemption yield, R is the real return (semi-annual rate) and J is the inflation rate (annual rate), then:

$$\left(1+\frac{Y}{200}\right)^2 = \left(1+\frac{R}{200}\right)^2\left(1+\frac{J}{100}\right)$$

$$\text{i.e.}\left(1\times\frac{R}{200}\right)=\left(1+\frac{Y}{200}\right)\Bigg/\sqrt{1+\frac{J}{100}}$$

$$\text{or } R=200\left[\frac{1+Y/200}{\sqrt{1+J/100}}-1\right]$$

The real rate of return on the index-linked stock is not simply Y − J, i.e. the money rate of return less the inflation rate.

For example if Y = 10 per cent, J = 6 per cent, R will be 3.97 per cent and not 4 per cent.

For a given stock, the real yield decreases as the projected inflation rate increases. For example, the real return on Treasury 2½ per cent 2001 is 3.6 per cent with inflation at 10 per cent and 4.3 per cent assuming inflation at 5 per cent.

10.19 Comparative analysis

In the same way that yield curves are calculated for conventional stocks, real yield curves can be plotted for index-linked stocks, albeit based on the limited number available in this market.

Since the real yield curve will go through most, if not all, the various real yields for the individual index-linked stock there is no point in examining relativities in position against the yield curve (as for conventional stocks). The particular index-linked stock to be purchased will depend on the term required, but also on the reinvestment real yield. For example if the real yield (assuming 5 per cent inflation) was 4.00 per cent on Treasury index-linked 2½ per cent 2013, but 3.75 per cent on 2½ per cent Treasury index-linked 2020, it is possible to calculate the real yield that would be needed on 2½ per cent IL 2020, purchased in 2013 on redemption of 2½ IL per cent 2013 in order for the overall real return from now until 2020 to be 3.75 per cent. The investor can then decide whether to initially invest shorter and purchase 2013 stock or to purchase the 2020 stock now. This is similar to the balance of term yield for conventional fixed-interest stocks discussed in Section 11.16.

10.20 Pricing futures

An investor has the alternatives of buying a fixed-interest stock and receiving the interest payments (on accrual of interest) or buying a futures contract and placing on deposit the cash which would otherwise have been used to purchase the fixed-interest stock.

Hence the basic equation for fair value for futures is:

$$\text{Futures price} + \text{Cash deposit interest} = \text{Stock price} + \text{Interest on stock}$$

$$\text{Futures price} = \text{Stock price} + \text{Interest on stock} - \text{Cash deposit interest}$$

The future may be higher or lower in price than fair value.

Carry is defined as the cost of financing a position in gilts. If the financing costs are greater than the return on the stock, there is a negative carry. Where the reverse is true it is positive carry.

Basis is used to measure the relationship between the gilt market and the futures price. It is the cash price (adjusted by the price factor) less the futures price. In a negative carry market, with futures prices at a premium to the cash price, the basis is negative as well.

Investors can arbitrage between cash and futures markets, and this helps the gilt and futures markets to stay in line. In practice the gilt future often tends to trade at a discount to its predicted price because:

1 There is a choice of gilts which can be delivered into the future.
2 Futures enable all investors to 'short' the market – previously this was only available to jobbers.
3 For most investors it is not possible to buy the future and to be short of physical gilts, whereas it is easy to hold gilts and sell the gilt future.

The long gilt future has been based on a notional 12 per cent twenty-year stock but investors can choose any stock of maturity between fifteen and twenty-five years to deliver into the contract. From September 1988 it is based on a notional 9 per cent stock. It is necessary to put each of the gilts which can be delivered on a common basis with this notional stock and this is done using a price factor. For the long gilt, the factor is the price of the issue to give a redemption yield of 9 per cent from the first day of the delivery month to maturity, divided by 100. On delivery, the futures price is multiplied by the price factor to give an invoice price for delivery. The factors assume clean prices and an accrued interest adjustment is necessary. Factors are an approximation and are only accurate when all deliverable issues have a redemption yield of 9 per cent. From the price factors it is possible to ascertain which of the gilts which can be delivered will be the most advantageous for delivery. This is called the cheapest deliverable stock.

11

Management of a fixed-interest and index-linked portfolio

11.1 Objectives

The effective and efficient management of any portfolio requires clear objectives, and the results achieved should be measured in the light of these objectives. The objectives can be quantitative or qualitative, and complex or simple. They may be to obtain a certain fixed return for conventional portfolios or a particular real return for index-linked gilt portfolios. Alternatively, or in addition, the aim may be to obtain a return of a certain amount in excess of a benchmark such as one of the FT–Actuaries Gilt Indices allowing for tax on income at some stated level. The objective may be in the form of a performance differential relative to a portfolio closely matched to the liabilities. However they are expressed, the objectives must be capable of practical interpretations in a portfolio.

11.2 Risk

There are a number of risk measures which can be employed. One is to ascertain the least risk position relative to the liabilities or cash flow requirements and compile the portfolio of gilt-edged securities which provides the closest match in cash flow terms to this. This would be the portfolio which would be used if there were no reserves available to mismatch the assets to the liabilities in any way. An investment manager would deviate from this 'matched' portfolio in order to try to make profits and the more that he deviates from the least-risk portfolio, the greater the risk of mismatching that he runs. It is not always possible to construct a matched portfolio without using artificial means such as futures, but it is still very useful to formulate the least-risk position from which departures can be measured.

The second measure of risk relates to the change in capital value of the portfolio to a change in interest rates. The purpose of this is to ascertain the capital value for a 'worst case' interest rate scenario, and also to see the likely capital appreciation given a 'best case' outlook for interest rates in a particular period. The overall fluctuations can then be examined to see if these possible capital variations can be tolerated given the reserves available and the nature of any liabilities. The method can be shown by looking at an investor who places all his assets in a one-year certificate of deposit at an interest rate of 10 per cent with a prime bank. His belief is that at no time during this twelve-month period will interest rates be higher than 14 per cent nor lower than 7 per cent. The greatest impact in capital terms on this asset compared with the expected levels would be if there was an immediate change in interest rates as soon as the certificate of deposit was purchased. If interest rates immediately fell from 10 per cent to 7 per cent just after purchase the portfolio would rise in value from 100 to 102.8, whereas if rates increased from 10 per cent to 14 per cent the value would fall to 96.5. If this amount of capital fluctuation cannot be tolerated, then it would be necessary to decrease the term of the portfolio and purchase shorter date CDs. Similar, if more complex, calculations can be done on portfolios of dated fixed-interest stocks.

11.3 Importance of income

Certain investors will have particular cash flow requirements in each year which can either be met from income and maturity proceeds or can be supplemented by sales of investments. The greater the constraints on investment policy by having to provide a certain level of cash flow in the form of income from fixed-interest stocks and maturity proceeds, the lower the assets available for investing to earn additional returns from exploiting expected interest rate changes or switching opportunities. If adequate reserves are available, then there is a case for allowing the manager to supplement the income flows on the portfolio with asset sales where necessary to provide defined levels of income, rather than placing a constraint on the investment income levels.

If securities are dealt in with accrued income separately specified, income can be received as accrued income on the sale of a security, and in effect income is paid away as accrued income on the purchase of a stock. In this way, the receipt of actual income payments on a six-monthly basis is not usually important as long as the defined cash flow is obtained in the required timespan.

11.4 The use of non-gilt stocks

Pension fund fixed-interest portfolios consist mainly of conventional and index-linked gilts. This is because this type of investor is not necessarily a long-term holder of gilts and places a premium on the high marketability of gilts. The opportunity cost which is given up by the much lower marketability of non-gilts which prevents an easy move into other asset classes when favourable opportunities arise, is larger than the extra potential return from the additional yields available on non-gilts. Some managers have used bulldogs in pension fund portfolios when they believe that the differential yield over gilts is temporarily high and corporate debt may be used in the future as the availability of long-dated gilt-edged stock decreases.

Insurance companies often have holdings of non-gilt-edged fixed-interest securities. Their liabilities have substantial elements which are based in monetary terms and hence are always likely to have a core holding of fixed interest assets. This core can consist mainly of non-gilt stocks since holdings are likely to be maintained in the long term and high marketability is not needed. The lower level of security in non-gilt stocks can be dealt with by a well-spread portfolio and an assessment of the capital and income cover for each asset. In this case the additional yield on non-gilts is seen as more attractive than the flexibility of gilts.

11.5 The place of overseas stocks

Holdings of non-sterling denominated stocks will usually depend on the breakdown of the liabilities by currency, and by the short-term outlook on currency and interest rates. If there are money-based liabilities in, for example, US dollars, then it is likely that there will be fixed-interest stocks also denominated in dollars. The type and amount of securities will depend on the regulations in each country, the reserves held compared with the contractual liabilities and the desired level of marketability. If there are no overseas liabilities then it is unlikely that a portfolio will contain long-term holdings of overseas fixed-interest assets. This is because in the longer term, any advantage of higher interest rates is likely to be offset by a compensating movement in the currency. It is difficult, if not impossible, for any major economy to permanently isolate itself from economic events in the rest of the world. However, in the short term currency swings can be very substantial and if these are correctly assessed, then the benefits can be exploited by holdings of bonds.

For example, an investor could have built up holdings of US dollar bonds in 1984 as the dollar strengthened and could have switched these to DM or Yen bonds for the period to the end of 1987 as the US dollar weakened. This type of policy recognizes the use of overseas fixed-interest stocks as a temporary home or 'safe haven' during currency fluctuations rather than as an investment in its own right.

11.6 The place of index-linked stocks

Index-linked stocks have been a feature only of the UK, Irish and Canadian investment scenes but in early 1988 commenced to be issued in the USA. During the high inflation era of the 1970s investors found that conventional portfolio assets were unable to even keep pace with inflation, and index-linked stocks offering a margin above the level of retail prices would have seemed to be relatively attractive if issued. Index-linked stocks have only been available in the low-inflation, steady-growth 1980s and investors have not generally been very enthusiastic towards such stocks. While it has been generally correct to invest in equities during most of the 1980s, it is difficult to understand why investors have found indexed stocks so unattractive. This may partly be due to their complexity and because it takes time for investors to materially alter their portfolios to incorporate new investment opportunities. Over time it can be expected that they will form larger percentages of portfolios (assuming that they continue to be issued to enable this to occur), as investors work out the after-tax returns on index-linked stocks using relevant inflation assumptions and compare these with the available alternative investments. Marketability of UK index-linked stocks has not generally been good, unless the purchase is of a tap stock.

Pension funds with final salary-type liabilities, and where there is the practice for some increases to pensions in payment to be paid to help offset the effects of inflation, have very few monetary-based liabilities. Most of the liabilities are linked to price or salary inflation and index-linked stocks are ideal to loosely match this type of liability. It is perhaps surprising that pension funds have had only about 3 per cent in index stocks and around 10 per cent to 15 per cent in conventional gilts for much of the 1980s. It is more logical for the non-equity element of pension plans to be indexed gilts (or other assets such as property) rather than conventional gilts, and over time changes in favour of index-linked gilts may occur.

Insurance companies with long-tail liabilities may use some indexed gilts to help offset the effects of inflation on this type of claim, but most prefer to use an element of equity investment to cover this aspect. Lloyds syndicates are, however, likely to use indexed gilts for certain types of liability because of their high after-tax returns to a Lloyds name (usually a top rate income tax payer).

The use of indexed stocks will vary according to the outlook for inflation and the break-even inflation rate for each investor. In theory, if the expectation of future inflation is greater than the break-even inflation rate implied by the current prices of conventional and indexed stocks, after account is taken of the investor's tax position, then the investor will purchase the index-linked stock rather than the conventional stock (assuming other factors such as the liability profile do not predominate).

11.7 Switching

There are a number of ways in which investors can attempt to maximize the overall return on their fixed interest and index-linked portfolios and these are usually referred to as forms of switching. Switches have been categorized into three types but the definitions are somewhat blurred between the types. The first is policy switching which involves a shift in the overall characteristics of the portfolio; the second is anomaly switching which maintains the main characteristics but makes a change in the individual stocks making up the portfolio; and the third is a miscellaneous category covering such items as switching between the gilt market and the futures market.

11.8 Policy switching

An investor needs to examine continually the characteristics of his portfolio in the light of his expectations for interest rates and the consequent change in the shape of the yield curve. The extent to which he will be able to implement changes as a result of this analysis will depend on his liability profile and his reserves. If these are not a constraint then the portfolio may be altered, with a change in its duration and its volatility. For example, if the yield curve is expected to maintain its present shape but all interest rates are expected to increase, then the portfolio may be shortened in duration by reducing the dates to maturity, and in addition, stocks with higher rather than lower coupons may be favoured further adding to the defensive characteristics of the portfolio. If interest rates are expected to fall substantially, and the investor is fairly confident about this outcome, then long-dated volatile stocks are likely to be the preferred choice. Forecasting changes in interest rates and in the general shape of the yield curve is likely to be the most important element in the mangement of a fixed-interest portfolio and the potential gains and losses from this are likely to be many times the size of the gains and losses from anomaly switches.

Expectations about movements in the inflation rate will mean a reappraisal of the relative amounts in fixed-interest and index-linked stocks and in the length of maturity of the portfolio. Decisions will depend on the break-even inflation rate implied by the current prices of index-linked and conventional stocks (taking into account the investor's tax rates). An increase in inflationary pressures will result in larger capital gains in longer rather than shorter-dated index linked issues and hence the policy move may be out of long-dated conventional stocks into long-dated indexed stocks, or just from short-dated index-linked into longer-dated index-linked stocks.

Currency movements are difficult to predict, particularly in the short term, but investors are forced to take some view on currencies if they wish to run an international portfolio, and to adjust the amount that they have in each country. Even if they are running only a domestic portfolio, currency considerations are still important and have an effect, not only on economic events, but also on the level of demand from foreigners for the UK fixed interest market. For example, if large foreign inflows are expected, stocks which are free of tax to foreign investors may show a better performance than ordinary stocks, and medium-dated stocks are more likely to be purchased than ultra-longs. This may flatten out any hump in the yield curve, which has been a feature of the yield curve at times in recent years. Depending on the expectations for interest rates, these factors may modify the overall policy for the portfolio.

The financial futures market enables an investor to see the market's estimate of future prices of financial instruments, which provides a guide to future interest rates, exchange rates and price level changes. Thus, even if an investor does not participate in the financial futures market, it is valuable in providing information to assist in policy switches.

Government funding policy can have an effect on the need to carry out policy switches. In1983 and 1984, the government seemed to restrict the issue of long-dated stock as corporate debt was encouraged. This assisted the performance of the longs and increased the hump in the yield curve in the medium-dated area of the market. In 1986 and 1987 the need for government funding in the gilt market was substantially reduced as the PSBR was decreased in real terms and most of the required funding by the government was by privatization equity issues. In 1988 and 1989 the government purchased gilt-edged stock from investors and the existence of the government as a buyer and the scarcity of long-dated stocks kept long-dated yields at lower levels than economic conditions would have suggested. Some investors used this situation to make policy switches. An increase in demand for stock not balanced by supply of added stock by the government would be a positive factor for the gilt market particularly favouring those areas of the maturity spectrum where stocks were already limited. Similar arguments can be advanced for index-linked securities where the existing supply is already small.

11.9 Anomaly switching

This generally refers to the sale of one security and the purchase of another similar stock with roughly the same coupon and maturity, which is expected to improve the return on the portfolio without materially altering the overall portfolio characteristics. Examples of an anomaly switch would be to sell Exchequer $12\frac{1}{4}$ per cent 1999 and to buy Treasury 13 per cent 2000 or to buy Treasury $13\frac{1}{2}$ per cent 2004/08 and to sell Treasury $11\frac{3}{4}$ per cent 2003/07.

The theory behind anomaly switching is that the positions of stocks relative to the yield curve or yield surfaces or to the computer model temporarily change from their normal positions and that it is possible to exploit these variations by selling those stocks that are 'dear' and buying those that are 'cheap'. As those investing in the market have obtained greater access to computerization, so the opportunities for profitable anomaly switching have decreased. A number of investors in gilts concentrate on policy switches and only use the techniques for anomaly switching to identify the cheap stocks in the area of the market in which they wish to invest.

Investors in debentures and loan stocks are usually unable to effectively pursue this form of switching due to the large difference between buying and selling prices and limited size of dealing. Some limited switching in bulldogs is possible where there is expected to be a marked change in the status (i.e. credit rating) of a stock. Switching between a bulldog and a gilt of similar coupon and maturity is possible depending on the expectations for the differentials between the yields on bulldogs and on gilts.

11.10 Miscellaneous forms of switching

The existence of a gilt future means that it is possible to switch between gilt stocks (the 'cash' market) and the future. This was discussed in more detail in Section 10.20, but the main principles are to assess the stock which is the cheapest deliverable for the future, and compare this with the expected fair value level for the future. If the future price is at a significant premium or discount to fair value, then switching opportunities occur between the future and the underlying stock.

Short-dated gilts with only a short time to maturity can be compared to other short-term, near-cash instruments, such as certificates of deposit, eligible trade bills and sterling commercial paper, to see whether switching opportunities are available. Investors may switch cash into gilt-edged stocks merely to obtain the benefits of the accrued income on a gilt. If the gilt market is firm, high coupon gilts will have a greater accrual rate on income than cash deposits, and the capital value of the gilt may be maintained. This is obviously more risky than holding cash because the capital value of the gilt can fall, but is nevertheless a way of exploiting short-term moves in the gilt market.

Methods of switching

11.11 Price differences

One of the first methods used for gilt analysis was price differences, which essentially is the difference in price between two stocks. Stocks move towards their maturity value at different rates, depending on time to maturity, current price and coupon. To avoid distortions from this effect, price differences can only be used for stocks with similar coupons, prices and times to maturity. The method had further problems in calculations for medium and long-dated stocks as stock went ex-dividend and caused a discontinuity (This was a problem prior to the quotation of all stocks on a clean basis from February 1986.) The method fell into disuse during the early 1970s when interest rate changes became more substantial and as increased computing power became available so that more sophisticated techniques could be used. Price differences are still used by some in the short-dated market, where prices are mostly near to par and where the intention is to reverse the switch within a few days.

11.12 Price ratios

Price ratios for an investor not subject to tax are the ratios of the clean prices of the two stocks (gross price ratio), while for an investor subject to tax the price used for each stock is the clean price plus the gross accrued interest since the last payment date less the net accrued interest (net price ratio). Price ratios are used for switching but care needs to be taken to understand their drawbacks. They have the advantage of showing the approximate scope for profit, but since they take no account of the income differences on two stocks, they are really suited to stocks of similar time to maturity and coupon. If a switch is made from one stock to another at an extreme in price ratios and the ratio returns immediately to a normal level with the investor reversing the switch, then one advantage of price ratios is that there is a tangible gain with more of the first stock than originally.

If the price ratios are used where there is a difference in coupons, the income difference between two stocks can make a major impact on performance. For example if the gross price ratio at the start of a year of Treasury $11\frac{3}{4}$ per cent 2003/07 against Treasury $8\frac{1}{2}$ per cent 2007 is 1.25, it is possible that the clean prices would move to leave the ratio at 1.25 at the year end. The performance of the two stocks would be very different because the holder of Treasury $11\frac{3}{4}$ per cent 2003/07 would have received £3.25 of additional income per £100 of nominal held. As the stocks move towards maturity the price ratio will fall and the rate of change in the price ratio is equal to the price ratio multiplied by the difference in flat yields (not coupons) of the two stocks. Hence it is important to compare actual price ratios over time with the trend expected in the price ratio.

The problems of income difference are small if the intention is to reverse the switch in a very short period of time.

11.13 Yield differences

Yield differences are plotted as the difference in gross redemption yield between two stocks, and consideration is then given as to whether the margin of yield justifies a switch between the stocks.

Although this technique is used by many fixed-interest investors, it does have a number of limitations which need to be taken into account:

1. The yield between two stocks will fluctuate but even at the extremes of the trading ranges may not be sufficient to justify the costs of making the switch.
2. There is no certainty that the stocks will continue to exhibit the same yield differences as in the past.
3. Although yield differences do, in effect, take account of income flows as well as capital changes (in contrast to price ratios), they do not reflect stock volatility. Hence, if the two stocks have different volatilities, the same change in yield will not produce the same capital change in each stock. If the volatility difference between the two stocks is substantial, then it is possible to make a switch from stock A to stock B with a gain in yield, at a later time from stock B back to stock A for a further gain in yield, only to end up with less of stock A than was held at the outset. Yield differences should be used where stocks have similar levels of volatility.
4. Yield difference analysis can be invalidated completely by changes in the yield curve or yield basis. This is an extension of the points made in (2) and (3) above.

11.14 Yield ratios

Yield ratios could be used rather than yield differences and may be useful to assess anomalies where there is a change in the yield basis. They are not in widespread use.

11.15 Position relative to yield curve

The cheapness or dearness of a stock can be measured relative to the yield curve or yield surface. This has the advantage that it is a single measure for each stock rather than the multiple measurements which result from yield differences where comparison is made against all other stocks. However, the yield curve will vary according to the method used and hence different investors can arrive at different answers. The yield curve is a plot of redemption yield against term to maturity, but redemption yield is also a function of coupon due mainly to the distortions introduced by tax systems. This suggests that measurements should take place against yield curves calculated with constant coupons (or a small range of coupons) or relative to a three-dimensional yield surface. Models of yield surfaces have become more common in recent years and anomalies are usually shown as deviations in price from those calculated by the computer model. Some use the concept of mean absolute deviation charts (described in a paper by Clarkson, *Transactions of the Faculty of Actuaries*, Volume **36**, (1978)) to try to identify whether the cheapness or dearness of a stock has reached an extreme level.

There is another sort of yield curve called a par yield curve. This in essence sets out to plot the coupons which would be needed at each maturity value in order to make the security price 100. Comparisons of changes in cheapness and dearness of individual stocks to a par yield curve are not really of practical use, since as the par yield curve alters due to moves in interest rates, only stocks with coupons the same as that implied by the par yield curve move in redemption yield by the same amount as the par yield curve interest rate move.

11.16 Balance of term yields

The methods described in Sections 11.11 to 11.15 do not involve making projections about the future. Balance of term yields look forward and compare buying a long-dated stock with investing in a shorter-dated stock, and on maturity reinvesting the proceeds in the long-dated stock. The balance of term yield shows the redemption yield of the longer-dated stock at maturity of the shorter-dated stock in order that the return on both stocks is similar. In order to carry out this type of calculation, it is necessary to make assumptions for the rate that dividends can be rolled up, as well as taxation rates. This roll-up rate could be the redemption yield for either stock, or the averages of the two, some arbitary rate, or a rate equal to the calculated balance of term yield. The yields take time to calculate and are not used as often as would be the case if readily available. Where they are calculated, a low balance of term yield will suggest the shorter stock is likely to be favoured whereas a high balance of term yield will mean that the terms favour the longer stock.

11.17 Performance returns

If an investor has sophisticated computer systems available it is possible for him to make comparisons between any two stocks. For example, if an investor wishes to achieve the maximum after-tax return over, say, a year and expects interest rates to fall 2 per cent with the yield curve shape staying constant, it is possible for him to ascertain which stock will produce the highest overall return over this period under this scenario and objective. The calculations will require far more assumptions than many of the other methods, but may bring added discipline to the investor's decision making processes. The method can also be used for portfolios of stocks as distinct from one stock although the sophistication currently available does not enable an investor to optimize the return by identifying which particular stock to buy. It can be expected that there will be substantial developments in this area over the next few years.

11.18 Yield differentials to gilts

Certain fixed-interest securities may be traded on the basis of a redemption yield differential to a certain gilt-edged stock. For example in the UK the redemption yield on bulldog and corporate stocks is shown relative to the redemption yield on Treasury 9 per cent 2008, even where the maturity date of the bulldog or corporate stock is not close to 2008. Graphs can then be plotted showing how this redemption yield differential changes over time, and investors may try to move into non-gilts when the differential is high and move back to gilts when it is low. Particular care must be taken with this type of analysis where the coupon and maturity of the non-gilt differs from that of the benchmark gilt, since changes in the shape of the yield curve can lead to changes in the calculated redemption price differential, even though the differential based on a true comparison with a gilt equivalent coupon and maturity may not have changed.

11.19 Passive management of gilt portfolios

Some investors believe that the extensive use of computer techniques within fixed-interest markets has eliminated much of the benefit from using resources to choose stocks. Consequently, such investors use either a 'buy and hold' type strategy where stocks are chosen only when cash flows occur as the most beneficial at that time, or stocks are chosen to replicate as closely as possible the movement of a particular index.

11.20 Switching of index-linked stocks

In theory, index-linked stocks provide further switching opportunities for investors, but the size of the market in the UK (approximately £10 billion) and the wide range of maturities means that switches are usually for policy reasons. Some choice can be made between maturities using similar techniques to balance of term yields for conventional stocks. Switching between conventional and index-linked gilts was discussed in Section 11.6.

Glossary

This glossary contains a number of expressions, many of which are explained extensively in the text of either this volume or our earlier book *A General Introduction to Institutional Investment*, Heinemann, 1986. If the explanations below are insufficient refer to the indexes of either volume, beginning with this volume, to locate relevant passages. Note that cross-references are not given *within* the Glossary although the use of the Latin phrase '*quod vide*' could have been used throughout. Some terms in the Glossary are relatively new and are not explained fully in the text because of publication deadlines.

Account day The (London) Stock Exchange year is split into dealing periods called accounts, generally of two weeks duration but occasionally of three. The account day is the day on which bargains struck in the preceding account are settled. This is not true of bargains in the gilt-edged market where settlement is usually the next business day.

Accrued income That part of the next interest payment of a bond relating to the period elapsed since the last payment was made.

Auction A method of issuing government stock used extensively in the US and occasionally in the UK.

Bank bill A bill of exchange bearing at least two 'first class' names, one of which is a London bank or acceptance house. They are discounted at the lowest rates because they are eligible for rediscounting at the Bank of England.

Basis point One hundredth of one per cent i.e. 0.01 per cent.

Bearer bond Bearer bonds are not registered and the owner's name does not appear on the certificate. Ownership rests in possession of the certificate. Interest payments must be claimed and are not sent as of right.

Big Bang 27 October 1986 was the deadline set for changes to the activities of the (London) Stock Exchange and, in particular, the role of brokers and jobbers. The eventual consequences were immense and are beyond the scope of this volume except in so far as the role of gilt market-makers is concerned.

Black Monday 19 October, 1987 when Wall Street and many other stock markets underwent downward corrective movement i.e. 'crashed'.

Black-Scholes formula Used in a theory of option pricing which calculates the value of an option based on the price of the underlying asset, the exercise price of the option, time to expiry of option, current interest rates, and market volatility.

Bought deal A new issue method whereby the lead manager buys an entire offer of securities on fixed terms and takes on the risk of selling them to the end investors.

Bulldog A sterling bond issued in the UK by a foreign borrower, either governmental or corporate.

Bullet loan A loan repayable in full on a specified future date.

CAP As part of interest exposure management an interest rate cap gives its buyer a guaranteed maximum funding cost by means of an agreement with a bank which, in return for the receipt of an up-front premium, agrees to reimburse any excess funding cost over an agreed rate.

Capital cover A measure of the security of a loan in the event of the winding-up of a company.

Cedel An independent company incorporated in Luxembourg operating a securities and precious metals clearing and safe custody system.

Central gilts office The facility for major participants in the gilt-edged market to have computerized balances in gilts and to effect book-entry transfers through computer terminals.

Certificate of deposit (CD) Certificates of deposit are receipts issued by banks and accepting houses as proof of a negotiable deposit of sterling. They are issued for a certain period at a stated rate of interest and are then freely tradable.

Clean price The quoted price of a bond excluding accrued interest.

Collar An arrangement between a bank and a customer whereby if the customer's funding cost is in excess of an agreed level the bank will reimburse him down to that level. If the customer's funding cost falls below a second agreed level, the customer pays the benefit to the bank. The customer pays a premium which depends on the width and level of the collar. A collar is often thought of as a cheap cap, since it provides the advantage of a cap at a lower cost, the penalty being that the floor may operate. The collar may also be used to hedge the yield on investments.

Commercial paper The modern form of bills of exchange which themselves are traceable as far back as the days of classical Greece.

Common stock The term used in the US for ordinary shares.

Conventional gilt A gilt which is not index-linked or any other form of special government issue.

Coupon Used in short for 'coupon rate', being the rate applied to fixed-interest and fixed-dividend securities which denotes the percentage rate per annum on the nominal issued capital which the issuer undertakes to pay to its holders.

Covenant A legal restriction on a borrower, imposed as part of the conditions of an issue, and binding over the life of the issue.

Cross default clause A clause associated with an issue of debt in which non-payment of interest on one form of debt triggers automatic repayment of all other debt.

Debenture A bond issued by a company that is secured through a trust deed or mortgage on specific assets of the borrower. It often includes restrictive covenants on the amount of total issuance. Debentures rank in priority to share capital and are usually repayable on a specified date or dates.

Discount house An institutional trader in short-term securities borrowing from banks and other institutions in order to finance a book of bills, CDs, local authority borrowings and gilts. They underwrite the whole of the Treasury bill issue each week and act as an intermediary between the Bank of England and the banking system.

Duration The discounted mean term of all coupons and maturity proceeds of a bond.

EMS The European Monetary System much loved by chancellors but abhorred by prime ministers, generally speaking.

Eurobond Fixed coupon bonds and floating rate notes issued by international organizations, denominated in various currencies and traded internationally.

Euroclear A clearance system for internationally-traded securities offering four interrelated services.

Eurosterling A bond denominated in sterling but issued 'offshore'. Easier to float and carrying much less onerous provisions than debentures for companies.

Ex-dividend Ex is Latin for 'without'. Stocks are quoted ex-dividend some weeks (approximately five in the UK) in advance of the dividend payment. A seller of the stock thereafter would retain the right to the dividend in question.

Federal budget deficit The US equivalent to the UK PSBR.

Federal Reserve Bank The US equivalent to the Bank of England.

Financial futures Forward markets in interest rates, currencies and certain other instruments.

Fixed charge A charge secured by debenture holders over specific assets of a company.

Flat yield The running or flat yield of a bond is the coupon divided by the clean price.

Floating charge An overall charge secured by debenture holders over the company's assets which only becomes specific on default.

Floating rate note An FRN is a negotiable interest-bearing security carrying a coupon which is usually indexed to one-month, three-month or six-month LIBOR. They are usually issued in bearer form.

Floor As part of interest rate exposure management an interest rate floor gives its buyer a guaranteed minimum deposit rate by means of an agreement with a bank which, in return for the receipt of an up-front premium, agrees to reimburse any shortfall in interest receipts from an agreed rate.

Forward/forward interest rate The interest rate to apply to a future loan (or deposit of an agreed currency sum) which will be drawn (or placed) for a fixed period commencing on an agreed future date.

Forward rate agreement A contract between a bank and its customer which determines the interest rate applying to a nominal loan (or deposit) from an agreed future date for a specified term.

Gearing A measure of the relative weighting of debt and equity on a company's balance sheet. Known in the US as leverage (pronouncing the first 'e' as in egg). Also used more colloquially to describe the sensitivity of investments to market movements. Thus options offer more gearing than their underlying cash stocks or shares.

GEMMs Gilt-edged market-makers, sometimes known as primary dealers. A company approved by the Bank of England to make a market in the government's debt. It undertakes to make prices in all gilts on issue. These companies have privileged access to the Bank and are able to participate in the interdealing system to trade gilts between themselves.

Gilt-edged securites Government-guaranteed bonds issued for the Treasury by the Bank of England. Gilts are bonds which pay interest half-yearly until redemption and may be either fixed-rate or index-linked.

Gross Domestic Product The total value of all goods and services produced within the particular country concerned. No deduction is made for depreciation or a reduction in capital stocks. GDP may be calculated at constant prices, at market prices or at factor cost. **Gross National Product** (GNP) includes net income from overseas.

Gross redemption yield The annualized return on a fixed instrument taking into account both the yield from income and the change in price to redemption date.

ICCH International Commodities Clearing House, the organization which administers and guarantees trades on commodities and futures exchanges such as LIFFE.

Immunization The actuarial process of protecting a fund from movements in interest rates.

Income cover A measure of a company's ability to service a fixed-interest security.

Index-linked gilt A gilt in which coupons payable and redemption values are linked to movements in the Retail Price Index.

Indexed fund A portfolio constructed to track the movements of a particular price index. Apart from the costs of rebalancing from time to time it is a low cost form of investment management. The investor has the comfort of knowing that the fund will perform in line with the chosen index but sacrifices the opportunity of outperforming or underperforming the market or sector as a whole.

Interbank market The means through which deposits are lent and borrowed via the banks and other institutions.

Interdealer broker A broker authorized by the Bank of England to deal between gilt-edged market-makers. He may not deal for brokers or clients.

Interest rate option A contract giving the buyer the right, but not the obligation, to fix the rate of interest on a notional loan or deposit for an agreed amount, for an agreed period, on a specific forward date. The buyer has no obligation to borrow from or deposit with the bank. On the expiry date the bank will make a payment to the customer to compensate for the extent, if any, to which the strike rate is more advantageous to him than LIBOR.

Jobber The name for a market-maker before Big Bang when dual-capacity was not permitted. A jobber could trade only with a broker and could not deal directly with a client. Whereas a broker relied on commission the jobber relied on his skill in adjusting prices according to supply and demand. The difference between the buying price and the selling price was known as the 'jobber's turn'.

Junk bond A high-yielding bond with limited capital and income cover, sometimes used in corporate takeovers and buy-outs.

Lead manager The principal firm in an underwriting syndicate for a new issue, typically of a Eurobond.

Leveraged buy-out (LBO) An expression from the US denoting the purchase of a corporation based heavily on the use of bonds, often junk bonds. The impact on gearing is significant. Leverage is the American term for gearing.

LIBID The rate at which a bank is prepared to *borrow* money from another (see LIBOR below).

LIBOR London Interbank Offered Rate is the rate at which one bank is prepared to *lend* to another and is expressed as a yield per annum.

LIMEAN The average of LIBOR and LIBID. The difference is of the order of $\frac{1}{8}$ per cent.

LIFFE London International Financial Futures Exchange.

LOCH London Option Clearing House.

Margin Amounts required in futures dealing as a cushion against potential losses.

Medium-term financial strategy (MTFS) The medium-term financial strategy was introduced as a central plank of Conservative government policy in the Budget of 1980.

Minimum lending rate (MLR) Minimum lending rate was introduced as a replacement for bank rate in 1972. On 20 August, 1981 it ceased to be used. It was briefly reimposed on 14 January, 1985.

Money broker A specialist intermediary in the deposit market. Also used to describe certain firms with specific responsibilities in the settlement of gilts including the lending of stock to ease the settlement procedure.

Negative pledge A clause associated with an issue of debt which prevents issue of more senior debt.

New owner clause A clause associated with an issue of debt which restricts the payment of retained earnings as dividends and, in particular, restricts the current year dividend in event of takeover.

Par yield curve Yield curve produced by assuming that the price of a stock is a function of the coupon, prevailing rate of interest and term to maturity and then finding the values for the coupon that correspond to a price of 100.

Passive management A notion of investment management that assumes that fund managers are able to add little value by their activities and which encourages the use of indexed funds.

Preference shares Used to describe stocks or shares ranking in some way before the ordinary shares either for payment of dividends or for capital in a liquidation. Preference shareholders are members of the company whereas debenture holders are not.

Price ratios The ratio of the clean price of two stocks monitored over time as a means of determining when to effect a switch between the stocks.

Primary dealer A market-maker authorized by the Bank of England to make continuous two-way prices in gilts.

PSBR Public Sector Borrowing Requirement. The central government borrowing requirement plus the borrowings of local authorities and public corporations.

PSDR Public Sector Debt Repayment – a negative PSBR.

Registered security All securities on the Stock Exchange other than bearer securities are 'registered' which means that the name of the owner is registered in the books of the company or borrower.

Reverse auction A method of repurchasing government stock recently introduced in the UK.

Roll-over Often used to describe the process of determining the rate of interest to be applied in the event that a loan or deposit be extended beyond the originally agreed term for a further period.

Sinking fund The regular application of amounts towards the reduction of the principal of a loan throughout its life.

Spens clause The clause in preference share trust deeds giving the shareholders rights, in the event of winding-up, in priority to other shareholders and to obtain repayment either at nominal value or, if higher, the average market price over the preceding six months. In more recent years the price is determined by reference to the yield on an equivalent gilt.

Spread The difference between the buying price and the selling price of a market-maker.

Swap (currency) A device for switching asset or liability exposure from one currency to another.

Swap (interest rate) A device for switching interest rate exposure from one form to another e.g. from a LIBOR-related formula to a rate fixed for the duration of a loan or deposit.

Switching The process of selling one stock and simultaneously reinvesting the proceeds in another stock.

Tap Surplus stock not subscribed by investors following a government gilt issue which is taken up by the Issue Department of the Bank of England and subsequently sold in response to bids from gilt-edged market makers.

Taplet A small tap, often a small issue of an existing gilt stock.

Technical analysis Market analysis based on patterns of price data.

Tickler clause A clause associated with an issue of debt which restricts disposal of assets of the company.

Traded option The right to purchase or sell stock at a specified price before a given date is called an option. If the right itself can be bought or written (sold) it is called a traded option.

Treasury bill Negotiable instrument issued by the UK government normally for three-month maturity and allotted by tender each Friday.

Volatility Technically this is a definition of the responsiveness of the price of a bond to a change in yield. It is also used more colloquially. There is also a rigorous definition in relation to market volatility used when valuing options.

Warrant A contract entered into by a company to issue on certain dates shares or stock at a specified price on application by the holders. The warrants usually originate as an attachment to loan stock and normally have the effect of reducing the rate of interest on the loan stock. Holders of warrants receive no income from them.

Withholding tax A tax on interest and dividend payments remitted abroad to foreign holders of securities.

Yankee bond The US equivalent of a bulldog.

Yield curve The result of fitting a mathematically-smoothed curve to stocks in a bond market. The y-axis represents yield and the x-axis term or volatility.

Index